SOCIOLOGY AS A SKIN TRADE

Essays towards a reflexive sociology

Sociology as a Skin Trade

Essays towards a reflexive sociology

JOHN O'NEILL

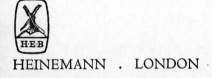

HEINEMANN . LONDON

Heinemann Educational Books Ltd
LONDON EDINBURGH MELBOURNE TORONTO
AUCKLAND SINGAPORE JOHANNESBURG
HONG KONG NAIROBI IBADAN NEW DELHI

ISBN 0 435 82660 3
ISBN 0 435 82661 1 (paperback)

© John O'Neill 1972
First published 1972

Published by Heinemann Educational Books Ltd
48 Charles Street, London W1X 8AH

Printed in Great Britain by Butler & Tanner Ltd
Frome and London

Contents

Acknowledgements

Sociology as a Skin Trade, appeared first in *Sociological Inquiry*, Vol. 40, Winter 1971.

Self-Prescription and Social Machiavellianism is a paper I presented at the Institut International de Sociologie, XXII Congrès, Rome, 15–21 September 1969. I wish to recognize the assistance of a Canada Council Travel Grant.

Public and Private Space was first published in *Agenda 1970: Proposals for a Creative Politics*, edited by T. Lloyd and J. T. McLeod, and published by the University of Toronto Press in 1968.

Violence, Language and the Body Politic first appeared in *The Canadian Forum*, January 1971. I would like to thank Abraham Rotstein for his improvements to this and other essays of mine.

Authority, Knowledge and the Body Politic appeared originally in the *Southern Journal of Philosophy*, Summer and Fall 1970.

Situation, Action and Language. This essay is adapted from two earlier versions which appeared in *Philosophy and Phenomenological Research*, vol. XXVIII, no. 3, March 1968, and *TriQuarterly*, no. 21, Winter 1971.

Marxism and Mythology was first published in *Ethics*, vol. LXXVII, no. 1, October 1966. Copyright © 1966 by the University of Chicago.

Embodiment and History in Hegel and Marx was originally published as 'Hegel and Marx on History as Human History', in the Proceedings of the XIVth International Congress of Philosophy, Vienna 1968. I wish to recognize the assistance of a Canada Council Travel Grant for the original presentation of this argument.

Between Montaigne and Machiavelli appeared in my earlier book, *Perception, Expression and History*: the Social Phenomenology of Maurice Merleau-Ponty, Evanston, Northwestern University Press, 1970.

The Hobbesian Problem in Marx and Parsons is to be published in *Explorations in General Theory in the Social Sciences*, edited by Jan Loubser *et al.*, New York, The Free Press. Copyright © 1972 by The Free Press, a Division of The Macmillan Company. This essay has benefited from several discussions with my colleague H. T. Wilson.

On Theory and Criticism in Marx appeared originally in *Situating Marx* Evaluations and Departures, edited by Paul Walton and Stuart Hall, London, Chaucer Press, 1972.

How is Society Possible? was a paper read at the Seventh World Congress of Sociology, Varna, Bulgaria, 20–26 September 1970. I wish to recognize the assistance of a Canada Council Travel Grant. The argument has also benefited from a careful reading by Kurt H. Wolff.

Reflexive Sociology or the Advent of Alvin W. Gouldner is adapted from a version first published in the *Canadian Review of Sociology and Anthropology*, Vol. 9, No. 9, May 1972.

Can Phenomenology be Critical? was first published in *Philosophy of the Social Sciences* Vol 2, No. 1, March 1972. I am grateful to my colleague J. O. Wisdom whose careful reading of this essay suggested a number of improvements.

Finally, I would like to recognize the very generous typing facilities which Dean John T. Saywell has put at our disposal in the Faculty of Arts, York University, as well as the patience and care which Mrs. Louise Turnpenny and her staff devote to making our scribble readable.

For my Teachers

Conclusion: A Note on Repressive Communication

A collection of essays has usually to be defended except where the intellectual status of their author leaves no question about the coherence of his thought. I have tried to shape these essays to meet a set of common problems. In doing so, I have gradually changed their general style to speak to the main issues in the everyday concerns of sociology. The attempt to reach a wider audience than one's colleagues seems to me to be an absolute necessity if one is to avoid contributing to the privatization of meaning which is a principal source of social control in a liberal society. I have in mind the paradox of the enormous accumulation of social science knowledge and publication which accompanies our present failure of political nerve.

The debate about the possibility of value-free knowledge turns upon the problem of trying to restore to knowledge its value as the basis of community by questioning the restrictive code of objectivist science. In a number of the following essays I have tried to show that the basic norm of liberal capitalism is contained in the pattern of scientific and technological rationality which legitimates a corporate agenda of the over-privatization of all social resources, including individual knowledge and conduct. I have developed this argument from the work of Hannah Arendt, Herbert Marcuse and C. Wright Mills.[1] But I also owe much to my teacher Paul

---

[1] C. Wright Mills, *The Sociological Imagination*, New York, Oxford University Press, Inc., 1959; 'Situated Actions and Vocabularies of Motive', *American Sociological Review*, vol. V (December 1940), pp. 904–913.

Baran,[1] to C. B. Macpherson[2] and what I have been able to make out of Hegel and Marx. In contemporary sociology I suppose I owe most to the works of Peter Berger and Erving Goffman for having explored further features of the consequences of repressive communication.

I am grateful to Claus Mueller for a recent formulation of the concept of 'repressive communication',[3] which suggested to me that my own essays have in part been concerned with its social and political framework but also with attempts to destroy repressive communication through the basic medium of 'body politics' such as my notion of sociology as a skin trade.

> Repressive communication operates on a number of levels. On the individual level, any incongruence between inner and outer language, between privatized and externalized meaning, any split in the symbols used, any incapacity to integrate symbolically one's biographic experience will not only result in a distorted monologue with oneself but also in distorted communication with others. This distortion constitutes the repressive nature of the communication.
>
> The common characteristic of repressive communication is that the internalized language system permits neither the articulation of subjectively experienced needs beyond the emotive level nor the realization of maximum individuation, or, thus implicit autonomy formation. On the psychic level, the language used represses parts of one's symbolic biography and inhibits the attainment of consciousness. On the class level the language used results in an incapacity to locate oneself in history and society.[4]

My thinking represents a blend of Marxism[5] with phenomenological concerns about language, embodiment, and intersubjectivity. Here

[1] Paul A. Baran, *The Longer View*, Essays Toward a Critique of Political Economy, edited and with an Introduction, 'Marxism and the Sociological Imagination' by John O'Neill, New York and London, Monthly Review Press, 1969.

[2] C. B. Macpherson, *The Political Theory of Possessive Individualism*; Hobbes to Locke, Oxford and the Clarendon Press, 1962.

[3] Claus Mueller, 'Notes on the Repression of Communicative Behavior', *Recent Sociology* No. 2: Patterns of Communicative Behavior, edited by Hans Peter Dreitzel, New York, MacMillan Company, 1970.

[4] Claus Mueller, p. 105.

[5] Jean Hyppolite, *Studies on Marx and Hegel*, translated, with an Introduction, Notes and Bibliography by John O'Neill, London, Heinemann Educational Books, 1969.

the principal influences have been Maurice Merleau-Ponty[1] and Alfred Schutz.[2] For anyone concerned with the nature of the construction of social reality, Marx will always remain a classical analyst of the deep structures of economic and social life. But it is hard to deny that Marxists, with certain notable exceptions, have failed to illuminate the connections between the levels of primary need and the levels of symbolic determination and freedom. The most serious rethinking in this respect has come from the critical theorists, and I have tried to develop my own version of these developments. For the same reason I have turned to the basic imagery of the body-politic. I have tried to demonstrate a dialectic of levels in the body-politic between its primary organic organization and its secondary want structures. Historically what has happened, I believe, is that traditional Marxist working class ideology remains tied to the symbolism of primary needs while the new levels of alienation experienced between the market and libidinal structures of the body-politic have produced the politics of street theatre, love-ins, and unisex, to name only a few of the responses of the new libidinal politics.

The test of the new body-politics will be whether it falls prey to the general privatization of media which destroys the genuine publicity of knowledge through its own instant responses, intermittent coverage, and rapid loss of memory. These effects are made more complex by the class-specific interpretational codes of revolutionary behaviour as well as the contrived gap between the generations. To the extent that liberal society achieves a one-dimensional reality, the exclusion of youth and the black and white poor makes irrational any attempt by the latter to create counter-repressive communications through marches, demonstrations, and strikes. In all this the sociologist is for the most part disoriented. The restricted code of functionalist sociology obliges him to interpret the revolutionary style of body-politics as irrational or at best a temporary strain in the process of new levels of adjustment. By the same token radical sociology needs to be aware of its own task of re-establishing a bond between affluent alienation and the primary alienation of the world's poor.

1 John O'Neill, *Perception, Expression and History*, The Social Phenomenology of Maurice Merleau-Ponty, Evanston, Northwestern University Press, 1970.

2 John O'Neill, *Making Sense Together;* an Essay on Social Ontology, forthcoming from Heinemann Educational Books, London, 1973.

A last thought which remains with me is whether these essays are not themselves prime examples of the mode of repressive communication. I have tried to grapple with this problem by gradually turning away from a style that is dictated, apart from any inherent inabilities of mine as a writer, by the standards of academic journals to a manner of expression which is more directly in pursuit of the reader. In the course of this I have become more aware of the work that goes into writing. I would like to think that my efforts that begin here in my study are much like those of workmen anywhere in the factories, the mines and the fields of the world. They hardly count for more but desperately risk being less.

PART ONE

On Private Troubles and Public Issues

The essays in this section are concerned with our experience of the separation between our private and public lives. I argue that liberal individualism is essentially a market vocabulary which must be seen historically so that we can understand its alternation between the release and constriction of individual action. This alternation is determined to suit the realization of a corporate agenda which shapes the middle-mass ecology and psychology of capitalist society. The projection of the corporate agenda as a normative culture simultaneously breeds the alienation of those who by income, age, sex and race are excluded from its mode of affluence. As I see it, the experience of sociology, its practice, its concepts of the self and institutional orders, is governed by a similar alternation of professional idiosyncrasy and public sentiment, which ties it to the contexts of corporate order, exploitation and violence.

1: Sociology as a Skin Trade

Sociology owes its fortune to the fact that nothing occupies man like himself. We are amazed as much by the misfortunes of others as by our own good fortune. Every need of ours involves someone else. The great tissue of human involvement which is woven out of our inability to live without the love and labour of others arouses a constant wonder in us. It is the framework of everything that is relevant to us.

Sociology is the study of people. It is a human pastime with pretensions to science. Sociology can be done in armchairs or buses, at sidewalk cafés or at university. Sociology belongs to familiar scenes, to neighbourhoods, gangs, and slums. In everyday life sociology belongs to the cunning of the salesman and the hustler, or to the proverbial barman and taxi-driver. This is an embarrassment to sociology once it aspires to science, affluence, and organization. Sociology when practised seriously is a profession, like the priesthood or prostitution. Sociologists generally profess not to like priests, though they are often more friendly to them than to social workers. This is a matter of professional pride. For some reason, sociologists prefer prostitutes to priests or policemen and have become their natural protectors. This is a matter of professional jealousy; it belongs to the battle for souls, or clients, as they are called nowadays. To the extent that sociological alibis give more comfort than confessions of sin, the world belongs to sociology and is rid of priests. No one notices that the sociologist, the policeman and the prostitute then proceed to divide the world between them in a three-penny opera of science and beggary.

Sociology has a natural fascination for young people painfully conscious of themselves and others. Sociology stirs the seriousness of

3

youth and awakens its sense of justice and awkward curiosity. At the same time, the complexity of social problems threatens to overwhelm young minds and to exhaust their natural idealism. For this reason youth is sometimes apathetic and even cynical. Many young people arrive at the university vaguely aware that they have been deprived of the natural protection of the home and family. They sense that home, school, and church lie on the social consciousness like those backward regions which are forced to send away their children to the city in search of jobs and excitement. In this sense all of today's youth, white and black, is seething in the ghettos, suburbs and colonies of the corporate business world. For young people the university has become the vital way-station in the civil rights movement which is essentially a youth movement, mindless of colour. Yet these events take the sociological profession by surprise. It is not comfortable at sit-ins, teach-ins, and ride-ins.

Today's youth is remarkable for its solidarity. It has a sense of community which resists commitment to the universal-achievement values of organizational society. Admittedly, the young community is as likely to choose pot as politics in order to express its own values. But whether marching or smoking, youth experiences a libidinal solidarity which challenges the repressive competitiveness of the market and ideological politics. Youth is a force for demystification. For this reason it delights in marches and demonstrations for the sake of their literal and palpable embodiment of arguments which cannot be captured in slogans or official replies. They remind us when marching against the Vietnam war of the evident truth that war is wrong because it separates lovers and kills young people who have no joy in regimentation. They remind old men that they operate a system which blows children to bits and is willing to starve and imprison others. They tell us that our children are the flowers of the earth and yet we set policemen to trample them.

It can hardly be doubted that today's youth would like to do something about the world. Indeed, students are interested in sociology because it is already part of their world and sociology has already insinuated itself into their civic consciousness. They do not need to be reassured in the opening chapters of their introductory texts that sociology is a science. Only sociologists worry about that in moments of professional anxiety. Whatever the reason, sociology is there in the world, ringing in everyday vocabulary, and enshrined in university calendars. Students, then, come to sociology expecting it to be relevant to their everyday lives. The major scenes of war, race, poverty, science, and bureaucracy are familiar to them. They already use a vernacular sociology created out of their experience with the system and confrontation. Yet, in the classroom today's students meet a quite alien scheme of relevances dictated by scientism, value-neutralism and professional sociologism.

So far the point of these introductory remarks is to convey how involved contemporary youth is with people. I want to emphasize that their concern with people is not just a charitable one, nor is it purely political. It is a libidinal and expressive concern which is partly religious, potentially political, but above all sociable. It is a belief that things go better with people than against them. It is a conviction which is troublesome to their elders. Strangely, it also is a belief from which they must be cooled out if they are to settle in as sociologists.

Students, however sullen-looking and apparently self-obsessed, come to sociology because they believe it is concerned with people and that it contributes to the understanding and practical improvement of human relations. They expect with the aid of some sociological training to find themselves in a position to 'work with people'. Now nothing is more likely to throw the sociological profession into turmoil than the persistence of this popular belief that sociology involves working with people. Students who will still believe this are called radicals and activists. They are regarded as throwbacks from the days when the academic establishment did not distinguish sex, socialism, and sociology. Sociology's status as a science was won very painfully and depends very much upon the segregation of those whose sympathies are with social work, or political and community action. Today there are signs that this conception of the professional role belongs more to the generation which worked its way up with sociology than to the contemporary generation of students who do not have the same status qualms about science or affluence. For it is not the professionally alienated or poorer sociology students who retain the activist and populist conception of sociology. The truth which the older generation of social science professionals must confront is the return of bad times and the inescapable involvement of sociology with the ills of society. Curiously enough, whereas the older professionals saw the priest as the spectre of bad times, nowadays the young sociologist regards the older technicians and professionals as the high-priests of the bureaucratization of spirit and imagination to which they attribute much of our social malaise.

Working with people creates a bewildering variety of practices which I shall call skin trades. People need haircuts, massage, dentistry, wigs and glasses, sociology and surgery, as well as love and advice. A vast number of people are involved in trades which fit out, adorn, repair, amuse, cajole, confine, and incarcerate other people. A special aura attaches to working with people. The work of the priest, judge, doctor, and missionary is regarded as holy. The work of the prostitute, the pickpocket, and undertaker is considered profane. In reality, these trades are all involved in dirty work with people. Alternatively, with the exception of the pickpocket, all of these trades may be regarded as holy occupations because of the sublimity of their purpose, to restore and make whole the person.

Working with people is a precarious undertaking and thus the skin trades are especially marked with the ambivalent aura of sacredness and profanity which surrounds the human body. For this reason, every society defines rituals of approach and avoidance to govern contacts between people, between the sexes and between trades. The vast symbiosis of social life is naturally represented as a body in which the spiritual functions are relieved for prayer and thought through the excremental services of the lower-orders. In this scheme of things, the skin trades have been traditionally low-caste, their services being required in order to keep the higher castes free from bodily impurities and thus holy. The lower castes cut hair, wash clothes, clean latrines and dress corpses. In the dutiful performance of these tasks, the lower castes exchange the possibility of mobility in this life for the certainty of it in the next life. This social division of labour is again expressed in the concentration of the skin trades in a locality of the city, for example, around ports, railway stations, and markets. With their teeming produce and swarming crowds, these areas symbolize the metabolism of social life. They are also the scenes of bar-fights, prostitution, hustling, miscegeny and missionary work. Ports, markets, and railway centres are the body orifices of society. As such they arouse the anxiety of the forces of law and order housed in the symbolic centre of the social organism. Once sociology enters the house of government it too becomes anxious about margins, disorder, and deviations.

Sociology is best thought of as a skin trade. This does not mean that sociology is not a profession and a science. It merely implies that sociology is obliged to claim the status of a science and a profession because that is the dilemma of the skin trades in the modern world. It suggests, too, that some of the scientific equipment of the sociologist, like that of the dentist, cosmetician, and pharmacist may be more related to status management than the real nature of his task. Consider the dentist's dilemma. As a mouth-miner he is employed in a dark hole filling cavities, stopping odours, uprooting and removing debris. To save face as a professional it is essential for him to spend more time on the surface than in mouth-mining. Thus the office decor, receptionist, nurse, and para-surgical front of the dentist's suite furnishes the necessary choreography of his professional activity. It enables him to reconstruct his mouth-work in the frame of the professional–client relationship.

Much of the sociological apparatus functions, I suggest, to support a ritual of decontamination between the scientist and his subject. It is essential that the sociologist view his subject only with professional eyes and that he resist the look in the eyes of the sick, the poor, and the aimless who turn his questions back upon him. In this way the erotic symbiosis of talk is reduced to the interview schedule or attitude survey in which the client comes clean before the professional *voyeur*. As the sociological apparatus increases in size and complexity it has to be housed in offices and institutes and its services can only be afforded by wealthy clients. This has the disadvantage of shutting sociology out of crowd scenes, disasters, and riots. It also demands standards of decorum from the sociologist which make it difficult for him to pass in the underworld of crime, sex, race, and poverty. The professional sociologist is curiously caught in his own caste.

In my view sociology is a symbiotic science. Its promise is to give back to the people what it takes from them. This is true of all culture but sociology more than any other discipline promises to make this a practical truth. This is not to say that sociology does not need the other sciences. On the contrary, it presupposes other physical and social sciences. But it has its own task in the need to articulate the connections between individual experience and the transvaluation of human sensibilities worked by the institutional settings of technology, science, and politics.

But, in its aspiration to become a science and to bestow professional status upon its members, sociology has uncritically assumed all the trappings of science. It has lodged itself in the bureaucratic organizations which are the institutional expression of the process of rationalization that has made the fortune of modern science and technology. The same processes of rationalization control the selection and organization of data collected for the sake of client projects parasitic upon the public life and concerns of the people. The apprentice sociologist is as much exploited by these projects as the people they are intended to benefit. He learns the collection and manipulation of data chosen as much for their machine-culinary properties as for any relevance to practical social or theoretical concerns. However, in exchange for domesticating his imagination with trivial generalizations or with the more frequent correlations which litter the sociological journals, the apprentice sociologist is assured of his acceptance to the sociological profession. He is all the more converted when he contemplates the power of professional method and organization which can produce an instant sociology of the Berkeley Free Speech Movement or of Watts, or of crime and violence in the streets, of poverty, or of affluence.

The most profound shock which the apprentice sociologist experiences occurs when he is confronted with the professional neutering of his sense of relevance and concern. This is achieved in a number of ways. Every freshman learns the distinction between facts and values. The effect of this distinction is to convince him that the classroom is a laboratory which can only be contaminated by his everyday knowledge of class, race, war, poverty, sex, and the body. To put it another way, many students come to sociology because its questions are raised for them in their everyday contact with one another, with the ghetto, the police, the military, and the administration. They have met 'the system' in their high schools, in their fights with university administrators, in the city-fathers, and in the sublime indifference of most people. They are not content with the abstract problem of how organizations handle uncertainty. They would like to know which in particular are the most powerful corporations. What is life like in these institutions? What is the ethnic composition of their labour force? What percentage of their production is destined for military purposes? What do their activities in colonial countries mean for the lives of those people? In short, they would like to know which organizations determine the distribution of comfort and security for some and poverty and danger for others. They know they cannot get answers to these questions from a sociology which relies on statistical data never intended to probe the consequences of organizational rationality.

These questions are often dismissed as the concerns of activists. This is short-sighted. Such questions really call upon sociology to re-examine its own sense of the relevance of things. They remind the professional sociologist that his own 'isms'—careerism, scientism, and opportunism—are showing through. They challenge the optimistic assumption of middle-range theory that somehow the data will pile itself up into the big answer to the big question with which no one meanwhile need concern himself.

There is no single road to sociological disenchantment. The fact-value distinction is only one of the devices for altering the student's sense of relevance. Another favourite is the method of 'sociological vertigo'. The strategy in this case is to confound the ethnocentrism of young students with a bewildering tour of the most exotic sociological and anthropological scenes. The purpose here seems to be to convince the sociology student that everything might be some other way—a terror usually reserved for students in introductory philosophy courses.

Nowadays such 'trips' are losing their power to convert students who live their lives experimentally and at short notice. In any case, once they discover that the sociologist's 'high' is on functionalism or social determinism and that he never understood what *they* meant by individualism and community, they turn off on the paid-piper. For the striking thing is that so many young students have thought through for themselves what it means to encounter other people as they are and to know them without needing the way in to be marked esoterically or the way out to be anything else than the time-in-between-people.

Each time one meets a class of sociology students one knows that sociology cannot escape into itself. This is possible only if we allow our jargon to turn meaning away from language and the world toward which it carries us. Yet sociology must speak in its own voice and according to its own experience. Much of what I have said may seem highly critical of professional sociology. If it were nothing more, then it would not serve young sociologists. What I mean to do is to awaken the sense of some of the root metaphors which apply to sociology as a 'trade', a 'craft', or a 'field'. These metaphors remind us of the care and sweat in doing sociology. At the same time, they remind us that sociology is only a way of earning a living and cannot presume to contribute more than others to the public good. It means that when we teach we take others into our care and in turn we must lend ourselves to what they need in order to grow and to become themselves. Young people are looking for work. We must show them the fields and how we care for them so that they will want to share the work. There is no way of legislating what sociologists should do even though we may be clear about what is urgent and important in their task. The practising sociologist must answer for himself and to his colleagues and to the rest of men.

In calling sociology a skin trade I want to restore its symbiotic connections with the body-politic and to situate it in relation to the exchange of organic needs and the utopian celebration of libidinal community which surpasses all understanding. This means that the rhetoric of scientism in sociology as well as its humanism must be tested against the commonsense relevance of everyday life. It is a reminder that society is richer than sociology and that for all our science the world is still the mystery and passion of being with our fellow men.

2: Self-Prescription and Social Machiavellianism

It is striking that at a time when individuals are more willing than ever to criticize and reject the control of such major social institutions as the industrial corporations, the universities and the police the dominant sociological imagery portrays society as a prison,[1] a puppet theatre, or an asylum.[2] Here we are told individuals willingly shut themselves up in order to act out institutional dramas of self-defeat remedied only by the inverted transcendence of underworld tricks of status inversion, of mental side-shows, mutterings, and making out.

To understand the sociological predicament of the individual, I propose to distinguish two related perspectives in the sociology of the self, namely, the models of the orientational structure of the self and the situational structure of the self. I shall refer to the 'orientational self' and the 'situational self' and I shall show that in contemporary sociological theory these two aspects of the self are polarized in a strange alternation between organizational bad faith and institutional madness.

What I have called the orientational self and the situational self represents two perspectives in the sociological theory of the self which, like so many of the paired concepts of sociology,[3] tend to suggest a false dualism of perspective when in fact they mean to

[1] Peter L. Berger, *Invitation to Sociology:* A Humanist Perspective, New York, Doubleday and Co. Inc., 1963.

[2] Erving Goffman, *Asylums:* Essays on the Social Situation of Mental Patients and other Inmates, New York, Doubleday and Co. Inc., 1961.

[3] Reinhard Bendix and Bennett Berger, 'Images of Society and Problems of Concept Formation in Sociology', in Llewellyn Gross (ed.) *Symposium on Sociological Theory*, New York, Harper and Row, 1959, pp. 92–118.

express a real existential dilemma that confronts us when we describe human behaviour and social experience.

The orientational self is the construction of a social psychology which takes the individual self to be the ontological basis of social processes and refers all explanation of social interaction back to its individual basis. The situational self is the counter-concept of a social psychology which assesses the logical priority of the social order and explains individual behaviour in terms of its openness to social patterns. The latter approach does not necessarily claim the ontological priority of society over the individual; it simply argues that the self is functionally, though not substantively, a social phenomenon. When either of these perspectives upon the self is advanced at the expense of the other, we are offered images of the self as either far more independent of social processes than it is in fact, or else much more determined by society than the phenomena of conflict, deviation, and change would indicate.[1]

Generally speaking, the sociological theory of the self tends to emphasize the institutional formation of the situational self. There are a number of reasons for this. Thus, historically, sociology owes its existence to the abstraction of levels of human behaviour irreducible to bio-physiological processes, for example, in Durkheim's classical demonstration of the relationship between the phenomenon of suicide and the processes of social solidarity. I suspect that Durkheim is also the source for the functional irony which is the style of much sociological teaching aimed at showing the institutional presuppositions of 'individual' behaviour. And surely, Merton's infamous paradigm of deviant behaviour[2] demonstrates, at least to undergraduate audiences, the pre-ordained nature of individual rebellion and anomie. Finally, given the political and moral restraints upon radical experiments with social and individual behaviour, the strategy of sociological research is more likely to contribute to the control of behaviour than to set up experiments in radical institutional or personal change.

---

[1] Dennis H. Wrong, 'The Over-socialized Conception of Man in Modern Sociology', *Psychoanalysis and the Psychoanalytic Review*, vol. 49, 2 (Summer 1962), pp. 53–69; Talcott Parsons, 'Individual Autonomy and Social Pressure: An Answer to Dennis H. Wrong', *ibid.*, pp. 70–79.

[2] Robert K. Merton, 'Social Structure and Anomie' in his *Social Theory and Social Structure*, New York, The Free Press, 1963.

These observations contain a paradox for the sociological imagination and its commitment to the values of self-identity and collective self-understanding. As Shils has argued, the sociological sensibility is a development that roughly corresponds with the growth of the moral personality of the individual, notwithstanding the latter-day vulgarity of mass society and its tendency to manipulative technocracy and alienation.[1] The paradox which confronts us is that the sociological sensibility which characterizes Western individualism and its active orientation contributes to drive man out of the social cosmos through massive shocks to his narcissism.[2]

In short, if we are to understand the active orientation of Western individualism it must be seen in terms of an alternation between transcendence and wounded omnipotence. The tendency to lose the dialectical tension between the situational and the orientational perspectives in the sociology of the self is perhaps due to the implicit scientism in the foundations of the modern sociological theory of action,[3] which has so far attempted the most systematic analysis of the cognitive and expressive structure of the self in Western society. The active orientation involves a complex of secular attitudes and institutions whose central value is the domination of man's natural and social environment. In these simple terms, the active orientation is closely identified with science, or rather scientism. Scientism involves an adherence to science in a manner which ignores the self-transformation of individual and social experience that is the consequence of the logic of scientific rationality and its technological domination of social processes.

It is fashionable to schematize Western experience in terms of the Parsonian variables regarded as properties of a social system which churns on its own axis. Alternatively, one may understand the Western world with Parsons' master, Max Weber, who saw very clearly that the pattern of rationality (the subordination of particularistic-ascriptive values to the values of universalism and achievement) is

1 Edward A. Shils, 'The Calling of Sociology', in *Theories of Society*, Foundations of Modern Sociological Theory, ed. by Talcott Parsons, Edward Shils, Kaspar D. Naegele, and Jesse R. Pitts, New York, The Free Press of Glencoe, 1961, vol. II, p. 1410.

2 Amitai Etzioni, *The Active Society*, A Theory of Social and Political Processes, New York, The Free Press, 1968, chap. I, The Active Orientation.

3 Talcott Parsons, Robert F. Bales and Edward A. Shils, *Working Papers in the Theory of Action*, New York, The Free Press of Glencoe, 1953.

not just an ideal–typical construction of the social scientist's understanding. It is rather the truth of subjectivity as it experiences itself in the institutions, the factories, hospitals, and schools of modern society which has broken the bonds of traditional sentimentality to create a vast machinery of individual rights, property, and contract whose meta-sociological significance is the self-transformation of human nature through the market as a generator of wants and sensibilities.

The existential questions of sociology need to be re-opened in every age, for there is a danger of repeating answers long after the original questions are forgotten. Today we are faced with the question of the social sources of rationality. For Reason no longer seems sure of its own calling. Thus Weber always had a nostalgia for the charismatic and inspirational sources in the genesis of ascetic rationality. If we understand him, Weber reminds us that Western rationality becomes an 'iron cage' as soon as it segregates itself from non-reason, pushing non-rational values and behaviour into the ghettoes of madness, crime, and disease. The confrontation of Reason with the madness it 'contains' is a necessary exercise; it forces upon us the justification of the limits of reason and non-reason, which brings the artist to the edges of his own sanity and the scientist to the margins of his own culture.

It is Goffman's great merit to have shown recently that sociological reason risks submission to the powers over madness and crime should it naïvely accept institutionalized definitions of social order, health, and insanity. In constructing the concept of 'total institutions', for example, Goffman introduces an understanding of the dialectic of alienation and commitment which grips both the authorities and the clientele of any institution. It becomes clear that sanity and insanity are the monopolies of neither side. By the same token sociological reason is neither on the side of the angels nor the devils; and yet it cannot stand by itself, except as the question which it is.

In the writings of Goffman and Berger we are offered a fresh solution to the dilemma of the orientational and situational self which destroys chill conformity in subliminal revolt, dream-work, and ecstasy. Here we meet individuals who still listen to their own bodies, who seek out life where the action is and who at every moment lay something of themselves and others on the line. These are the handicapped, the stigmatists, con-artists, circus performers, hustlers, sexual, racial and social passers whose world offers a mirror to the three-penny opera of legitimate society. Never has social life appeared more dangerous, more potentially self-destructive than in Goffman's world of face-to-face encounters. In these primal scenes of sociology the individual must account for himself in the knowledge that others anticipate the slightest deviation in standards of spontaneity, cleanliness, tidiness, generosity, hospitality, credibility, and courage.

In scenes where every individual is committed to the line he projects but where standards of trust and support have similarly to be projected to sustain the action, society is precariously suspended in the rituals of face-work, self-abasement, pride, and forgiveness: 'the coolness exhibited by Antonia in submitting to the target role requires for its field of action the marksman efforts of Hemingway.'[1] Each of us is what he can be for others, every man a mark and operator,[2] and thus an element of calculation enters every special transaction from the simplest greeting to the small print in a contract which may marry us or confine us to a mental institution. We connive at our own downfall and only the man whose dreams and stars have been 'cooled out' can hope to 'graduate'.[3] In Goffman the social order is merely a desperate holding action against the crisis of trust which underlies face-to-face interaction. Whatever the outrage there is a conspiracy between the agent and his victim to support the action for the sake of the identities it generates.

'To prescribe activity is to prescribe a world; to dodge a prescription can be to dodge an identity.'[4] In view of the organizational practice of imputing an identity to its members, whether patients, prisoners, employees, or students, the only recourse allowed to the individual is absenteeism, or defaulting on a prescribed self. The individual can transcend his situation and its official prescription only through the creation of an organizational underlife whose 'conways' allow him to expand his self image in ways not provided for in the institution.

1 Erving Goffman, *Interaction Ritual*, Essays on Face-to-Face Behavior, New York, Doubleday and Co., Inc., 1967, p. 208.

2 Erving Goffman, 'Cooling the Mark Out: Some Aspects of Adaptation to Failure', *Psychiatry*, vol. XV (November 1952), pp. 451–463.

3 Burton R. Clarke, 'The "Cooling-out" Function in Higher Education', *American Journal of Sociology*, vol. LXV (May 1960), pp. 569–576.

4 *Asylums*, p. 187.

Consider the case of the patient in a modern hospital whose entire bureaucratic and rational order functions only in terms of the stripping of his self from all personal effects and even affects at a time when his 'case' needs more emotional support than usual. Under such circumstances the patient is likely to risk his record as a good patient, and possibly as a curable one, by a number of infringements of the rules governing, say, possession of personal belongings, in order to preserve a link with the wider world of freedom and discretion with which they are associated. Under similar conditions, in prisons, schools, and factories, the individual resorts to a variety of responses ranging from simple 'make-do's' to elaborate and ingenious techniques for 'working the system', acquiring 'stashes', or 'messages', or anything that enables an individual to 'make out' under adverse conditions, short of breaking out or breaking down.

Goffman concludes his observations on the variety of individual responses to organizational control with the recommendation that for sociological purposes the self is best defined as a 'stance-taking entity, a something that takes up a position somewhere between identification with an organization and opposition to it'.[1] The sociological self survives as the seat of an expressed distance which allows for the possibilities of transformation and detachment and thus opens up the permanent possibility of organizational sabotage, daydream, and ecstasy. Nevertheless, I suggest that Goffman's account of role distance, upon which Berger builds so much, is ultimately a bitter testimonial to Goffman's relentless undermining of the 'touching tendency to keep a part of the world safe from sociology'.[2]

In Berger the gloomy scenarios of Goffmanic-Goffdepression are transformed into blithe fantasias of the sociological spirit. Berger says:

It is as relief from social determinism that we would explain the sympathy that we frequently feel for the swindler, the impostor or the charlatan (as long, at any rate, as it is not ourselves who are being swindled). These figures symbolize a social Machiavellianism that understands society thoroughly and then

---

[1] *Asylums*, p. 320.
[2] Erving Goffman, *Encounters*, Two Studies in the Sociology of Interaction, Indianapolis, The Bobs-Merrill Company Inc., 1961, p. 152.

untrammeled by illusions, finds a way of manipulating society for its own ends.[1]

There is more to Berger's qualification of social Machiavellianism than a mere disclaimer of the bad luck involved in becoming even an occasional victim of its practice. For, at bottom, whatever we may say, we cannot live a lie or a falsehood without corroding and dividing the self. Nor can we endure without the feeling of being 'at one' with ourselves and others, at least in the world of primary relations, as Berger himself points out in an extremely valuable comment on Goffman's model of social interaction.[2] For if the need to establish a distance between ourselves and every social situation or social role in which we find ourselves ever becomes a universal need then it is difficult to see how we could ever establish the grounds of self-identity. In fact it is just this awful experience which the schizophrenic reports. His sense of evil in himself and in others overwhelms his sense of personal identity.[3]

Despite his better knowledge of the naïve intersubjectivity which is the ground of our trust in social reality,[4] Berger proposes to seek authenticity in treating what others take to be an essential identity as a convenient disguise. 'In other words, "ecstasy" transforms one's awareness of society in such a way that givenness becomes possibility.'[5]

'The sense of possibility' advocated by Berger reminds one of the same quality in Musil's *Man without Qualities*. The man without qualities or essences lives in a world of 'qualities without man' in which people are unable to connect with their own feelings and identity. The possibilitarian is potentially a crackbrain, a dreamer, a fool, and a god who risks the possibilities of reality in the reality of possibility. One day he receives a slap in the face or someone goes off with his mistress.

1 Peter L. Berger, *Invitation to Sociology*, p. 134.

2 Peter L. Berger and Thomas Luckmann, *The Social Construction of Reality*, New York, Doubleday and Co., Inc., 1967, pp. 205–206, note 15.

3 Ronald D. Laing, *The Divided Self*, A Study of Sanity and Madness, Chicago, Quadrangle Books, 1960.

4 Alfred Schutz, 'The Social World and the Theory of Social Action', in *Collected Papers*, edited and introduced by Arvid Brodersen, The Hague, Martinus Nijhoff, 1964, vol. II, p. 14, cf. Harold Garfinkel, 'Common Sense Knowledge of Social Structures: the documentary method of interpretation in lay and professional fact finding', *Studies in Ethnomethodology*, New Jersey, Prentice Hall, 1967.

5 Peter L. Berger, *Invitation to Sociology*, p. 136.

And since the possession of qualities presupposes that one takes a certain pleasure in their reality, all this gives us a glimpse of how it may all of a sudden happen to someone who cannot summon up any sense of reality—even in relation to himself— that one day he appears to himself as a man without qualities.[1]

In both Goffman and Berger the situational and orientational structures of the self are preserved in a precarious internal dialectic of revolt and detachment, in alternating fits of depression, 'aways'[2] and ecstasy. Goffman's inmates undermine their world and stratify themselves and their stigmata in a parody of legitimate statuses, turning against one another, the blind leading the blind into a phantom solidarity with the young, white, handsome, and hetero-sexual world of healthy affluence.[3] Berger's sociological ecstatics, the lost tribe of marginals, ethnics, and intellectuals, scorn their folkways, are too cosmopolitan for familiar scenes of birth, marriage, and death to move them, and their alienated presence is the only way they have of showing they have left 'home' and 'made it', as gangsters, 'career' sociologists, or existentialists.

Just as the history of American crime is in many ways the history of American society as a business society, so there is a plausible analogy between the institutions of the prison and mental hospital as 'total' institutions and the bureaucratic institutions of legitimate social action. Indeed, the two are not worlds apart if only because the sick role is society's last chance of seducing the deviant into recommitting himself to social gatherings, objects, and loyalties.[4] Illness and madness are merely plays within a play.

Nowadays the social drama of self-identity is acted out as a play put on by the inmates of a prison which no longer has any walls because it can count upon us to imprison ourselves for crimes in which we are the victim and the criminal, police, judge, and exe-

[1] Robert Musil, *The Man Without Qualities*, translated from the German and with a foreword by Eithne Wilkins and Ernest Kaiser, New York, Coward-McCann, Inc., 1953, vol. I, pp. 4 and 39.

[2] Erving Goffman, *Behavior in Public Places:* Notes on the Organization of Social Gatherings, New York, The Free Press, 1963, pp. 69–75.

[3] Erving Goffman, *Stigma*, Notes on the Management of Spoiled Identity, New Jersey, Prentice-Hall, Inc., 1963, pp. 122 and 128.

[4] Philip E. Slater, 'On Social Regression', *American Sociological Review*, vol. 28, 3 (June 1963), pp. 339–364.

cutioner. And if there is any light in this prison, it is only the illusion of life outside as it is seen from inside the walls.

In the obsessive imagery of society as a prison or puppet theatre we have a symbolization of the contemporary sociological answer to the existential question of the bases of freedom and order. The modern individual faces the challenge of self-identity in the organizational dramas of prisons, mental hospitals, factories, wars, concentration camps, and purges.

In all these horrors the perfect victim is man himself. For with the death of God man alone can expiate the threat to the insecurity of modern progress which has strangely no past and no future and is thus obsessed with conformity.

3: Public and Private Space

Political imagination is shackled by the corporate organization of modern society. The traditional antitheses of individual and state, state and society, public and private rights, conflict and order, no longer serve to orient men's private lives toward their political contexts. Modern society is increasingly consensual and apolitical; it generates a comfortable reality which tempts us to identify the rationality of its industrial metabolism with the whole of rationality and thus to disengage ourselves from the critical tasks of reason. The tendency to identify technological rationality with social rationality is the major threat to the survival of the political imagination.[1] It underlies the liberal abdication of politics in favour of the market economy. By contrast, the subordination of technological rationality to social rationality is the programme of a genuine Marxist political economy.

Political economy remains nerveless so long as it rests upon a concept of government which does not question the social distribution of resources between the public and private sectors of the economy. No modern government can retain power which fails to control industrial technology and the power of large corporations to shape the national ecology and psychic economy of individuals. The corporate economy stands between the state and the individual. Its power to determine the life-style of modern society must be recognized as the principal subject of political economy. The critique of the

[1] Herbert Marcuse, *One-Dimensional Man*, Studies in the Ideology of Advanced Industrial Society, Boston, Beacon Press, 1964. For the distinction between technical or 'functional' rationality and 'substantial' rationality see Karl Mannheim, *Man and Society in an Age of Reconstruction*, London, Routledge and Kegan Paul, 1940, pp. 51–60.

forces working to produce what Herbert Marcuse has called one-dimensional society must avoid the elitist fiction that mass society is the cause of our political troubles as well as the liberal illusion that pluralistic countervailing power is the only viable formula for political conduct.[1] At the same time, the basic organizational form of modern industrial society is so closely tied to such a small number of corporate and bureaucratic structures that the ideas of pluralism can hardly be said to exercise a qualitative effect upon the system.

In a specific sense advanced industrial culture is *more* ideological than its predecessor, inasmuch as today the ideology is in the process of production itself. In a provocative form, this proposition reveals the political aspects of the prevailing technological rationality. The productive apparatus and the goods and services which it produces 'sell' or impose the social system as a whole. . . . The products indoctrinate and manipulate; they promote a false consciousness which is immune against its falsehood. And as these beneficial products become available to more and more individuals in more social classes, the indoctrination they carry ceases to be publicity; it becomes a way of life. It is a good way of life—much better than before—and as a good way of life, it militates against qualitative change. Thus emerges a pattern of *one-dimensional thought and behaviour* in which ideas, aspirations, and objectives, that, by their content, transcend the established universe of discourse and action are either repelled or reduced to terms of this universe. They are redefined by the rationality of the given system and of its quantitative extension.[2]

One-dimensional society is characterized by a systematic linkage between the subordination of public space to private space through the agency of the corporate economy and an ideological privatization

1 '*To be socially integrated in America is to accept propaganda, advertising and speedy obsolescence in consumption.* The fact is that those who fit the image of pluralist man in pluralist society also fit the image of mass man in mass society. Any accurate picture of the shape of modern society must accommodate these ambiguities.' Harold L. Wilensky, 'Mass Society and Mass Culture: Interdependence of Dependence?' *American Sociological Review*, vol. 29, 2 (April 1964), p. 196.

2 Herbert Marcuse, *One-Dimensional Man*, pp. 10–11. For an empirical confirmation of the ideological content of the consumer orientation, see Sanford M. Dornbusch and Lauren C. Hickman, 'Other-Directedness in Consumer-Goods Advertising: A Test of Riesman's Historical Typology', *Social Forces*, vol. 38, no. 2, pp. 99–102.

of individual sensibilities which reinforces corporate control over the allocation of social resources and energies. One-dimensional society has its roots in the liberal concept of society as a field in which the private pursuit of economic interests produces public benefits without political intervention. The emergence of a 'social universe', which is, strictly speaking, neither public nor private, is a modern phenomenon that arises from the public significance accorded to the business of making a living and has no counterpart in the ancient world. It is a phenomenon which has forced upon us the hybrid term 'political economy' and with it the challenge to rethink the relation between the public and private domains in modern industrial society.

Public and Private Space

In the Graeco-Roman world the boundary between the public and private realms was clear and men were conscious of the threshold between public and private life. Although the ancient city-state grew at the expense of the family household and kinship group, the boundary between the public and private realms was never erased. Indeed, the definition of the public realm as an area of freedom and equality presupposed the recognition of 'necessity' in the household economy.[1] The needs of maintenance and reproduction defined the social nature of man and the family, and the sexual and social division of labour between man and woman, master and slave.

In the modern period this ancient boundary between public and private realms was dissolved with the emergence of 'society' and the liberal concept of mini-government. A whole new world—the social universe—emerged between public and private life. The public significance of the social universe has its roots in the subjectivization of private property and the subordination of government to a minimal agenda in the social equilibration of individual and public interests. The seventeenth century reduced the political domain to the narrow limits of 'government' in order to exploit the boundless domain of possessive individualism, which Professor C. B. Macpherson has described as the central impediment of modern liberal-democratic ideology.

> Its possessive quality is found in its conception of the individual as essentially the proprietor of his own person or capacities, owing

[1] Aristotle, *Politics*, 1252 a.2.

nothing to society for them. The individual was seen neither as a moral whole, nor as part of a larger social whole, but as an owner of himself. The relation of ownership, having become for more and more men the critically important relation determining their actual freedom and actual prospect of realizing full potentialities, was read back into the nature of the individual. . . . Society becomes a lot of free individuals related to each other as proprietors of their own capacities and of what they have acquired by their exercise. Society consists of relations of exchange between proprietors. Political society becomes a calculated device for the protection of this property and for the maintenance of an orderly relation of exchange.[1]

The liberal practicality shied away from any utopian conception of the public domain and was content with an order that seemed to emerge through non-intervention in the natural processes, or rather in the metabolism, of society. As Hannah Arendt has argued, this extraordinary identification of society with its economy may be traced in part to the liberal devaluation of politics.

What concerns us in this context is the extraordinary difficulty with which we, because of this development, understand the decisive division between the public and private realms, between the sphere of the polis and the sphere of household and family, and, finally, between activities related to a common world and those related to the maintenance of life, a division upon which all ancient political thought rested as self-evident and axiomatic.[2]

All the spaces of the modern world are absorbed into a single economy whose rhythms are linear and mechanical. The architecture of public and commercial institutions, the furnishings of the home, and even the styles in which we clothe our bodies, threaten to destroy the dialectic between the things that are to be shown and the things that are to be hidden. The results vary from the inhuman naked space of the typing-pool to the democratic open spaces of Toronto's

[1] C. B. Macpherson, *The Political Theory of Possessive Individualism: Hobbes to Locke*, Oxford, The Clarendon Press, 1962, p. 3. The liberal concept of 'society' provoked the counterconcept of 'organic society' in Conservative and Marxian thought which have more in common than either has with liberalism. Karl Mannheim, *Essays on Sociology and Social Psychology*, New York, Oxford University Press, 1953, chap. II, 'Conservative Thought'; also chap. 6 below.

[2] *The Human Condition*, Chicago, University of Chicago Press, 1958, p. 28.

new City Hall where the shocking exposure of secretarial knees produced demands for privacy in the design of working areas. Even more desperate is the loss of the values of privacy in the very sanctuary of the home. Le Corbusier has called the modern house 'a machine to live in', a machine that mechanizes living in a mechanical world. In a strange, disordered repetition of ancient symbolism, the modern household is hooked into the centre of the universe through its television navel and suspended by an aerial (*universalis columna quasi sustinens omnia*) between heaven and hell. 'The Kwakiutl believe that a copper pole passes through the three cosmic levels (underworld, earth, sky); the point at which it enters the sky is the "door to the world above". The visible image of this cosmic pillar in the sky is the Milky Way.'[1] Through the picture-frame windows of the modern house the metabolism of family life is projected into the public realm and from there it completes its circuit back into the home through a magical aether populated by waxes, deodorants, soapsuds, and tissues.

In one-dimensional society desire born of necessity is no longer domesticated. Now the whole of society is organized to satisfy domestic passions. And this is an arrangement eminently suited to the ethic of individualistic-familism and the socialization of the members of society into their 'calling' as consumers whose needs are the self-imposed agency of social control. It is this continuity of psychic and socio-economic space which grounds the coherent fantasy of consumer sovereignty at the same time that it fills the air with the noise and filth that are the by-products of the commercial narcosis.[2]

[1] Mircea Eliade, *The Sacred and the Profane*, New York, Harcourt, Brace and Company, 1959, p. 35.

[2] 'To behold, use or perceive any extension of ourselves in technological form is necessarily to embrace it. To listen to radio or to read the printed page is to accept these extensions of ourselves into our personal system and to undergo the "closure" or displacement of perception that follows automatically. It is this continuous embrace of our own technology in daily use that puts us in the Narcissus role of subliminal awareness and numbness in relation to these images of ourselves. By continuously embracing technologies, we relate ourselves to them as servomechanisms. That is why we must, to use them at all, serve these objects, these extensions of ourselves, as gods or minor religions. An Indian is the servo-mechanism of his canoe, as the cowboy of his horse, or the executive of his clock.' Marshall McLuhan, *Understanding Media: The Extensions of Man*, New York, McGraw Hill, 1965, p. 46.

Metabolism and Political Economy

In the period between the decline of the feudal family order and the rise of modern nation-states geared to a fully industrialized economy there emerged a microcosmic version, in the Court circle and the salon of high society, of the tragic alienation of the individual in a universe hidden from God and abandoned to the play of social forces.[1] Whether it is through the identification of the individual with his title at Court in the *ancien régime* or with his occupational status in the modern corporation, the modern individual encounters a bureaucratization of private sensibilities, a wasteland between the boundaries of the heart and the public presentation of the self.[2] The rise of modern society is the history of the decline of feudal community, the growth of the nation state, industrial technology, and political democracy. But it is also the paradox of the affinity of individualism for conformism through the erosion of the communal bases of the family, the guild, the village, and the Church.[3] The emergence of the 'total community' has its origins in the growth of rationalism in economics, politics, and religion. In each of these areas modern individualism receives its impulse from the subjectivization of the bases of the feudal community and a simultaneous assimilation of the individual into the abstract community of market society.

Thus, from the viewpoint of this enlightened political economy which has discovered the *subjective* essence of wealth within the framework of private property, the partisans of the monetary system and the mercantilist system, who consider private property as a *purely objective* being for man, are *fetishists* and *Catholics*. Engels is right, therefore, in calling Adam Smith the *Luther of political economy*. Just as Luther recognized *religion* and *faith* as the essence of the real *world* and for that reason took up a position against Catholic paganism; just as he annulled *external*

[1] Lucien Goldmann, *Le dieu caché: Etude sur la vision tragique dans les pensées et dans le théâtre de Racine*, Paris, Librarie Gallimard, 1955.

[2] Locke shows no awareness of the alienation of man in society, unlike Hobbes, who, nevertheless, has no solution for it. It is Rousseau who first attempts to link the experience of alienation with social criticism.

[3] Robert A. Nisbet, *Community and Power*, New York, Oxford University Press, 1962. Cf. Karl Marx, *Communist Manifesto*, Gateway Editions, 1954, p. 12. Marx's sketch of the breakdown of feudalism is brilliantly developed in Karl Polanyi, *The Great Transformation*, Boston, Beacon Press, 1957.

religiosity while making religiosity the *inner* essence of man; just as he negated the distinction between priest and layman because he transferred the priest into the heart of the layman; so wealth external to man and independent of him (and thus only to be acquired and conserved from outside) is annulled. That is to say, its *external* and *mindless objectivity* is annulled by the fact that private property is incorporated in man himself, and man himself is recognized as its essence. But as a result, man himself is brought into the sphere of private property, just as, with Luther, he is brought into the sphere of religion. Under the guise of recognizing man, political economy, whose principle is labour, carries to its logical conclusion the denial of man. Man himself is no longer in a condition of external tension with the external substance of private property; he has himself become the tension-ridden being of private property. What was previously a pheno-menon of *being external to oneself*, a real external manifestation of man, has now become the act of objectification, of alienation. This political economy seems at first, therefore, to recognize man with his independence, his personal activity, etc. It incor-porates private property in the very essence of man, and it is no longer, therefore, conditioned by the local or national *charac-teristics of private property* regarded as existing outside itself. It manifests a cosmopolitan, universal activity which is destructive of every limit and every bond, and substitutes itself as the *only* policy, the *only* universality, the *only* limit and the *only* bond.[1]

The identification of the metabolism of the household with the national economy, which results in the hybrid concern of 'political economy', is the outcome of the alienation of private property and labour from their anchorages in use-values. In their endlessly repro-ducible forms, as the exchange-values of capital and labour power, private property and labour enter the public realm and subordinate the public realm to the needs of market society. The emancipation of labour is the precondition of the substitution of exchange-values for use-values which leads to the subordination of all fixed forms of life and property to the accumulation and expansion of wealth. In the remarkable passage from the *Economic and Philosophical Manuscripts* quoted above, Marx explains how private property becomes the subjective impulse of industrial activity through its definition as

[1] *Karl Marx: Early Writings*, T. B. Bottomore, trans. and ed., London, C. A. Watts and Company, 1963, pp. 147–148.

labour-power. The Physiocrats identified all wealth with land and cultivation, leaving feudal property intact but shifting the essential definition of land to its economic function and thereby exposing feudal property to the later attacks on ground rent. The objective nature of wealth was also in part shifted to its subjective basis in labour, inasmuch as agriculture was regarded as the source of the productivity of land. Finally, industrial labour emerged as the most general principle of productivity, the factors of production, land, labour, and capital, being nothing else than moments in the dialectic of labour's self-alienation.

Private Opulence and Public Squalor

Marx's expectation that capitalism would collapse because of the conflict between the technological rationalization of its economy and the irrationality of its social and political structure remains unfulfilled. The question is whether the Marxian diagnosis is as irrelevant as the phenomena of welfare and affluent capitalism[1] are taken to suggest. Certainly, the metabolism of the corporate economy absorbs more than ever the public and private energies of modern society. Under the banner of a neo-feudal ideology of corporate responsibility,[2] a new psychic serfdom to brand-loyalties and occupational status immunizes monopoly capitalism from the processes of social and political criticism. It is increasingly difficult to discuss the nature of the good society where everyone is mesmerized by the *goods* society.

In the North American context, there are historical and environmental factors which contribute to the equation of politics and abundance.

The politics of our democracy was a politics of abundance rather than a politics of individualism, a politics of increasing

[1] For a careful appraisal of the relations between welfare capitalism and the affluent society, see T. H. Marshall, *Sociology at the Crossroads*, London, 1963, Part Three, 'Social Welfare', and Richard M. Titmuss, *Essays on the 'Welfare State'*, with a new chapter on 'The Irresponsible Society', London, Allen and Unwin, 1963.

[2] It has been argued that the corporate exercise of political power is in principle continuous with the natural-law tradition of the separation of sacred and profane power and its institutionalization in the countervailing powers of feudal nobility. St Augustine's 'City of God', understood as the theory that in every age there is a moral and philosophical framework which constrains power, has been claimed as the model of corporate politics. Adolf A. Berle, *The Twentieth Century Capitalist Revolution*, London, Macmillan, 1955.

our wealth quickly rather than dividing it precisely, a politics which smiled both on those who valued abundance as a means to safeguard freedom and on those who valued freedom as an aid in securing abundance.[1]

The ideological roots of the affluent society have been traced by John Kenneth Galbraith to the hold upon the liberal mind of certain imperatives which flow from the 'conventional wisdom'. Adam Smith, Ricardo, and Malthus were clear enough that the mass of men were powerless against the class of property owners. But in view of the factors of scarcity, against which any proposal for social redistribution could only mean a relapse into barbarism, it seemed that the mutual interests of the rich and the poor lay in the expansion of industrial activity. However, in the conventional wisdom the imperative of production remains just as imperious as it ever was, despite intervening changes in the modern economic environment which have made abundance a technological possibility, if not a sociological certainty.

These—productivity, inequality and insecurity—were the ancient preoccupations of economies. They were never more its preoccupations than in the nineteen thirties as the subject stood in a great valley facing, all unknowingly, a mountainous rise in well-being. We have now had that mountainous rise. In a very large measure the older preoccupations remain.[2]

The paradox of the affluent society is that it has exhausted the liberal imagination in a 'solution' of the problems of inequality and insecurity through a mindless expansion of production.

The instrument of this paradoxical situation is the corporate organization[3] of the economy whose success in controlling its economic

---

[1] David M. Potter, *People of Plenty: Economic Abundance and the American Character*, Chicago, University of Chicago Press, p. 126.

[2] J. K. Galbraith, *The Affluent Society*, Boston, Houghton Mifflin Company, p. 77.

[3] 'By and large, corporations have been able to exert sufficient pressure on governments, and on social institutions generally, to stabilize the field in their favour. *This stabilizing of the environment is the politics of industry.*' J. Porter, *The Vertical Mosaic: An Analysis of Social Class and Power in Canada*, Toronto, University of Toronto Press, 1965, p. 269 (my italics). The weakness of government planning in America has been attributed to the competitive nature of its political institutions which weaken it relative to the more monolithic structure of business. A. Shonfield, *Modern Capitalism: The Changing Balance of Public and Private Power*, New York, 1965, Oxford University Press, p. 353.

environment has won for it political acceptance from its employees and the stabilizing support of state-administered anti-depressants for those moments in which the soulfulness of the corporation threatens to reach a low-point. The power of the corporation to control its environment assumes a variety of forms, ranging from its ability to control price–cost relationships, levels and composition of investment, the nature of research and innovation, the location of industry with its effects upon local communities and, of course, its power to influence governmental intervention, and, last but not least, the power to shape the physical and socio-psychological environment of the consumer public. In each case, these powers of the corporation are of enormous social and political consequence.[1]

In the face of the reality of corporate power, Galbraith's theory of countervailing power is hardly more than a figleaf for corporate respectability and liberal prudishness. It is in any case a desperate gesture in view of Galbraith's own understanding of the corporate practice of integrating its production and sales efforts through the generations of wants. By engineering consumer response, the corporation is able to get an *ex post facto* ratification of its commitment of social resources as determined by the corporate agenda. While paying lip-service to consumer sovereignty in the final allocation of social resources, the corporation can in fact assume the conventional distribution of social resources between the public and private sectors of the economy. This presumption is a political reality inasmuch as the demand for public services presently arises out of the needs of low-income groups who are powerless to compete away social resources from the private uses of higher-income groups. It is only in the context of the unequal distribution of income, which remains as much as ever a defining characteristic of affluent capitalism, that one can properly understand the imperative of production or, rather, of *relative overproduction for the private sector*, which in turn promotes the secondary imperatives of consumption and other-direction. Despite the heralds of the age of high mass consumption, the fact is that monopoly capitalism is a production system continually

1 Carl Kaysen, 'The Corporation: How Much Power? What Scope?' and Norton Long, 'The Corporation, Its Satellites and the Local Community', in Edward S. Mason, ed., *The Corporation in Modern Society*, Cambridge, Mass., Harvard University Press, 1961, pp. 85–105, 202–217.

faced with the problem of deficient consumption structurally related
to the class distribution of income.[1] Because of this conventional
restraint upon the economic space of the capitalist system, it is
necessary to invade the psychic space of workers and consumers through
raising levels of expectation or through deepening levels of credit.

There are, of course, attempts to expand the economic space of the
capitalist system through extensions of the public sector, overseas
operations, and the conquest of outer space. But in no case do these
extensions result in a significant alteration of the flow of social
resources between the public and private sectors. The commanding
position of the corporation in the face of governmental efforts to
redistribute social income is evident from the relative stability of
corporate profits after taxes as a share of national income during the
last forty years.[2] In effect, the government merely uses the corporation to collect its taxes and is therefore dependent upon the corporate
economy's agenda having been substantially realized before it can
undertake its own programme. Indeed, it must be recognized that the
determination of the balance between the public and the private
sectors of capitalist society depends increasingly on the identification
of welfare and warfare. The American war psychosis is an obvious
manifestation of the increasingly militarized production imperatives
of the corporate economy. The significance of the social unbalance
created by military spending is lost when considered simply as a
proportion of total gross national product. From this perspective, the
one-tenth of GNP absorbed in military expenditure seems negligible
and easily enough absorbed in alternative expenditures. However, once
it is realized that military expenditures represent half of total federal

[1] Gabriel Kolko, 'The American "Income Revolution"', in Philip Olson, ed.,
America as a Mass Society, New York, Free Press of Glencoe, 1963, pp. 103–116,
J. Porter, *The Vertical Mosaic*, pp. 125–132, for an evaluation of the validity of the
middle-class and middle-majority in Canada.

[2] Irving B. Kravis, 'Relative Shares in Fact and Theory', *American Economic
Review*, December 1959, p. 931, quoted in Paul A. Baran and Paul M. Sweezy,
Monopoly Capital: An Essay on the American Economic and Social Order, New York,
Monthly Review Press, 1966, p. 148. There is consistent empirical evidence of
long-run tax-shifting by corporations. Two recent studies emphasize the long-run
maintenance of a stable after-tax rate of return on investment despite substantial
increases in corporation income tax, E. M. Lerner and E. S. Hendrikson, 'Federal
Taxes on Corporate Income and the Rate of Return in Manufacturing 1927–1952',
National Tax Journal, vol. IX (September 1965), pp. 193–202; R. E. Slitor, 'The
Enigma of Corporate Tax Incidence', *Public Finance*, vol. XVIII(1963), pp. 328–352.

government expenditures,[1] it is clear that the issue is neither negligible nor easily corrigible. It is not negligible because it represents the impoverished conception of the public domain in capitalist society. Nor is it easily corrigible, since to find alternative paths of governmental spending involves a reconsideration of the balance between the public and private sectors which would expose the poverty of the liberal ideology.

The institution of advertising can now be understood as the essential means of expanding the economic space of capitalism in a manner compatible with the liberal ideology. What Galbraith calls the 'dependence effect' is in reality a political option which, if unrelated to the class structure of capitalist society and its effects upon the distribution of social resources between public and private uses, appears as the myth of an evil genius.

> Were it so that a man on arising each morning was assailed by demons which instilled in him a passion sometimes for silk shirts, sometimes for kitchenware, sometimes for chamber pots and sometimes for orange squash, there would be every reason to applaud the effort to find the goods, however odd, that quenched the flame. But should it be that his passion was the result of his first having cultivated demons, and should it also be that his effort to allay it stirred the demons to even greater and greater effort, there would be question as to how rational was his solution. Unless restrained by conventional attitudes, he might wonder if the solution lay with more goods or fewer demons.
>
> So it is that if production creates the wants it seeks to satisfy, or if the wants emerge *pari passu* with the production, then the urgency of the wants can no longer be used to defend the urgency of the production. Production only fills a void that it has itself created.[2]

It is not the dependence effect as such which is responsible for the irrationality of consumer behaviour. For in every society wants are largely cultural acquisitions. The real problem is the nature of the social order which determines the content and pattern of wants. A society which fails to maintain the necessary complementarities between private and public goods and services drives itself even deeper

[1] In a record US budget of $135 billion for the fiscal year 1967 $72·3 billion were allocated to military expenditure, a sum exceeded only by the figure of $81·3 billion spent in 1945. *Globe and Mail*, Toronto, 25 January 1967, p. 1.

[2] J. K. Galbraith, *The Affluent Society*, p. 153.

into the accumulation of private amenities in order to compensate for the public squalor which this very process leaves in its wake.

The automobile becomes the true symbol of the North American flight into privacy.[1] It has hollowed the cities and drained the countryside, melting each into the atomized living-space of suburbia; it is the instrument of urban congestion and rural uglification. At the same time, the automobile is perfectly geared to the values of technical rationality, private ownership, individual mobility, sex equality, and social rivalry—pre-eminently the values of the liberal ideology and the stock-in-trade of the corporate economy. The automobile is eminently the equilibrator of the tensions in corporate culture: it is a family headache and a family joy, an air-pollutant indispensable for trips into the fresh air of the countryside, an escape mechanism from all the problems with which it is structurally integrated.

The role of the automobile in modern society makes it evident that we can no longer consider machines from the purely technological standpoint of the mastery of nature. We must take into account the interaction between machinery and the social relations between men not only in the context of machine production but in the wider context in which machinery patterns our style and ecology of life. Short of such an understanding, we find ourselves hallucinating the conquest of distance while all the time the road which opens up before us is the distance between a humane living-space and the little boxes which house our automobiles.

[1] Housing would illustrate the problems of over-privatization and the impoverishment of the public sector just as well as the automobile to which it must be related. The housing situation is especially illustrative of the tendency to privatize even explicitly public functions. 'Public money totalling hundreds of millions of dollars has been advanced as National Housing Act loans for middle- and upper-middle-income families, to help them buy houses. But few lower-middle-income families and no poor families can get these loans . . . many persons in Europe look on the Canadian system as socialism for the rich, private enterprise for the poor. The North American welfare approach to public housing singles out low-income tenants as conspicuous recipients of public bounty. It hives them off in ghettos for the poor. The European approach, on the other hand, treats housing as a public utility. It contains a big public sector, in which non-profit housing is provided to persons in a broad income range—not merely the poor. It also contains a large area in which private enterprise operates freely and profitably.' G. E. Mortimer, 'Canada's Leaky Housing Program', *Globe and Mail*, Toronto, 5 January 1967, Women's Section, p. 1.

But any criticism of the automobile is likely to be dismissed as quixoticism. For the power to respond to such criticism has been sapped through the cultivation of psychic identification with the automobile as an extension of individual personality. Even where slightly less elongated extensions have been preferred by four-wheeled man, the apparent rationality of that choice actually only deepens the commitment to private as opposed to public transportation alternatives. The result is a chain-process in the privatization of other social resources integrated with the automobile culture at a time when more than ever we need to break that circuit.

The difficulty of intervention on behalf of the public domain is nowhere better seen than in the light of the potential hue and cry against interference with the individual's freedom to buy, own, and drive, wherever and whenever, that capsule which seals him off from physical and social reality while making him completely dependent upon it. Likewise, the course of public intervention in regard to the automobile is indicative of the impoverished conception of government in liberal society. The result so far is the confusion of the growth of public space with the extension of public highways which breeds more automobiles and accelerates the dislocation of urban spaces in favour of suburban locations. Commuting by means of private transportation becomes the only link between living spaces and working spaces. Finally, the rationale of this living arrangement is given a coherent projection through television advertisements in which the enjoyment of suburban values can be 'seen' in the happy use of the automobile to take children to school, mother to the stores, father to work, and the dog to the veterinarian, without anyone even wondering how everything got so far away.

Alienation and the Sublimation of Politics
There is a trend in industrial society towards the interpretation of freedom and equality in terms of consumer behaviour rather than as political action about the nature and conditions of production and consumption. 'Equality for the working-classes, like freedom for the middle-classes, is a worrisome, partially rejected, by-product of the demand for more specific measures.'[1] In the context of corporate capitalism, the rhetoric of freedom and equality no longer swells into

1 Robert E. Lane, *Political Ideology: Why the American Common Man Believes What He Does*, New York, Free Press of Glencoe, 1962, p. 60.

a coherent political ideology as it once did as a strategy of bourgeois and proletarian emancipation. Just as the terrible freedom of market society has not always been tolerable to the middle class without escapes, so the working class response to market society has varied from class struggle to the becalmed acceptance of inequality softened by improvements to the social basement. This ambivalence in the response to the symbolism of freedom, equality, and reason must be understood in terms of the changing social contexts from which these nations derive their meaning and significance. Robert A. Nisbet has commented upon the changing contexts of individuality.[1] He observes that when we speak of 'the individual' we are dealing with an ideal type or moral abstraction whose symbolic currency depends upon the existence of an institutional context which is favourable to its assimilation in everyday life. The liberal image of man, its possessive individualism, is the result of the imputation of the properties of market society to the interior life of the individual. The liberal theory of society and the individual was plausible just so long as the historical situation which liberalism presupposed effectively linked its vocabulary of motives with typical contexts of action.[2] However, once the evolution of market society moves in the direction of corporate society, the vocabulary of liberalism merely evokes lost contexts, arousing a nostalgia haunted by the loss of meaning.

The loss of a meaningful, social or public context for the ideals of individualism, freedom, and equality is reflected in the alienated and confused symbolism of David Riesman's *Lonely Crowd* or Paul Goodman's *Growing Up Absurd*. Each of these works confronts us with the paradox that society may be free without individuals being free. The liberal identity of individual and social interests, or, rather, the liberal perception of the challenge and opportunity offered to the individual by society, has withered away into a conviction of the absurdity of society and the idiocy of privatization which is its consequence. For want of a genuine public domain, in which the

[1] *Community and Power*, chap. 10, 'The Contexts of Individuality'. Compare C. B. Macpherson's discussion of 'social assumptions', *The Political Theory of Possessive Individualism*, chaps. 1, 2, 3, 6.

[2] C. Wright Mills, 'Situated Actions and Vocabularies of Motive', in *Power, Politics and People: The Collected Essays of C. Wright Mills*, I. L. Horowitz, ed., New York, Ballantine Books, 1963, pp. 439–452.

political and social activities of individuals can achieve a focus and historical perspective, men abandon politics for the civic affairs of suburbia or the 'bread and butter' questions of unionism. By shifting awareness toward improvements in consumption styles, these tactics deflect attention from the social imbalance which results from the pursuit of intra-class benefits that leave whole sectors of the population outside of their calculus. This tactic is further strengthened by the ideological acceptance of social improvement through the escalation effect of an expanding economy upon all classes rather than through any radical redistribution of class income or the extension of chances of individual mobility between classes.

As individual awareness is increasingly shifted toward a concern with consumption, economic knowledge is reduced to a concern with prices in abstraction from the corporate agenda which determines prices. The result is a loss of any coherent ideological awareness of the political and economic contexts of individual action. However, this does not represent an end of ideology. It is simply the nature of the dominant ideology of individualism shaped by the context of corporate capitalism. In order to break the tendency to monetize all individual experience, and in order to shift individual time perspectives away from short-term consumer expectations, it is necessary to institutionalize more universal goals of collective and long-term value. Such a requirement falls outside the pattern of instant satisfactions projected by the consumer orientation. The latter substitutes the thin continuity of progress for the solid accumulation of social history. The result is the paradox upon which Robert E. Lane has commented. 'Is it curious', he asks, 'that a nation that has so emphasized progress should have no sense of the future? I do not think so,' he replies, for 'progress is a rather thin and emotionally unsatisfactory continuity. It is the continuity of differences, the regularity of a rate of change, almost a rate of estrangement.'[1] Any concern with social balance, institutional poverty, and waste, or the interaction between politics, economics, and culture presupposes a collective and historical framework; but this is foreign to the liberal ideology of individual agency and its moralistic acceptance of inequality and failure within a natural order of social competition and private success.

In a society where individual interests are so privatized that people

[1] *Political Ideology*, p. 290.

fear and denigrate public activities, common effort is likely to be
viewed only as a substitute for private effort. Moreover, any comparison between public and private enterprise will be moralized in
favour of the fruits of individual effort owing to the very real
struggle involved in the acquisition of private pools, homes, and
education. The loss of community functions resulting from the
privatization of social resources makes individual accumulation
appear all the more 'rational'. In reality, the individual is driven
toward this pattern of privatization not from genuine choice but
because he is deprived of alternatives whose systematic provision
would require a public sector powerful enough to compete with the
private economy. The provision of alternatives to the patterns of
production and consumption in the corporate economy never gets
beyond the platitudes of 'variety' and consumer sovereignty which
are virtually meaningless once attention is diverted from increasing
the size of the goods basket to questions about the quality of a single
item in it, such as bread.[1] The 'efficiency' of private enterprise must
be discounted by the loss of social energy involved in trying to choose
a reasonable (unmagical, unwrapped, uncut) loaf of bread, and reaches
an absurdly low point once the individual retreats to 'home-baking',
or, indeed, any kind of hobby which is a *substitute* for satisfaction in
the private economy. The rise of para-social, political, and economic
activities is an indication of individual withdrawal from 'society'. It
is the expression of an abstracted individualism that is the ideological
alternative to political action on behalf of a world that men can have
in common. This loss of a common world separates society into
a corporate hierarchy and a multitude of individuals who are turned
in upon themselves in the competition to maintain occupational
status and at the same time other-directed in their attempt to
rationalize their loss of community in the pursuit of the good life—
family-style. Where there is no common world between working life
and private life the individual's public life is reduced to shopping
expeditions, church attendance, and movie-going, all homogenized

---

[1] 'I say we make the foulest bread in all the world. We pass it off like fake
diamonds. We advertise it and sterilize it and protect it from all the germs of life.
We not only have failed God, tricked Nature, debased Man, but we have cheated
the birds of the air with our corrupt staff of life.' Henry Miller, 'The Staff of
Life,' in *The Intimate Henry Miller*, with an introduction by Lawrence Clark Powell,
New York, Signet Books, 1959, pp. 73–74.

to suit family-tastes, which are, of course, presensitized to the appeal of the 'goods life'.

It is in keeping with the liberal ideology of individualistic familism that tensions are personalized and at best call for individual therapy. Any attempt to relate private troubles to institutional contexts, which would suggest public or political action, is regarded as projection, the evasion of difficulties best tackled within the four walls of the home, if not in one particular room. The result is that men lack bridges between their private lives and the indifference of the publics that surround them.

Nowadays men often feel that their private lives are a series of traps. They sense that within their everyday worlds, they cannot overcome their troubles, and in this feeling they are often quite correct. What ordinary men are directly aware of and what they try to do are bounded by the private orbits in which they live; their visions and their powers are limited to the closeup scenes of job, family, neighbourhood; in other milieux, they move vicariously and remain spectators. And the more aware they become, however vaguely, of ambitions and of threats which transcend their immediate locales, the more trapped they seem to feel.[1]

It is the task of the political and sociological imagination to conceive men's private troubles in the contexts of public concern and to furnish bridging concepts which will enable individuals to translate their private uneasiness into public speech and political action. It must undertake to shift the contexts of freedom, equality, and reason away from the private sector and out of the household into a public domain which will constitute a genuine common world. And this is a task which must be articulated in a conception of government which is bold enough to seek understanding and responsible control over the human and social values generated but largely dissipated in the corporate economy which enforces the privatization of men's lives. Such a positive conception of government would help to create a public domain in which men share common assumptions about their moral and physical environment and exercise them in a concern for truth of speech and beauty of form in public places—places cleared of their present monuments to financial cunning and the fear of the future that wastes private lives.

[1] C. Wright Mills, *The Sociological Imagination*, New York, Grove Press, 1961, p. 3.

PART TWO

On Language and the Body Politic

The corporate agenda is realized through the rational organization of its mode of production and its social relations. However, the 'rationality' of modern organization is indifferent to the nature of human values and is thus able to pursue destruction as easily as production. The paradox of the corporate agenda is that it produces poverty in the midst of plenty and war in the midst of peace. The organization of the paradoxes of war and poverty distorts knowledge and language into the forms of pseudo-rationality and objectivity. In these forms the cultural alienation produced by the corporate agenda compounds the alienation of its poor. At the present time, the legitimacy of corporate rationality is subject to counter-cultural attack. I have tried in the following essays to express the symbiosis between corporate rationality and its violence. In a positive way, I have argued for the re-invention of the language of commonsense knowledge and values contained in the medium of the body politic.

4: Political Delinquency and the Iron Mountain Boys

The experience of modern societies has altered our perception of violence. This, however, is not simply a question of finding fresh formulas for the levels of destructive power contained in modern armoury and warfare. At 8.15 on the morning of 6 August 1945, America entered history as a stone age society swinging an atomic bomb. The bomb dropped on Hiroshima had more power than twenty thousand tons of TNT, if there is any meaningful unit of the destructiveness of TNT that can be carried through such multiplication. The heat from the explosion was sufficient to print the shadows of men and buildings into the stone around them.

Modern social science literature bulges with studies of rates of mortality, disease, unemployment, mental illness, crime in America and elsewhere. The old style literature of this sort is cast in a model of prediction and control. What science it contains withers for lack of an adequate political framework to make any sense of the implications of its findings. But there is also a new style of social science literature in which the old assumptions of humanism and political democracy as the will to turn knowledge to welfare are totally lacking. This new literature, which makes use of the game metaphor, treats alike war-games and peace-games in a strange third world beyond the conventional borders of fact and value. The *Report from Iron Mountain*[1] adopts what is called a 'military contingency' model (p. 12) for its study of the possibility and, note, the desirability of

[1] *Report from Iron Mountain on the Possibility and Desirability of Peace*, with introductory material by Leonard C. Lewin, New York, Dell Publishing Company, 1967.

peace. The government-sponsored group conducting the inquiry into the conditions of peace resolutely separated themselves from any wishful thinking regarding either the likelihood or the desirability of achieving peace as a goal for American society.

The *Report from Iron Mountain* is remarkable for the way in which it steals all ideological thunder, blending it into the single value of the *stability of American society as a war machine*. We are to contemplate this goal, leaving aside for the moment the cost in human lives among those whom America chooses to turn upon and forgetting the costs in alternatives to war whether in America or abroad. Section Two of the *Report* considers the feasibility of a reconversion of the American war effort (presently one-third of the total Federal budget) to non-military forms of production. It is immediately obvious that military production is not simply a residual element in the American economy. It is intricately integrated with the various levels of specialization in the production process, as well as with occupational and geographical inflexibilities which defeat any notion of marginal and progressive reconversion. The *Report* rejects out of hand any argument that the problems of the national economy can be solved in terms of analogies drawn from local programmes and subsidiary re-organizations (p. 19). It rejects with hardly less ceremony the arguments of liberal economists that a combination of fiscal tools and the expansion of consumer needs even in the hallowed section of public health, education, and welfare could feed the vacuum left by the removal of the war-machine. The argument against the liberals is a simple one, just as it is the utter abnegation of any liberal conception of the nature of social and economic behaviour. Fiscal controls basically reflect the economy and do not motivate it. Of themselves they are powerless to transform a billion dollars' worth of missile production per year into their equivalent production of domestic and public sector consumption. Such proposals are empty liberal talk without consideration of the political acceptability and political implementation of such a conversion of the American economic and social order.

The major weakness in all 'disarmament scenarios', according to the *Report*, is their basic misconception of the social nature of war. War is not a consequence of innate aggression, nor of the existence of armaments. On the contrary, men are aggressive and armaments are stockpiled because 'war itself is the basic social system, within

which other secondary modes of social organization conflict or con-
spire' (p. 29). This basic postulate of social structure is proven by
the historical record which shows that most societies in history as
well as in today's world have been and still are warring societies.

Once this is correctly understood, the true magnitude of
the problems entailed in a transition to peace—itself a social
system, but without precedent except in a few simple pre-
industrial societies—becomes apparent. At the same time, some
of the puzzling superficial contradictions of modern societies
can then be readily rationalized. The 'unnecessary' size and
power of the world war industry; the pre-eminence of the
military establishment in every society, whether open or concealed; the exemption of military or paramilitary institutions
from the accepted social and legal standards of behaviour required elsewhere in the society; the successful operation of the
armed forces and the armaments producers entirely outside the
framework of each nation's economic ground rules: these and
other ambiguities closely associated with the relationship of war
to society are easily clarified, once the priority of war-making
potential as the principal structuring force in society is accepted.
Economic systems, political philosophies, and *corpora jures* serve
and extend the war system, not *vice versa*.

It must be emphasized that the precedence of a society's war-
making potential over its other characteristics is not the result
of the 'threat' presumed to exist at any one time from other
societies. This is the reverse of the basic situation; 'threats'
against the 'national interest' are usually created or accelerated
to meet the changing needs of the war system. Only in com-
paratively recent times has it been considered politically expe-
dient to euphemize war budgets as 'defense' requirements. The
necessity for governments to distinguish between 'aggression'
(bad) and 'defense' (good) has been a by-product of rising
literacy and rapid communication. The distinction is tactical
only, a concession to the growing inadequacy of ancient war-
organizing political rationales.

Wars are not 'caused' by international conflicts of interest.
Proper logical sequence would make it more often accurate to
say that war-making societies require—and thus bring about—
such conflicts. The capacity of a nation to make war expresses
the greatest social power it can exercise; war-making, active or
contemplated, is a matter of life and death on the greatest scale

subject to social control. It should therefore hardly be surprising that the military institutions in each society claim its highest priorities.

We find further that most of the confusion surrounding the myth that war-making is a tool of state policy stems from a general misapprehension of the functions of war. In general, these are conceived as: to defend a nation from military attack by another, or to deter such an attack; to defend or advance a 'national interest'—economic, political, ideological; to maintain or increase a nation's military power for its own sake. These are the visible, or ostensible, functions of war. If there were not others, the importance of the war establishment in each society might in fact decline to the subordinate level it is believed to occupy. And the elimination of war would indeed be the procedural matter that the disarmament scenarios suggest.[1]

War, then, is not something which disturbs the peace of the world nearly as much as the prospect of dislocating the stability of the American industrial order. It is a commonplace that the American economy is the richest in the world, understood in the sense it has the greatest capacity of any industrial order to produce an economic surplus. The American economic order has by definition the world's greatest inventory problem. It therefore has the world's largest waste production in which military production of all kinds is the major component. We should not gloss over the ways in which war production leads to advances in medicine, transportation, as well as a variety of improvements to materials and fabrics. The ironies of war, however, are minor themes compared to the logic of war as the foundation of social organization. A society only has an identity in so far as it can defend its claims to existence. Its claim to existence can be defended by inventing a threat to its existence, provided the society substantiates the existence of the enemy in its own preparations for war, which in turn lend reality to the enemy. The nature of military technology is superbly remote and distant in its power to reach and sustain an equally remote and abstract enemy. Meanwhile the consequences for personal and socio-economic organization are positively galvanizing for the war system, quite independently of individual instincts for aggression or the recruitment of the dregs of society. Indeed, the historical record

[1] *Report from Iron Mountain on the Possibility and Desirability of Peace*, pp. 29–31.

may be appealed to in order to show the dangers of internal collapse from want of an outside threat to the social order.

> The existence of an accepted external menace, then, is essential to social cohesiveness as well as to the acceptance of political authority. The menace must be believable, it must be of a magnitude consistent with the complexity of the society threatened, and it must appear, at least, to affect the entire society (p. 47).

Having rejected any socio-economic alternative to war, the *Report from Iron Mountain* considers only the question of the credibility of war surrogates. It toys with the idea of space programmes on the order of an 'invasion from Mars', but rejects these in the light of the failures of 'flying saucers' to capture the popular imagination. I suppose now the non-event of Apollo I, despite the attempts of communicators to dramatize the possibility of a Russian collision or spying, would also deter the Iron Mountain people. Only the failures of the space programme seem to arouse human interest, which is curious when one recalls the attempts of clergymen and poets, not to mention would-be youth counsellors, who tried to sell the turned-off generation with the success, hard-work, and team-spirit behind the space-shots. The truth is that the space-programme, like any ride in an elevator, hardly stirs the imagination. The *Report* prefers to avoid the sterility of the future in favour of the nightmares of the primitive history of social control. In passing there is a consideration of environmental pollution as a political substitute for war, though it fails to pass the credibility test.

> It may be, for instance, that gross pollution of the environment can eventually replace the possibility of mass destruction by nuclear weapons as the principal apparent threat to the survival of the species. Poisoning of the air, and of the principal sources of food and water supply, is already well advanced and at first glance would seem promising in this respect; it constitutes a threat that can be dealt with only through social organization and political power. But from present indications it will be a generation to a generation and a half before environmental pollution, however severe, will be sufficiently menacing, on a global scale, to offer a possible basis for a solution.
>
> It is true that the rate of pollution could be increased selectively for this purpose; in fact, the mere modifying of existing

programmes for the deterrence of pollution could speed up the process enough to make the threat credible much sooner. But the pollution problem has been so widely publicized in recent years that it seems highly improbable that a programme of deliberate environmental poisoning could be implemented in a politically acceptable manner.[1]

The basic need to guarantee the social stability of the American economic order leads the *Report* to conclude that serious thought should be given to 'the reintroduction, in some form consistent with modern technology and political processes, of slavery' (p. 20). In addition, a moral equivalent to war, which would also provide circuses for the unemployed and alienated, might be found in the development of 'blood games', for example, the ritual institution of a manhunt 'for purposes of "social purification", "state security", or other rationale both acceptable and credible to postwar societies' (p. 71). Enter pigs, students, Guardsmen, and hard hats.

All this may sound fantastic. That is not the mood of the *Report from Iron Mountain*. Its authors consider the outcome of peace unlikely but dangerous enough to merit study. With all the more reason they recommend the proper study of war which, merely for having served us so well to date, cannot be presumed to do so in future without self-conscious cultivation. The *Report* is in many ways a paradigm of the modern literature on violence. It is a recipe for the production of domestic and international violence—the blueprint for numerous other scenarios of collective psychosis, bloodletting, ecological destruction, and faceless cynicism.

For the Iron Mountain Boys violence is sexy, though this is not immediately obvious in a society which is more horrified by naked bodies making love than by bodies strewn across the highway in automobile accidents or maimed in war. Indeed, many parents would rather see their children in uniform than in long hair or nothing at all. In conventional society, the body appears only in the postures of violence, rape, competitive sport, and the rituals of hygiene. In these scenes the body is the medium of white politics, class, and racialism. It is the theatre of repressive individualism. Today, the human body is the basic political organization of our times. It suffers mobilization for foreign wars, exploitation, starvation, and asphyxiation in the cities. It is the victim of racial violence and genocide. Modern living

[1] *Report from Iron Mountain on the Possibility and Desirabilities of Peace*, pp. 66–67.

becomes a way of death striking political fear into the very genetic roots of humanity. This is the political root of the generation gap.

We owe to Freud a remarkable insight into the nature of *politics as juvenile delinquency*, although the phrase belongs to Norman O. Brown.

> Politics made out of delinquency. All brothers are brothers in crime: all equal as sinners. 'To expand the population, Romulus followed the model of other founders of cities; he opened an asylum for fugitives. The mob that came in was the first step to the city's future greatness.' 'The remission of sins which makes us citizens of the Heavenly City was faintly adumbrated when Romulus gathered the first citizens of his city by providing a sanctuary and immunity for a multitude of criminals.' The Heavenly City is also only an asylum for fugitives. Or as social contract thinkers see it, the social contract establishes corporate virtue as an asylum for individual sin, making an immoral society out of immoral men; men whose national inclination according to Hobbes and Freud, is murder. The social contract establishes the general will to counter the will of each —that general will which Freud called the super-ego. The super-ego is supra-individual; even as the crime, so also conscience is collective.[1]

What we must understand in order to renew or rejuvenate the body politic is the affinity between the politics of repressive individualism and the structure of possessive individualism,[2] otherwise known as the Weberian thesis of the affinity between the Protestant ethic and the spirit of capitalism. The development between Hobbes and Freud represents the deepening of the psychological basis of the containment of violence in the liberal social order. The abstract doctrines of liberty, property, and equality are the weapons with which the sons of the revolution destroyed the patriarchal and monarchical authority of seventeenth-century England and eighteenth-century France. The attack on monarchy was consciously an attack upon the patriarchal family and its property system, as is clear in Locke's attack upon Filmer's *Patriarcha* in his *First Treatise of Civil Government*, or in Burke's great classic of English political language,

[1] Norman O. Brown, *Love's Body*, New York, Vintage Books, 1966, pp. 15–16.
[2] C. B. Macpherson, *The Political Theory of Possessive Individualism*, Hobbes and Locke, Oxford at The Clarendon Press, 1962.

his *Reflections on the French Revolution*. It is for this reason that communism is the ultimate programme of delinquency, as we see from its emergence in the Levellers' and Diggers' arguments during the Putney Debates.[1] But the liberation of the sons only leaves them free to rape and dominate mother earth under the pain of bodily labour, which satisfies the guilt of political and theological revolution. The revolt of the sons against their own oral/anal dependency upon the patriarchal genital bond releases a vast escalation of the excremental and metabolic processes of capitalist society: the project of self-made man.

What the psychoanalytic paradox is asserting is that 'things' which are possessed and accumulated, the property and the universal condensed precipitate of property, money, are in their essential nature excremental. Psychoanalysis must take a position not only as to the origin of the money complex but also as to its ultimate validity. Vulgar psychoanalytical exegesis limits itself to the argument that the category of property originates in infantile manipulation of the excremental product. But the real point is that property remains excremental, and is known to be excremental in our secret heart, the unconscious. Jokes and folklore and poetic metaphor, the wisdom of folly tell the secret truth. The wisdom of folly is the wisdom of childhood. What the child knows consciously, and the adult unconsciously, is that we are nothing but body. However much the repressed sublimating adult may consciously deny it, the fact remains that life is of the body and only life creates values; all values are bodily values. Hence the assimilation of money with excrement does not render money valueless; on the contrary, it is the path whereby extraneous things acquire significance for the human body, and hence value. If money were not excrement, it would be valueless.

But why particularly excrement? Possession, according to psychoanalysis, gratifies bodily Eros concentrated in the anal zone. But the concentration of libido in the anal zone reflects the attachment to the anal zone of the infantile narcissistic project of becoming father of oneself. The project of becoming father of oneself, and thus triumphing over death, can be worked out with things, and at the same time retain bodily meaning, only

---

[1] *The Political Theory of Possesive Individualism*, pp. 157–159. Macpherson qualifies the radicalism of the Levellers by clarifying their sociological presuppositions.

if the things produced by the body at the same time nourish it. Possessions are worthless to the body unless animated by the fantasy that they are excrement which is also aliment. Wealth brings so little happiness, said Freud, because money is not an infantile wish; the infantile wish which sustains the money complex is for a narcissistically self-contained and self-replenishing immortal body. Therefore only if excrement were aliment could the infantile wish sustaining the money complex be gratified.[1]

Marcuse has formulated the basic processes of social control in an attempt to put Freudian instinct theory in the context of capitalist culture. The crux of Marcuse's formula is to bring together Marx's concept of economic surplus with Freud's theory of instinctual suppression. The result is that civilization, culture and freedom, in so far as they presuppose an economic surplus, institutionalize self-domination in the instinctual and psychic being of the individual. In Hegel's master-slave dialectic, the pattern of domination leads through the slave's labour and the world or work to the rise of the proletarian consciousness. Although he labours for another, the slave learns to work with objects whose independence now submits to his production, though not to his free consumption. By the same token, the master's independence of things becomes his dependence upon the slave's cultivation. Thus out of the slave's recognition of the value of life and his fear of death, expressed in the submission to things and daily cares for the sake of life, the dialectic of domination and servitude opens up the cycle culture as the objective mediation of self-expression and the world.[2] The world becomes the field of conscious *praxis* whose goal is freedom and mutual recognition. However, Marcuse argues that corporate capitalism is able to contain the master–slave dialectic through the technique of the neutralization of domination which produces a one-dimensional reality that destroys critical thought by closing the universe of discourse.[3] The language of administration, operationalism, and functionalism

[1] Norman O. Brown, *Life Against Death*, The Psychoanalytical Meaning of History, New York, Vintage Books, 1959, pp. 292–293.

[2] Herbert Marcuse, *Five Lectures*, Psychoanalysis, Politics and Utopia, translations by Jeremy J. Shapiro and Shierry M. Weber, Boston, Beacon Press, 1970.

[3] Herbert Marcuse, *One-Dimensional Man*, Studies in the Theology of Advanced Industrial Society, Boston, Beacon Press, 1964, chaps. 3 and 4.

destroys all critical responses in the happy consciousness of affluent society.

To be sure, Marx held that organization and direction of the productive apparatus by the 'immediate producers' would intro-duce a *qualitative* change in the technical continuity: namely, production toward the satisfaction of freely developing indi-vidual needs. However, to the degree to which the established technical apparatus engulfs the public and private existence in all spheres of society—that is, becomes the medium of control and cohesion in a political universe which incorporates the labor-ing classes—to that degree would the qualitative change involve a change in the *technological structure itself*. And such change would *presuppose* that the laboring classes are alienated from this uni-verse in their very existence, that their consciousness is that of the total impossibility to continue to exist in this universe, so that the need for qualitative change is a matter of life and death. Thus, the negation exists *prior* to the change itself, the notion that the liberating historical forces develop *within* the established society is a cornerstone of Marxian theory.

Now it is precisely this new consciousness, this 'space within', the space for the transcending historical practice, which is being barred by a society in which subjects as well as objects consti-tute instrumentalities in a whole that has its *raison d'être* in the accomplishments of its overpowering productivity. Its supreme promise is an ever-more-comfortable life for an ever-growing number of people who, in a strict sense, cannot imagine a quali-tatively different universe of discourse and action, for the capacity to contain and manipulate subversive imagination and effort is an integral part of the given society. Those whose life is the hell of the Affluent Society are kept in line by a brutality which revives medieval and early modern practices. For the other, less underprivileged people, society takes care of the need for liberation by satisfying the needs which make servitude palat-able and perhaps even noticeable, and it accomplishes this fact in the process of production itself.[1]

As Marcuse sees it, corporate capitalism succeeds in creating a total containment of the contradictory forces within itself. Its macro-madness seen from within appears rational inasmuch as the destruction of wealth produces employment otherwise unavailable

[1] Herbert Marcuse, *One-Dimensional Man*, pp. 23–24.

and unnecessary production can be sold through the creation of equally unnecessary needs. Here we have the vision of social equilibrium so desperately sought after in the *Report from Iron Mountain*. Indeed, what is even more shocking to critical reason is that this irrational economic order is able to appear quite beneficient through a technique of splitting behaviour and fantasy in the packaging of its goods. To consider a trivial example, the girl who is not free to resist the mini-skirt fashion can be sold her sexual or feminine liberation with it in a vicarious fantasy of admiration and conquest which is split off from the everyday mini-scenes in which nothing happens to her or the men around her. This example in turn serves to understand Marcuse's further analysis of the nature of the processes of *repressive desublimation* which characterize the cultural style of domination in the context of monopoly capitalism.

The Pleasure Principle absorbs the Reality Principle; sexuality is liberated (or rather liberalized) in socially constructive forms. This notion implies that there are repressive modes of desublimation, compared with which the sublimated drives and objectives contain more deviation, more freedom, and more refusal to heed the social taboos. It appears that such repressive desublimation is indeed operative in the sexual sphere, and here, as in the desublimation of higher culture, it operates as the by-product of the social controls of technological reality, which extend liberty while intensifying domination.[1]

Through its technique of neutralized domination, monopoly capitalism is able to deepen its penetration into the individual's psychic space in ways that seem perfectly compatible with the liberal sovereignty of the individual. This technique is in turn a socially acceptable way of living out the collapse of genuine individual privacy while extending the economic space of the capitalist system but not altering the class coordinates of the capitalist system.

A dying culture destroys everything it touches.
Language is one of the first things to go.
Nobody really communicates with words anymore.
Words have lost their emotional impact, intimacy, ability to shock and make love.

1 *Ibid.*, p. 72.

C

Language prevents communication.

> CARS LOVE SHELL
> How can I say
> "I love you"
> after hearing:
> "CARS LOVE SHELL"

Does anyone understand what I *mean*?

Nigger control is called "law and order". Stealing is called "capitalism".

A "REVOLUTION" IN TOILET PAPER
A "REVOLUTION" IN COMBATING MOUTH ODOR!

A "REVOLUTIONARY" HOLLYWOOD MOVIE!
Have the capitalists no respect?

But there's one word which Amerika hasn't destroyed.
One word which has maintained its emotional power
and purity.
Amerika cannot destroy it because she dare not use
  it.
It's illegal!
It's the last word left in the English language:

FUCK!!!

One bright winter day in Berkeley, John Thomson crayoned
on a piece of cardboard "FUCK WAR", sat down with it and was
arrested within two minutes. Two more people sat down with
signs saying "FUCK WAR". They were arrested.

The Filthy Speech Movement had been born.[1]

The poet of the body politic is Norman O. Brown. Jerry Rubin
is the playwright of body politics, the creator of revolutionary
street-theatre. Cassius Clay, Eldridge Cleaver, and Frantz Fanon
are the political artists of black soul politics. Between them they
have taught us to understand the deep political structures of sex,
language and the body. They have reduced conventional politics to
biological warfare in order to renew love's body. Brown sweeps
away conventional reality as illusion, mystification, and dream. We

[1] Jerry Rubin, *Do It!*, Scenarios of the Revolution, with an introduction by
Eldridge Cleaver, New York, Simon and Schuster, 1970, pp. 109–110.

re-enact our past, the primal scene, all politics is infantile regression, the overthrow of genital tyranny defeated by identification with the father's penis which is our soul enslaving our body. The head of the state is the erection of the body politic (Pierre and Tricky Dick) sublimated in his official person.

> Erect is the shape of the genitally organized body: the body crucified, the body dead or asleep; the stiff. The shape of the body awake, the shape of the resurrected body, is not vertical but perverse and polymorphous; not a straight line but a circle in which the Sanctuary is in the Circumference, and every Minute Particular is Holy; in which
>
>> Embraces are Comminglings from the Head even
>> to the Feet,
>> And not a pompous High Priest entering by a
>> Secret Place.[1]

The aim of the revolution is revelation, to take words out of the market place, to renew the word, to renew vision, to declare the Pentagon a public urinal.

Norman O. Brown drives radical thought to the limits of cynicism and madness in order to pass through the cave culture of the Protestant ethic and the spirit of capitalism. It is important not to misunderstand Brown's demystification. It is not a substitute for action, as Marcuse has argued.[2] All action is set in a culture and thus the destruction of symbolism is itself an historical and political deed. Marcuse criticizes Brown for not specifying the mediations between sex and politics and thus running the danger of bad surrealist dialectics. The suppression of the real divisions and boundaries between the sexes, between mine and thine, may only result in a nightmare of repression.

The argument between Marcuse and Norman O. Brown is the Left version of the generation gap. Marcuse's civilization of self, person, and property baulks at Brown's communism based upon the theory of libidinal use-value. Meantime, while the ideological Left tortures history to deliver the revolution (and when it comes misses it—in Russia, China, and Cuba—due to the law of uneven develop-

[1] *Love's Body*, p. 137.
[2] Herbert Marcuse, 'Love Mystified: A Critique of Norman O. Brown', *Negations*, chap. VII, with a reply to Herbert Marcuse by Norman O. Brown.

ment) or puzzles over whether the proletariat is any longer a revolutionary agency, Jerry Rubin is in the revolutionary business, casting parts for thousands of middle-class kids, in street scenes that pack them in in Berkeley, Chicago, and Washington. His techniques are exaggeration and the co-option of the police, the Pentagon, the House of Unamerican Activities, NBC, Wallace and colour TV. Rubin has turned the revolution into a youth movement which has survived the failure of the civil rights movement by making pot *the* civil rights issue of America and the real bond between blacks and whites in their struggle against the Pigs and the *status quo*.

Jerry Rubin is a consummate street artist engaged in constructing Apocalyptic scenarios in which the world of business and politics is consumed in its own fires. Rubin builds take-out kits for the revolution, do-it-yourself methodologies of Freudian revolt and revelation. Sample:

> 22: *Money is Shit—Burning Money, Looting and Shoplifting*
> *Can Get You High*
> The Stock Exchange official looks worried. He says to us, "You can't see the Stock Exchange."
> We're aghast. "Why not?" we ask.
> "Because you're hippies and you've come to demonstrate."
> "Hippies?" Abbie shouts, outraged at the very suggestion. "We're Jews and we've come to see the stock market."
>
> > VISION: *The next day's headlines:*
> > NEW YORK STOCK MARKET BARS JEWS.
>
> We've thrown the official a verbal karate punch. He relents.
>
> The stock market comes to a complete standstill at our entrance at the top of the balcony. The thousands of brokers stop playing Monopoly and applaud us. What a crazy sight for them —longhaired hippies staring down at them.
> We throw dollar bills over the ledge. Floating currency fills the air. Like wild animals, the stockbrokers climb all over each other to grab the money.
> *"This is what it's all about, real live money!!! Real dollar bills! People are starving in Biafra!"* we shout.
> We introduce a little reality into their fantasy lives.

*   *   *

While throwing the money we spot the cops coming. The cops grab us and throw us off the ledge and into the elevators. The stockbrokers below loudly boo the pigs.

We find ourselves in front of the stock market at high noon. The strangest creeps you ever saw are walking around us: people with short hair, long ties, business suits and brief cases.
They're so serious.
We start dancing "Ring Around the Rosey" in front of the Stock Exchange.
And then we begin burning the things they worship: dollar bills!
Straight people start yelling: "Don't! Don't do that!"
One man rushes to get a burning $5 bill out of Abbie's hand, but it's too late. The money is *poof!*
A crowd assembles; emotions are high. The police come to break it up. We split into the subway.

Three weeks later *The New York Times* reports: "The New York Stock Exchange last night installed bullet-proof glass panels and a metal grillwork ceiling on its visitors' gallery for what an exchange spokesman said were 'reasons of security'.
"Last August 24 a dozen or so hippies threw dollar bills from the gallery—a display many exchange members do not want to see repeated."[1]

Rubin's method is political theatre in which it is essential for the audience to participate in the staging of their own myths. By participating in the Amerikan myth the yippies succeed in making Amerika strange to itself in ways that the politics of alienation and withdrawal could never do.

"Up against yourselves, motherfuckers"

Rubin gathers the Coca-Cola tribes of Amerika in the cities, in the streets, and in the parks in order to resurrect the body-politic and to expose the obscenity of the American dream in its own naked youth.
Language is the world around us and others to whom we speak. Language transforms the world with the gifts of poetry, myth, and science. It is the coin of our dreams. But language is also our curse, more cruel than sticks and stones hurling 'Nigger', 'Jew', 'Commie', at people we have never known. Language is the instrument of

1 Jerry Rubin, *Do it!*, pp. 117–119.

mystification, stereotypes, and ideologies. Philosophers, it is said, talk a great deal, without saying very much. The complaint in this might be put another way. Philosophers have said a great deal without talking enough, as they once did in the days of the *Symposium*. What I mean by this is that the theory of language and meaning is inseparable from the erotic contexts of talk and togetherness through which we come to make sense. Understood in this way Truth, Beauty, and Goodness are inseparable and are to be looked for in the eyes of those with whom we talk or in the hearts of those who listen to us or read what it is we are trying to say.

Language is our first world, the world of names, of our first steps, the world of infantile pleasure and playfulness which becomes the world of reality as we tie the names of things into the syntactic structures of space and time, fantasy and reality, good and evil within the boundaries of home, play, and the outside world. Language like its own infantile erotic base is polymorphously perverse—playfully metaphorical. Yet, like all other libidinal activities of man, language learns to subordinate itself to the reality-principle, and to become technical, logical, and scientific. Language like culture in general is therefore always a neurotic compromise between the pleasure principle and the reality principle. Consequently cultural revolution must always be the work of poets and artists and can never be trusted solely to Marxists and social scientists.

5: Violence, Language and the Body Politic

The experience of violence tests in us the sense of our own humanity. It may provoke in us the cry of our own anger, rage and sorrow felt for the very first time. In some it will lead to despair and silence. Terror commits its deepest injury when it tempts us to silence. Yet it is not easy to say what we feel in the face of terror for at such times to speak at all is to depend upon the very human motives and situations which terror destroys. Thus terror hollows and empties our language, threatening it with destruction and ultimate silence.

How, then, are we to speak of terror and violence which obliterate the human landscape and wither the look of man? We need to dwell among men to begin to understand how it is we find violence among our other experiences like love or disappointment, joy and anger. We know about violence just as we know about famine and floods, or the coming of the jumbo jet and thalidomide babies. We know that there is violence in the streets in which white and blacks and police and students are involved in our own towns, in Berkeley, Tokyo, Paris and London, even Toronto. What child does not know of Vietnam? What parent does not know of Hiroshima, Auschwitz and Biafra? Our common awareness of violence easily draws distinctions within the forms and modes of violence as it affects our daily practices. We distinguish war and revolutions, political violence and criminal violence. We also distinguish personal violence and institutional violence, the blow on the head and the hunger and disease which results from foreign exploitation. We know of these things from life in the family, from the hurts of love and in general, from the very business of living that ties the world together in a patchwork of wealth and misery. We know of racial violence, urban and colonial violence and what we know in general of these is not much less than the experts whom these phenomena support.

We have then, through everyday language a capacity for living with violence. Even Hiroshima was not experienced in the same way by everyone and so there were some left to help, and to pray and to rebuild. Indeed, the phenomenon of violence is curiously revealing of the nature of human space and human time, that is to say, of the human world as the frame and flesh of violence and imagination. Every day we turn away a poor man. Every day we ride through ghettos on overhead expressways, in automobiles for which the exploitation of the world's natural resources is the primary symbol of affluent pride and colonial indignity. Every evening we watch living death and destruction on news reels just as all day long, day in and day out, we and our children, but especially our children, watch hours of violent action as the medium of a primitive sense of right and wrong, the code of criminal justice. And yet we celebrate, as we must, the great tissue of human understanding woven out of our common need of each other's love and labour. We need to believe that the contiguity of space is human, that our neighbour fares no worse than ourselves.

Violence is not simply any threat to the stability of the political and social order. For in everyday politics, change and reform are as much sought after as stability and entrenchment. Under ordinary circumstances we do not speak of violence to convey the expectation of the legitimate enforcement of political mandates. We understand the power of government and we trust that it will carry out its will with due regard for humanity and with provisions for appeal. Nor are these conventional understandings in any way naive. They are the very fabric of political order. For this reason they are provided for in the institutions of law, parliamentary practice, democratic election and the freedom of speech and publicity. The conviction that government is not naked force, that justice is not terror, and that democracy is not merely a sham elitism is not to be regarded as a mere article of political faith unless it can be shown that none of the institutions of political life serve their purpose and there is no public domain in which this faith can be acted upon through political deeds and public speech to which men attend.

The concern with violence is mere sensationalism when it is not understood in terms of an analysis of the fabric of the social order which generates violence and its onlookers. For we should not overlook that we are the consumers of violence as much as its producers, though not in the same way and with the result that there is a certain order in the variety of concerns with violence. Violence is tragic when it is not willed yet unavoidable. In every other case it is comic, mad, and utterly senseless feeding upon its own frustration. Historically, violence has ranged anywhere from political slapstick to the cold war games of mega-destruction. But the experience of our century is with a scale of violence that overwhelms social science knowledge and reduces it to fictional extrapolations of the origins and consequences of violence in utopian orders beyond genuine political experience.

The tendency of social science knowledge to produce fictional states or utopias in order to make sense of its own production arises from the failure to comprehend the political context of knowledge, speech, and action. This is the task of political phenomenology and it is in this sense that we might turn to Hannah Arendt's essay *On Violence* for what it can teach us about the foundations of political life. This is an exercise which will, I think, reward our concern to create a political culture able to domesticate the massive forces of modern technology and to comprehend the symbiosis of modern rationality and violence.

It would be easy to dismiss Miss Arendt's essay as a conventional attempt at orientation in an academic world which for its own violence now looks more like the world beyond its walls. For at first sight, Miss Arendt seems to pose the threat of world destruction as a mere pretext for the discussion of student rebellions and the violence of Marxist rationalism. Yet it is clearly impossible for her to have anything very revealing to say about the empirical contexts and developments on topics of such range in the short compass she allows herself. But we must remember that Miss Arendt has already written at length in *The Human Condition* of political foundations and modern world destruction as a problem in the very nature of modern knowledge.

With this in mind, I propose to read Miss Arendt's essay *On Violence* as a phenomenology of the basic vocabulary of politics, motivated by the tendency of violence to destroy the foundations of political speech and to undermine the realm of politics. And I propose this reading conscious that it is not to be found there entirely except as a further exercise in political imagination, hopefully within the spirit of her own reflections and without conceit.

The modern age is built upon the paradox that its expansion of technological, economic, and social activity has produced a massive world alienation, an attitude of world-domination and universal migration motivated by what Weber called 'innerworldly asceticism'. The release of these forces was preceded by the collapse of the ancient and feudal conceptions of the world as a political realm of public deeds and public speech resting upon the citizen's or the lord's control of his own household and its private economy. So long as the household economy was embedded in the political order, men's labour served to produce objects whose value was subordinate to the social values created by the thoughts, deeds, and speech of political man. The modern world, however, is built upon an inordinate expansion of individual utilities which subordinates labour or production to a cycle of consumption and destruction disembedded from the political order. This is the source of the modern conception of 'society' as a field solely of individual interests which inspired Hobbes' nasty vision and whose essentially contradictory features were later explored by Hegel and Marx.

Marcuse has argued that affluent slavery is fun mediated by the techniques of repressive desublimation—the executive pink shirt. This is an argument which is tempting to Miss Arendt inasmuch as the resulting smoothness of progress and the inevitable widening of the gap between contrived and human needs invites violence as the only possible means of interrupting a course of events that threatens to automate dehumanization. Although this is only a remark she makes in passing, it must be pointed out that it serves more to identify the violence of affluent student youth or American despair than the violence of workers' strikes or of the ghetto and colonial poor.

Miss Arendt has herself pointed to the pain of bodily labour as the essence of modern experience affecting the masses. Her account in fact resembles Marx's description of the alienation of the worker not just from his product, but from his other sensory and intersubjective possibilities. Labour's desire to break with the privatization of experience through bodily pain is surely the most basic cause of the revolutionary violence which Miss Arendt considers essential to the cause of humanity. The problem is that the pain of labour and its daily and world routine of misery, hidden in the mines, ships, and factories, finds no expression, not even by the workers themselves. For we should not be deceived into believing that Marxism, or the languages of conventional politics and social science speak in the voice of the workers. Here the workers are to be neither seen nor heard. For this reason their very appearance surprises us and is a threat to the political order which nearly always responds to them with violence. Moreover the frustrations of labour are aggravated in an affluent culture where the over-privatization of social resources worked by monopoly capitalism results in a stylization of the issues of power, class, and public indifference. The result is a fun-culture riddled with violence, racism, and colonial wars. The basic class conflict underlying the social order of monopoly capitalism is further distorted through the techniques of repressive desublimation into the sentimentalities of charity, social reform, and colonial aid which are the vicarious counterparts of affluent fun-culture and its white liberal politics. In such a context, it becomes very difficult to speak of justice and outrage which calls for unavoidable violence because these are responses that have been made 'irrational' through the passive 'rationalization' of motives worked upon the card carrying members of the fun-culture whose political future has been mortgaged by this same process. It belongs to this same context that violence is made to appear 'senseless', just as the exploitation which causes it, for want of any adequate sociological analysis, is considered 'unnecessary'. This is so in part because cynics consider the class system can be sustained without overt exploitation, and for the rest because the 'solution' of the production problem reduces exploitation to a problem of improved patterns of social consumption.

Violence however, can also be made part of the 'realism' of capitalist fun-culture. By this I mean that the split between domestic peace and international violence can be reproduced as the split in the animal and rational nature of man. The colonies, ghettos and now the prehistory of man provide marvellous scenarios for the dramatization of the destructive potential of a superficially harmless fun-culture. Since Miss Arendt has not, in my opinion, been sufficiently sympathetic to colonial and racial violence or its romantic interpreters, something more may be said of it as an expression of the pain of labour outside of the fun-culture.

Fanon and Cleaver have shown how well the rhetoric of mind–body dualism is suited to the expression of racial exploitation and colonial revolt and thus how the language of violence is essential to the body politic.

Eldridge Cleaver, black soul on ice, understands instinctively the contemporary reversal of the ideal and material orders in North American civilization. Since Cassius Clay affected poetry, the Word is no longer white property to teach blacks the lesson of submission, the great white dualism of class and the mind–body split. Worse still for American white male supremacy, it was a black muscle-man who betrayed their fears, Muhammad Ali spouting poetry, floating like a butterfly, stinging like a bee. But Cleaver himself understands deepest of all the demon of Black poetry, the blinding White Circle of the Black soul.

A cult of death need of the simple striking arm under the street lamp. The cutters from under their rented earth. Come up, black dada nihilismus. Rape the white girls. Rape their fathers. Cut the mothers' throats.

In his allegory of the Black Eunuchs, Cleaver looks into the face of his own anger and what he sees there should give us pause lest we speak too easily of reform or revolution. He sees the hatred between whites and blacks so twisted into the roots of the black family that there can be no love that isn't broken by the black's lust for a white woman or the black woman's secret admiration for the white man unbroken by the system. In a racist context the class struggle roots itself in the individual's split-self, dividing the black male and female against themselves and destroying the natural unit of a black society, a black nation or homeland. Thus the black man suffers a socially imposed self-hatred of his manhood compounded by the stereotypification of the black as brute strength, body without mind. In terms of this analysis the black revolution can only succeed if it involves a deep psychic transformation, the rebirth of black pride, of the black spirit, of the black family and black culture. This is not to deny the place of violence in the black revolution. But I think Cleaver means to say that there is much potential violence that is the violence of twisted souls who must also pass through their own dark night before the blood flows in the streets and before anyone can be sure his is building the new Africa.

The same profound diagnosis of the black experience is developed in Frantz Fanon's essays on colonial social structure and the psychology of slavery and revolt. Fanon makes it clear that the way oppression works is through the black man's dreams, through his sexual and family life and through taste of self-hatred and oppression. Here too the medium is his language which teaches him the contours, the touch and taste of self-hatred and oppression. Here too the medium is the message. Language, knowledge, beauty, power, money, the land are all white and the black man who uses or looks upon any of these instinctively warns himself off, as a thief, a violator, a brute negativity. To be in the world at all is for the black man to leave his home and his woman and even his senses for the white man's world. This is a daily routine, a journey of the soul made every time the black man leaves the ghetto for work in the morning, passing a policeman, a home or any white man whose look tells him there is another way but it is not for blacks. Fanon has the marvellous gift of revealing the structure of racial neurosis as a landscape, a country, a language, a dream, a vision of the body in which black and white confront each other as themselves. In the white man's neurosis the black man figures as the force of life that is drying up on himself. In his own dream the black man dreams of white civilization.

Miss Arendt remarks on the irony of interpreting the violence generated by the world's most complex industrial technology as due to man's basically animal need for violence which, if frustrated by culture, then takes such 'irrational' forms as world destruction rather than the more natural periodic displays of war and violence. It is in her reply to the attempt to place the definition of the uses of violence in the hands of the new political zoologists such as Lorenz, Ardrey, Rubin and Hoffman that Miss Arendt's conception of *the essentially human nature of violence* is set forth.

The tendency of technological rationality to generate social and political values is the basic feature of modern politics. At the same time, it is the source of the wars, revolutions and violence that constitute the contemporary crisis of political authority. We should not fail to understand her argument on the human or humanizing nature of violence. The attempt to reduce violence to an irrational factor, to deprive it of any place in the vocabulary of politics, can only be successful where the processes of dehumanization have reduced men

to abject slavery and victimage. It is only where men see no prospect
of action that their sense of injustice and rage at alterable human
conditions atrophies or is turned against themselves. In short,
violence and rage must be understood as integral motives so long as
the institutions of political conduct are open to human initiative and
the call for freedom and justice. Miss Arendt warns against the
tendency to place the human emotions in opposition to 'rationality'
when in fact these emotions only become 'irrational' when they
sense reason itself is distorted. Indeed, much of what outrages
contemporary rationality is nothing but the outrage of a more
humane reasonableness driven to expose the sham of establishment
rationality. It is in this context that we must understand the
rhetoric of creative violence, that is to say, as the attempt to connect
with the humane roots of reason which are progressively destroyed
by technological rationality and the myth of progress.

Miss Arendt is critical of the attempt to reduce violence to a
biological concept which is then reintroduced as a dangerous metaphor in the vocabulary of revolutionary politics. Here I think she
is not always in touch with the language of revolution which belongs
to a general cultural revolution and is first of all the work of poets
and artists who restore language and perception to playfulness, to
say what is unspeakable, to make the word flesh once more. In this,
the language of revolution reaches naturally for the language of the
body because its experience is the awareness of the body starved,
brutalized, and ready to kill or be killed.

The eroticism of modern economic and political life is the fundamental feature of the major events or happenings which move the
body politic. The counterparts of the happy, healthy, integrated
executive and his suburban family are the long-haired visionaries of
flowers and rainbows who are the soul-brothers of sit-ins, lunch-
ins, ride-ins, and love-ins which are the renewal of the libidinal body
politic. The phenomena of violence in the ghettos, mass demonstrations and sit-ins in the offices of authority are all grounded in
the basic logic of the body politic not to endure the unendurable,
not to suffer inhuman denials of recognition and in ultimate crises
to 'come together' so that the authorities can 'see' what they are
doing to the people. The underlying logic is a logic of demonstration
that is pre-ideological and rests upon the simple faith that men have
in the renewal of justice and community. It is a simple logic which

challenges the constitutional alienation of the authority of the body-politic. For once the injustice of life in the ghetto goes beyond the limits of tolerance, then the ghetto becomes a natural armoury of stones, bottles, sticks, crowds, with which to beat the conventional police-system. Once the inanity of administrative authority is exposed it is defenceless against the belly-laugh, the clap-in or sing-in. Where is the official who will explain to children and to young men and women with flowers the necessity of the war that will cripple them or blow them to bits?

It may be that we are engaged in a new meta-politics in which the Burkean identification of temporality and political community is destroyed in the politics of the generation gap and the street happenings of the 'new mutuants'. The new style of political demonstration destroys the polis as an organization of needs and wants, of life and against death, by pushing death into the erotic economy of male–female, black–white, rich–poor, expert–layman organization. The politics of unisex, nudity, camp and pop art exhibit the reversibility of organization, artist and audience, leader and mass whose own self-improvization and abandonment is the supreme anti-political act. Leslie Fiedler has spoken of the flight from *polis* to *thiasos* ('the movement'). This involves a new direction of political knowledge which surpasses the Victorian misgivings of Lionel Tiger's genetic code of male-bonding no less than Fiedler's own anxiety over the post-Jewish antics of the anti-male. The new politics is Dionysian, achieving form only in the moment of self-destruction. Because it maintains control through improvization, the new politics cannot presume upon any rationalization or ideological interpretation of sensory experience. Its audience is therefore part of the art, the music, the lesson, and the political platform. The new politics invents a destruction of vicarious experience in becoming children, playing with toys, dressing up, mocking, loving, and raging in the streets. Its destruction of vicarious experience is simultaneously the creation of community groups, circles, and games in which experience is opened to feeling, magic, and mysticism in the search for a workable and communicable truth. The way of this truth is often stark and violent. It differs from the established truth in its search to become a truth, founded upon the gift and the exigency of the human body.

These observations, however, imply no endorsement whatsoever of the use of biological metaphors which propose violence as the cure for a sick society, sick with white guilt and black rage. Violence may serve as a means to the dramatization of the political condition. The risk in resorting to violence is that it proposes itself as a solution to racial and ethnic differences caught in the deadlock of interests which liberal society refuses to give a genuine political definition.

So long as these interests lack the vocabulary of class politics their actions can be reduced to crimes against property or decency as purely criminal or police concerns. This anti-political character of violence regarded from the standpoint of law and order in turn feeds back into such violence driving it into terrorism in ever more desperate attempts to expose the political and social segregation of the issues of poverty, race, and war. This cycle is only aggravated where the establishment power is organized in bureaucracies which increasingly privatize the contexts of meaning and action at the expense of the political realm. The result is a certain pathological symbiosis between bureaucratic rationality and the resort to vocabularies of creative violence, internal migration, and communal utopias which destroy genuine political speech and public action.

Bureaucracy destroys the political realm because it treats individuality as equality and thereby destroys its sense as uniqueness which brings into being the necessity for human speech and expression. Bureaucracy stylizes differences as fads or fashions creating the political paradox of conformist freedoms. Corporate capitalism in particular parodies human initiative through the engineering of responses to the inevitability of annual novelties. It drowns the question of who a man is in the litanies of what he has or can acquire in order to construct an image. These effects of bureaucracy are perfectly geared to the liberal minimization of the public realm of common action once inspired by collective identity and tradition in which character and history interweave. The modern world systematically destroys the special and temporal dimensions of public conduct through the privatization of the resources of action and its codes of meaning and motivation.

In North America, religion, politics, and business are alike in being serious business. There is no joy in them, and thus their very seriousness is inverted into the vulgarities of worship, democracy, and money-making. We must, however, understand that profanity or vulgarity can only be what it is in the light of its fall from the sacred. Politics, religion, and business are equally holy works of man. It is the task of the rebel, the clown and the practical joker to remind us of the dialects of the holy and the profane, of godhead and manhood.

The vocation of western knowledge for domination establishes modern science as the paradigm of social and political knowledge. Its behavioral assumptions invent plausible utopias of colossal world violence and destruction while alienating the human responses of outrage and violence as appeals against their injustice and insanity.

Modern violence is of such an enormous scope and impersonality that it strains every metaphor of language by which we might tie events to their authors and victims. There is the massive horror but there is no one to speak about; only the author's guilt in his own survival which reduces his language to the barest medium of factual account and reporting. And this is perhaps necessary in order to save language from delirium in the effort to speak at all of modern violence, to be faithful at once to what happened and to the necessity of rediscovering the human face, the minds and hearts of those buried or crippled by these experiences. The scene of violence, the camp, the bomb, the riot, overwhelm the categories of character, intentionality, and action so that not even the writer can situate himself, far less construct a conventional story. Modern armies obliterate a village or town before they can enter it and when they do, the villages are empty or littered with dead and maimed bodies with no other story to tell than the ravages of overkill and napalm whose meaning is reduced to the scene itself.

Language is the soul of our lives together. Today we must work to restore language, to speak where violence puts an end to speech. Miss Arendt's essay *On Violence* begins the work of renewing political speech, defining its basic words and the contexts of public and private usage which generate their meaning.[1] In this task the only resources we have are the same words which condemn a man to death, or prejudice and exploitation. There are times when words take refuge in songs, jokes, and prayers. But the soul of language is never broken while men still have on their lips, the words of 'freedom', 'justice', 'faith', and 'revolution'.

[1] For Maurice Merleau-Ponty's phenomenological approach to the problem of violence, see chap. 8 below.

6: Authority, Knowledge, and the Body Politic

A political community has always to find a symbolic expression of its beliefs concerning the sources, mechanisms and threats to the orderly relationships between its members. The symbolism of the body politic is a recurring expression of the nature of order and disorder in the political community. From the plebeian secession from Rome to latter-day sit-ins, the imagery of the body politics survives in the vocabulary of popular politics. The body politic represents a fundamental structure of political life which may be appealed to in times of deep institutional crisis where it is necessary to reconstitute the grounds of political authority and social consensus.

> A sound leader's aim
> Is to open people's hearts,
> Fill their stomachs,
> Calm their wills,
> Brace their bones
> And so to clarify their thoughts and cleanse their needs
> That no cunning meddler could touch them:
> Without being forced, without strain or constraint,
> Good government comes of itself.
>
> —Lao Tzu

Here I shall attempt to trace the crisis of political authority in terms of an argument based upon the dialectic between commonsense and expert knowledge and three structures of the body politic which I label as follows:

(1) The Organic Body Politic.

68

(2) The Sensible Body Politic.

(3) The Libidinal Body Politic.

In constructing a typology of the body politic I have not intended to abstract the history of political thought, far less to encapsulate the history of western politics. My approach is phenomenological in the sense that I understand the forms of the body politic as existential structures of political experience. I do not mean to suggest that the patterns I have distinguished are mutually exclusive. Indeed, it is the overlap and tension between them which must be understood. For in each of the three levels of the body politic there is a distinct mode of values differentiated in terms of biological needs, social wants, and libidinal expression which function as a criteriology of the ultimate grounds of political authority and social consensus.

Hannah Arendt has discussed the historical sources of the crisis of authority in the West in terms of the conflict between the rule of knowledge and the violence of knowledge.[1] According to Arendt's first argument, the tendency of philosophy to become tyrannical arises from its sense of the hostility of the polis toward philosophy. In Socrates' death we witness the resolution of the conflict between the salvation of the polis and the independence of philosophy. Yet with the death of Socrates, Plato seems to have become sceptical of the persuasive power of truth without the coercion of myth. The result is that ultimately the authority of reason in the body politic rests upon the sanctions of an after-life.

As Arendt observes, there are other arguments in Plato which attempt to ground the standards of political truth apart from scepticism and misanthropy. Arendt comments upon Plato's attempts to find a principle of legitimate coercion drawn from the model of existing social relationships such as those between the shepherd and his sheep, and the physician and his patient. But she remarks that these arguments either ground authority upon confidence in expert knowledge or else assume the natural hierarchy implicit in the relationships discussed.

Now I think that a careful consideration of the use of the body politic analogy in Plato and Aristotle might reveal a tension between a commonsense politics and an 'expert' politics which is vitally relevant to the problem of authority and consensus.

[1] Hannah Arendt, 'What is Authority?' *Between Past and Future, Six Exercises in Politicial Thought*, London, Faber and Faber, 1954.

The Organic Body Politic

To the Greeks the human body offered a symbol of the political order because of a certain analogy between the harmony that must be embodied in the life of the individual and the order that must be incorporated in the members of the body politic. It will be re-called that when Socrates is challenged to define justice and its effects upon the soul, he suggests the strategy of studying justice in the state since the life of a community is simply the life of its members 'writ large'. This strategy served from the outset to define the nature of political order as an organic unity which rather than being the creation of a contract is necessarily presupposed by any kind of con-tractarian association. We can no more imagine the state coming into being piecemeal than we can imagine an arm or a head growing into a body. There is, of course, a distinction in Plato and Aristotle between the 'becoming' and 'being' of the polis (πολις . . . γιγνομενη μεν του ζην ενεκεν, ουσα δε του ευ ζην).[1] This distinction involves the transition from the 'first city' whose principle of order (at the organic and sensible levels) rests upon the natural division of labour which arises out of individual differences and the comp-lementarity of human needs. However, at this level the distinctly political form of association is not yet evident for life does not yet aim beyond food and shelter. It is only when human needs pass beyond the distinctly animal level, when human nature becomes second nature, that the knowledge of good and evil becomes the constituent principle in the (libidinal) organization of the polis. In other words, the body loses its natural affinity for its own harmony and must subject itself to the organization of the soul to maintain its life. This transition involves a specialization of function in the body politic for which there is seemingly no analogy in the natural body. While the health of the body requires that each of the organs perform its function, there is no special organ charged with the health of the body. Furthermore, the nature of the health of the body as well as of any particular organ is not naturally an object of concern, still less of knowledge, in the natural state of man.

The transition to the polis is a transition in the order of art or moral knowledge. The nature of this transition involves us in ques-tions which are central to the nature of Platonism and, as Hannah Arendt has argued, even to modern political thought. For in adopt-

[1] Aristotle, *Politics*, I.2.

ing the analogy of the body politic we seem to have confounded its basis in the natural body. Once the transition is made from the 'first city' it may seem that the body no longer furnishes an analogy with the polis for it has no counterpart to the ruling function in the state. On the other hand, it may be argued that the ruler only knows by artifice what the body 'knows' by nature. Again, the ruling function, precisely because it lacks a counterpart in the body, is the most easily abused function, having no natural limit. It is because of the organic unity of the body that when one of its members suffers we speak, says Plato, of the *man* having a pain in his finger and the best organized community would express a similar concern for its members.[1] Without pressing the difficulties in the analogy any further, we are prone to think of man having a function as such, much as it is the function of the eye to see, and that the healthy performance of man's function provides a criterion for the justice and health of the political community.

> Are we then to suppose, that while the carpenter and cobbler have certain works and courses of action, Man as Man has none, but is left by Nature without a work ($εργον$)? Or would not one rather hold, that as eye, hand, and foot, and generally each of his members, has manifestly some special work; so too the whole Man, as distinct from all these, has some work of his own?[2]

I suggest that the analogy of the body politic is not incidental to the Platonic discussion of the intrinsic grounds of authority and reason in the polis. Indeed, it provides a foundation for the Platonic transition from a poetic politics based upon the Form of the Beautiful to an expert politics based upon the Form of the Good. Arendt observes that Plato first sought for the intrinsic grounds of the authority of reason. In the allegory of the Cave the philosopher goes in search of the truth of being without any thought of returning to impose the truth of his vision upon other men. It is only under the compulsion to return to earth that the philosopher reinterprets his contemplative vision of the Forms of Beauty, Goodness, Truth, and Justice, in terms of an analogy with practical and technical arts.

Plato's discussion in the early books of the Republic in which he differentiates the first and second cities, or the organic and libidinal

1 Plato, *Republic*, V, 462.
2 Aristotle, *The Nicomachean, Ethics*, I, 1097 b.

levels of the body politic, is guided by the Form of the Beautiful. It is only in the Sixth Book that Plato turns away from a politics of being to a politics of practicality based on instrumental standards of fitness.

> For the original function of the ideas was not to rule or other-wise determine the chaos of human affairs, but in 'shining brightness', to illuminate their darkness. As such, the ideas have nothing whatever to do with politics, political experience, and the problem of action, but pertain exclusively to philosophy, the experience of contemplation, and the quest for the 'true being of things'. It is precisely ruling, measuring, subsuming, and regulating that are entirely alien to the experiences underlying the doctrine of ideas in its original conception. It seems that Plato was the first to take exception to the political 'irrelevance' of his new teaching, and he tried to modify the doctrine of ideas so that it would become useful for a theory of politics. But useful-ness could be saved only by the idea of the good, since 'good' in the Greek vocabulary always means 'good for' or 'fit'. If the highest idea, in which all other ideas must partake in order to be ideas at all, is that of fitness, then the ideas are applicable by definition, and in the hands of the philosopher, the expert in ideas, they can become rules and standards, or as later in the *Laws*, they can become laws.[1]

The development of the *Republic*, therefore, involves a transforma-tion in the concept of order as an aesthetic standard, whose measure is the exemplification of the Beautiful, to a technical standard of fitness under the rule of the Good. In drawing attention to the body analogy in Plato, I am suggesting that the *Republic* involves a triple structure of political experience in which the needs of the organic body politic (the first city) play into a dialectic of transcendence (the libidinal body politic envisaged under the Form of the Beautiful) and alienation (the sensible body politic brought to order under the Form of the Good).

The Sensible Body Politic

The alienation of political authority in the sensible body politic becomes manifest in modern society. What I call the sensible body politic is not an explicit concept in any of the writings from which

---

[1] *Between Past and Future*, pp. 112–113.

it is drawn. It is a construct drawn from writers as different as Edmund Burke, Adam Smith, and Karl Marx. The justification for taking these authors together is that they share a concept of authority which is opposed to all legal and rationalistic formulations of the nature of social consensus and solidarity. They believed that the foundations of the social order are prior to the state and rest upon the natural division of social labour and the complementarity of human needs.

Clearly, I do not mean to suggest that Burke, Smith and Marx shared the same political philosophy. But I do think that what each arrived at is very much determined by the very solid grasp they had of the social and historical bases of political authority. Long before Durkheim, who is usually credited with this finding, Burke and Smith made it clear that the social order is a sentimental order written in the hearts of men through custom, long habit and tradition.

Burke and Adam Smith demonstrated that the social order rests upon a natural sympathy that men have for one another which is the ground of their being moved by the rules of approbation and disapprobation. This is not to say that man's natural sympathy cannot be corrupted, particularly in the quest for power and wealth. But I think Smith and Burke regard this as the exceptional case, at least on the eve of market society. In Burke the social order is not the product of calculation. It is a sentimental order which rests upon habits of thought and feeling that may be abused by law and contract but can never be established by them.

Our political system is placed in a just correspondence and symmetry with the order of the world and with the mode of existence decreed to a permanent body composed of transitory parts, wherein, by the disposition of a stupendous wisdom, moulding together the great mysterious incorporation of the human race, the whole, at one time, is never old or middle-aged or young, but, in a condition of unchangeable constance, moves on through the varied tenor of perpetual decay, fall, renovation, and progression. Thus, by preserving the method of nature in the conduct of the state in what we improve we are never wholly new; in what we retain we are never wholly obsolete. By adhering in this manner and on those principles to our forefathers, we are guided not by the superstition of antiquarians, but by the spirit of philosophic analogy. In this choice of inheritance we have given to our frame of polity the image of a relation in blood, binding up the constitution of our country with our dearest domestic ties adopting our fundamental laws into the bosom of our family affections, keeping inseparable and cherishing with the warmth of all their combined and mutually reflected charities our state, our hearths, our sepulchres, and our altars.[1]

Burke attacked the abstract, metaphysical and mathematical conception of political reason which he found in the Jacobins. He did so because he believed they ignored the moral constitution of the body politic, operating upon it without due regard for its 'great conservatories and magazines of our rights and privileges'. There is a certain pathos in Burke's attempt to delimit politics and the business of life to a small part in the great partnership of science and art which binds the past and future generations of mankind in an eternal society. For Adam Smith was just then demonstrating that what society lost in consuming its own past it gained in the universality of its trade and industry. This change in perspective has been described by Hannah Arendt in terms of a reversal of the order of politics and economics which separates modern 'society' from the ancient world. The substance of this transition is the social importance attached to the metabolic processes of the reproduction and expanded production of wealth. The result of the social significance attached to making a living is that man is driven back into the most isolating of his experiences, namely, the bodily pain of labour.

The development of the modern age and the rise of society, where the most private of all human activities, labouring, has become public and been permitted to establish its own common realm, may make it doubtful whether the very existence of property as a privately held place within the world can withstand the relentless process of growing wealth. But it is true, nevertheless, that the very privacy of one's holdings, that is, their complete independence 'from the common', could not be better guaranteed than by the transformation of property into appropriation or by an interpretation of the 'enclosure from the common', which sees it as the result, the 'product', of bodily activity. In this aspect, the body becomes indeed the quintessence of all

1 Edmund Burke, *Reflections on the Revolution in France*, edited with an introduction by Thomas H. D. Mahoney, Indianapolis, The Bobbs-Merrill Company, 1955, p. 38.

property because it is the only thing one could not share even if one wanted to. Nothing, in fact, is less common and less communicable, and therefore more securely shielded against the visibility and audibility of the public realm, than what goes on within the confines of the body, its pleasures and pains, its labouring and consuming.[1]

As the industrial revolution took hold, Burke's majestic conception of the sensible body politic yields to Marx's portrayal of the twisted bodies of the proletariat. Arendt mistakenly understands her own argument upon the significance of bodily experience in the modern world as a critique of the world Marx made.[2] In fact, it was Marx who first expressed the nature of the social experience of industrialization and class struggle in terms of the alienation of the human senses and the enforced privatization of experience derived from the separation of labour and ownership of the means of production. To Adam Smith the reduction of human sensibility to a simple dexterity was the price exacted in return for the magical abundance of the social division of labour. Marx departs from Smith in his focus upon the institutional preconditions, in particular, property and social class, which undermine the natural social consensus which Smith believed to be generated in a market society. However, Marx does not ignore the dramatic expansion of the human world and human sensibility which interacts with economic development, as may be seen from the *Communist Manifesto*. But from Hegel, Marx understood that the development of human sensibilities under capitalist conditions involved a terrible alienation of the human senses in all individuals, not just the working class. While conceding the expansion of human possibilities through industrial development, Marx attacked the distortion of the sense of reality and value which derives from the emphasis in capitalist society upon *having* at the expense of *being*.

In an extremely important passage Marx draws out the interrelationship between the doctrines of Adam Smith and Luther, in what is in fact an anticipation of the celebrated Weberian thesis on the Protestant ethic and the spirit of capitalism. Here it is important

1 Hannah Arendt, *The Human Condition*, Chicago, University of Chicago Press, 1958, p. 97.
2 John O'Neill, 'Marxism and Mythology', *Ethics*, vol. LXVII, no. 1 (October 1966), pp. 38–49. Chap. 10 below.

to draw attention to the redefinition of human sensibility and the world which is effected through the transvaluation of property and acquisitiveness under capitalism. Just as Luther rid the world of priests by making every man a tortured priest, says Marx, so capitalism consumes the substance of the world by reducing all human properties to the property of being wealthy (Marx seems to have liked such puns).

But as a result man is brought within the orbit of private property, just as in Luther he is brought within the orbit of religion. Under the semblance of recognizing man, the political economy whose principle is labour is really no more than consistent implementation of the denial of man, since man himself no longer stands in an external relation of tension to the external substance of private property, but has himself become this tensed essence of private property. What was previously being *external* to oneself —man's externalization in the thing—has merely become the act of externalizing—the process of alienating. If then this political economy begins by seeming to acknowledge man (his independence, spontaneity, etc.); and if, locating private property in man's own being, it can no longer be conditioned by the local, national, or other *characteristics of private property* as of *something existing outside itself*; and if this political economy consequently displays a *cosmopolitan* universal energy which overthrows every restiction and bond so as to establish itself instead as the *sole* politics, the sole universality, the sole limit and sole bond, then it must throw aside this *hypocrisy* in the course of its further development and come out *in its complete cynicism*. And this it does—untroubled by all the apparent contradictions in which it becomes involved—by developing the idea of *labour* much more *one-sidedly* and therefore *more sharply* and *more consistently* as the sole *essence of wealth*; by proving the implications of this theory to be *anti-human* in character, in contrast to the other, original approach;[1]

The Libidinal Body Politic

Much now has been written upon the Marxian conception of alienation.[2] So far very little has been done towards the formulation

[1] Karl Marx, *Economic and Philosophic Manuscripts of 1844*, translated by Martin Milligan, Moscow, Foreign Languages Publishing House, pp. 94–95.

[2] John O'Neill, 'The Concept of Estrangement in the Early and Late Writings of Karl Marx', *Philosophy and Phenomenological Research*, vol. XXV, no. 1 (September 1964), pp. 64–84. Chap. 9 below.

of a positive theory of non-alienation. In what follows I suggest that the Marxian theory of alienation may be conceptualized with respect to the positive and negative experiences of the human body within the framework of the organic, sensible, and libidinal levels of the body politic.

The libidinal body politic is a work of art. It presupposes the constructs of the organic and sensible body politic but aims at a mere distinctly human form of political life. The imagery of the libidinal body politic is above all the vehicle of radical politics. It promotes autonomy and creativity rather than subordination and specialization. It identifies freedom with creativity and regards these as the criteria of the health and sanity of the body politic.

The core insight contained in the theory of the libidinal body politic is the identification of politics and psychology. Just as Marx exposed the moral psychology underlying classical political economy, so we owe to Freud the analysis of the relations between the organization of the psychic economy and the political order of the family and social censorship. The basic insights of Marx and Freud sensitize us to the processes of sublimation through which the individual 'makes out' under the restraints of the political and economic order, which defines everyday reality. In the encounter between the individual and society the individual learns to subordinate the pleasure principle to reality-testing, work and social commitment.

What is basic in Marx and Freud is that human culture, politics and economics are related to the human body, or the humanization of the body. This, I think, is a constant, whatever the differences between Marx and Freud with regard to the historical origins and resolutions of the alienation of human sensibility and desire. Actually, I think Marx and Freud hardly disagree in their conception of the end-state of the libidinal body. As I understand it, Marx and Freud regarded the humanization of the body as a polymorphous pervertible play of the human senses, liberated from the dominance of genital sexuality which is tied through the family to economic organization and the politics of class and adulthood.

There are, of course, differences between Marx and Freud. But I think they are complementary differences. Marx focused his attention upon the historical and sociological structures of repression, exploitation, and alienation and related these to role-behaviour and ideology. Freud starts from the side of the individual organization of libidinal energy and relates culture and social institutions to the sublimation of pre-genital sexuality.

Disagreement between Marx and Freud arises over the nature of the space in which human action occurs, whether as work or dream. It is essential to the Marxist position that all our 'practical-sensuous activity' occurs in a social space which is the ground of institutions, historical development, and political reform.[1] The alternative is that we inhabit a self-furnished inner-space bound to others only through collective fantasies.

> The difference between a neurosis and a sublimation is evidently in the social aspect of the phenomenon. A neurosis isolates; a sublimation unites. In a sublimation something new is created —a house, or a community, or a tool—and it is created in a group for the use of a group.[2]

The Freudian theory of sublimation and repression involves an intensification of repression in response to the guilt aroused by the primal rebellion. The result is that the arbitrariness of the Oedipal authority is impersonalized and rationalized in the law of society outside of which there can be no life. However, to the extent that the repression stems from economic necessity, the increasingly machine-machine nature of modern industry opens up the possibility of desublimation.

The paradox of modern corporate culture is that it panders to the libidinal body, titillating and ravishing its sensibilities, while at the same time it standardizes and packages libidinal responses to its products. In North America the libidinal body politic is the creature of the corporate culture and its celebration of the young, white, handsome heterosexual world of healthy affluence. In this sense the libidinal body politic is an unhealthy distortion of the political life of the community since it fails to cope with the poor, the sick, the aged, the ugly, and the black. Everything which fails to con-form to its image of suburb-inanity has to be segregated and pushed

---

[1] John O'Neill, 'Public and Private Space', in T. Lloyd and J. T. McLeod, *Agenda 1970: Proposals for a Creative Politics*, Toronto, University of Toronto Press, 1968, pp. 74–93. Chap. 3 above.

[2] Geza Roheim, *The Origin and Function of Culture*, Nervous and Mental Disease Monograph, No. 69, New York: Nervous and Mental Disease Monographs, 1943, p. 74.

into the ghettos of race, poverty, crime, and insanity. It is therefore natural that political struggles over integration in the affluent-racist context of corporate capitalism take on the imagery of white rape, black power, and youthful protest at the jaded juvenilism of the corporate world.

Today we observe an articulation of the body politic in the simple and commonsense demands of people everywhere for self-respect, for freedom of speech and movement and for hope which makes for dreams and laughter. Mrs Rosa Parks could have walked to almost any place in the small town of Montgomery. But on Thursday afternoon, 1 December 1955, she took a freedom ride. And soon people were on the march. In 1960 four college freshmen sat down at the lunch counter at Woolworth's in Greensboro, North Carolina. These actions typify the non-verbal rhetoric of the body politic which revitalizes the *esprit de corps* of oppressed peoples. As such these simple acts of riding, sitting, eating and loving constitute the civil foundations of the rebirth of the Negro central nervous system celebrated in the dithyrambs of black Hip during the long nights of unborn freedom.[1]

Nowadays we are witnessing a genesis of political community which instinctively reaches for the language of the body politic, enriching it with its own rhythm and sound.

From the moment that Mrs Rosa Parks, in that bus in Montgomery, Alabama, resisted the Omnipotent Administrator, contact, however fleeting, had been made with the lost sovereignty —the Body had made contact with its Mind—and the shock of that contact sent an electric current throughout this nation, traversing the racial Maginot line and striking fire in the hearts of the whites. The wheels began to turn, the thaw set in, and though Emmitt Till and Mack Parker were dead, though Eisenhower sent troops to Little Rock, though Autherine Lucy's token presence at the University of Alabama was a mockery— notwithstanding this, it was already clear that the 1954 major surgical operation had been successful and the patient would live. The challenge loomed on the horizon: Africa, black, enigmatic, and hard-driving, had begun to parade its newly freed nations into the UN; and the Islam of Elijah Muhammad, amplified as it was fired in salvos from the piercing tongue of Malcolm X

---

[1] Eldridge Cleaver, *Soul on Ice*, New York, McGraw–Hill Book Company, 1968.

was racing through the Negro streets with Allen Ginsberg and Jack Kerouac.

Then, as the verbal revolt of the black masses soared to a cacophonous peak—the Body, the Black Amazons and Super-masculine Menials, becoming conscious, shouting, in a thousand different ways, 'I've got a Mind of my own!' and as the senator from Massachusetts was saving the nation from the Strangelove grasp of Dirty Dicky, injecting as he emerged victorious, a new, vivacious spirit into the people with the style of his Smile and his wife's hairdo; then, as if a signal had been given, as if the Mind had shouted to the Body, 'I'm ready!'—the Twist, super-seding the Hula Hoop, burst upon the scene like a nuclear ex-plosion, sending its fallout of rhythm into the Minds and Bodies of the people. The fallout: the Hully Gully, the Mashed Potato, the Dog, the Smashed Banana, the Watusi, the Frug, the Swim. The Twist was a guided missile, launched from the ghetto into the very heart of suburbia. The Twist succeeded, as politics, reli-gion, and law could never do, in writing in the heart and soul what the Supreme Court could only write on the books. The Twist was a form of therapy for a convalescing nation. The Omnipotent Administrator and the Ultrafeminine responded so dramatically, in stampede fashion, to the Twist precisely be-cause it afforded them the possibility of reclaiming their Bodies again after generations of alienated and disembodied existence.[1]

The contemporary crisis of authority represents a crisis in the political economy of segregation by wealth, race, and knowledge which is at the same time a crisis of identity and community. Cleaver challenges contemporary political analysis to relate the con-cepts of power, authority, and justice to a demystified conception of political truth emerging from the life-world of economic, psychic, and sensuous exploitation. Not that Cleaver or Fanon, especially Fanon,[2] ignore the need for detailed institutional analyses of the politics of poverty, racism, and colonialism. But like their cool counterparts, Marx and Freud, beneath the analysis there is the pulse of sensuous being and the authority of sweet reasonableness whose voice is justice and whose medium has always been the people.

[1] Eldridge Cleaver, *Soul on Ice*, pp. 195–197, 202.

[2] Frantz Fanon, *The Wretched of the Earth*, preface by Jean-Paul Sartre, translated by Constance Farrington, London, Penguin Books, 1967; *Black Skin White Masks*, translated by Charles Lain Markmann, New York, Grove Press, Inc., 1967.

7: Situation, Action and Language

In this essay I shall restrict myself for the most part to Sartre's essays collected in the volumes, *Situations*,[1] since what follows is intended largely as an introduction to *Situations* IV,[2] and in particular to the long essay therein on Sartre's relation to Merleau-Ponty. The ultimate purpose of the discussion is to suggest that there is perhaps a greater similarity in the views of Sartre and Merleau-Ponty on the phenomenology of action, expression, and history than is likely to appear if one relies upon a number of conventional interpretations of Sartre and then turns away in order to study Merleau-Ponty. I am aware, of course, that the two friends became enemies over their differences. But I am suggesting that Sartre's tribute to Merleau-Ponty and his later work in the *Critique de la Raison Dialectique* represents an ultimate comprehension which was always present. It has been argued that Sartre's identification of consciousness and imagination condemns individual consciousness to a comedy of errors, degeneration,

---

[1] *Situations* I–III, Paris, Gallimard, 1947–1949. Essays from *Situations* I and III translated by Annette Michelson have been published as *Literary Essays*, New York, Philosophical Library, 1957, and most of *Situations* II translated by Bernard Frechtman as *What is Literature?* New York, Philosophical Library, 1949. Quotations are from the English translations.

[2] *Situations* IV, Paris, Gallimard, 1964, translated by Benita Eisler, *Situations*, New York, George Braziller, 1965. There is a fascinating history of an alternating conception of environment as a deterministic force (*milieu*) and as a beneficent shell or field (*ambiance*) to which the thought of Heidegger, Sartre, Marcel, and Jaspers might be related. I refer to the essays of Leo Spitzer, '*Milieu* and *Ambiance*: An Essay in Historical Semantics', *Philosophy and Phenomenological Research*, Vol. III (1942–1943), pp. 1–42 and 169–218.

and self-enchantment. Similarly, Sartre's conception of individual freedom as any awareness of the conflict between *L'être-en-soi-pour-soi* and the being that lacks being opens up an abyss which individual freedom can never overleap.[1] Together these views involve the diffi-culty that the flux of individual consciousness and the futility of its passions resist identification with any historical process which aims at the realization of political values willed as such for all men. The Sartrean individual is crippled by the burden of a radical freedom which is essentially indifferent to the structures of language, history, economy, and society.

In my own view much of the critical literature has concentrated upon the antithetical nature of Sartre's philosophy of action because it has dealt only with its epistemological and/or ontological ekstasis, but has not attempted to understand these as secondary structures within the temporal ekstasis which is the diasporatic unity of all the intra-mundane multiplicities of being. Time is the opening in being, through which there can be meaning (*sens*) which is neither trans-cendental nor opaque, but rather a schema of the practical truth or physiognomy of things. Thus time is the hollow in being in which is conceived the value of being-in-itself for the being who lacks being or self-coincidence. Time is the arrow of being, the dialectical surge which continuously sweeps up its starting points into fresh, but equally distant, totalizations of the human act.

> Thus Temporality is not a universal time containing all beings and in particular human realities. Neither is it a law of develop-ment which is imposed on being from without. Nor is it being. But it is the intra-structure of the being which is its own nihila-tion—that is, the *mode of being* peculiar to being for itself. The For-itself is the being which has to be its being in the form of Temporality.[2]

We shall not properly understand Sartre's concept of situation as a matrix in which the act is born in a revelation and recovery of being unless we preserve its temporal ekstasis. Situation is a secondary structure which can be made and unmade in the temporalization of

[1] Iris Murdoch, *Sartre, Romantic Rationalist*, New Haven, Yale University Press, 1959.

[2] *Being and Nothingness*, translated by Hazel E. Barnes, New York, Philosophical Library, 1956, p. 142.

an original project which is never present in a global view, but reveals being at the place where being opens to gesture, expression, and conduct. It is thus the appropriation of a world that is present to a being which undertakes to make itself through acts which polarize the world as value and instrument—that is, the human world.

The structure of the human world is essentially linguistic. It is through language that we assume reponsibility for events either in the past or future which are the necessary but otherwise insufficient conditions of the *act*; hence the unities of time, place, and action.[1] It is the task of the play and the novel, as employed by Sartre, to recuperate the mysterious depth which the decision to act opens up in the commonplace world which otherwise bears us away from our acts and covers them over as soon as they are done. Literature is action because of the intentional structure of the word, and its situations are correlative with the historical structure of the world. There are, however, at the extreme limits two literary techniques which are alien to the intention of the authentic novel. Though they seem to be opposites, naturalism and *l'art pour l'art* are in practice two species of objectivism, i.e., an unsituated perspectivism which produces a decomposition of time and duration. Writers who employ either technique construct novels according to what Sartre calls the eidetic imagery of bad faith—handing over the freedom of their characters to the past, or moving them like creatures who have pawned their future in order to maintain their author's omniscience. The true novelist draws the reader into the situation of his characters as an accomplice to actions which unfold with the characters and polarize the flow of events as acts polarize the scenes in a play.

The technique of the naturalist or neo-realist does not, according to Sartre, produce genuine novels. The naturalist fails because he attempts to construct the novel out of events which have only a Humean history and never any intrinsic meaning. But then it might be argued that Hume is the first philosopher of the Absurd, as Camus, Hemingway and Dos Passos are the great novelists of the Absurd. What each reveals to us is that man's customs are merely veils which hide the abyss between man and nature. None of our routines ever succeeds in establishing a 'qualitative ethic'. Outside of the idea, we experience only a sequence of radically contingent events which,

[1] F. Jameson, *Sartre, The Origins of a Style*, New Haven, Yale University Press 1961.

turn up without qualitative adhesions, yet with a density of their own in the feelings. Although the philosophy of the Absurd scrupulously avoids the orientations of bad faith, Sartre nevertheless denies the status of the novel to Camus' *The Stranger*, as he does for similar reasons to Hemingway's *Death in the Afternoon*. In each case, Sartre's objection is that the technique of these writers is not to use words to integrate the absurd into a human order, but to juxtapose a transparent sequence of events and an order of meaning correspondingly opaque. Similarly, in Dos Passos, the technique of accumulation by conjunction is employed to represent events which borrow prefabricated meanings through the public declarations of the characters. But in Dos Passos ('the greatest writer of our time') the characters maintain a hybrid existence between their own lived time and the collapsed time of reported events into which they are driven in the conflict between character and the destiny which is their lot in capitalist society.

The lack of transcendence in the writings of the naturalists, which has its source in their metaphysical decomposition of time, is likewise the defect of an author such as Mauriac, who views his characters *sub specie aeternitatis*, a technique which also fails to grasp the nature of lived time essential to the novel as the unfolding of action.

A novel is a series of readings, of little parasitic lives, none of them longer than a dance. It swells and feeds upon the reader's time. But in order for the duration of my impatience and ignorance to be caught and then moulded and finally presented to me as the flesh of these creatures of invention, the novelist must know how to draw it into the trap, how to hollow out in his book, by means of the signs at his disposal, a time resembling my own, one in which the future does not exist. If I suggest that the hero's future actions are determined in advance by heredity, social influence or some other mechanism, my own time ebbs back into me; there remains only myself, reading and persisting, confronted by a static book. Do you want your characters to live? See to it that they are free.[1]

Characters whose future is congealed in the gaze of the author are reduced to *things* which have a *destiny* but no life that the reader can share from the inside.

The fate of Mauriac's characters is revealed in his use of third-

[1] *Literary Essays*, p. 7.

person statements. The latter function ambiguously to designate the other, viewed solely from the outside, and simultaneously, while preserving a certain *aesthetic distance*, to draw us into the intimacy of the subject on the basis of shared experience. But in Mauriac's use the ambiguity of the third person loses the dimension of aesthetic distance and is employed to set us up in judgment over the characters. Suddenly, out of his own omniscience, Mauriac gives us the key to his characters. Thereafter, 'Therese's "pattern of destiny", the graph of her ups and downs, resembles a fever curve; it is dead time, since the future is spread out like the past and simply repeats it'.[1] In Mauriac there are no time-traps, objects have no resistance or impenetrability, and conversations never stumble, meander, or grope towards meaning—everything is lucid. But lucidity is the novelist's sin of pride. It is the denial of the principle of relativity which applies both to physical and to fictional systems (the novel as a whole, as well as the partial systems of which it is composed, the minds of the characters, their psychological and moral judgments). In short, 'novels are written *by* men and *for* men. In the eyes of God, Who cuts through appearances and goes beyond them, there is no novel, no art, for art thrives on appearances. God is not an artist.'[2]

Sartre's conception of action and the novel may be further illustrated by turning to his comments upon the novels of Nathalie Sarraute and André Gorz which, like those of Nabakov, Waugh, and Gide, represent an attempt to use the novel against itself in order to reflect upon the genuine nature of the novel. The result is what Sartre calls the *anti-novel*,[3] understood as a creaive experiment which explores the novel as a metaphysical trap for the storyteller and the reader. Sarraute takes as her theme the realm of the *commonplace*, much like Dos Passos. The trick of the novelist is to shuffle off the problem of the relation of the individual to the universal by resorting to the commonplaces of character, moral opinion, and of art, especially the novel itself. Through such devices the threat of subjectivity is contained within the realm of the objective. Feeling is centrifugal and consensual, feeding upon the exchange of generalities, in flight from itself.

Sarraute subjects the novel to a confrontation with its possibility of inauthenticity. Gorz, however, pushes the novel into an extreme

---

[1] *Ibid.*, p. 19.   [2] *Ibid.*, p. 23.
[3] *Situations*, p. 195.

situation in which the words have yet to inhabit its principal character. We witness the birth of an order in which every moment involves the risk of a regression. The pages of the book murmur to us, but they do not speak in the first person for the very reason that they are in search of a self.

> What reassures us, however, is that we perceive, behind the hesitations of life and language, an arid, trenchant and frozen passion, a steel wire stretched between the lacerations of the past and the uncertainty of the future. An inhuman passion ignorant of itself, an uneasy seeker, a lunatic silence within the heart of language. It bores a hole through the reader's time, dragging this stream of words behind. We shall have faith in it.[1]

The experiment undertaken in Gorz's novel is the search for the *act* which justifies the shift from the third person to the first person. Otherwise we all remain kidnapped by the other. 'They spoke of us as "He" years before we were able to say "I". We had our first existence as absolute objects.'[2] It is this circumstance which causes us to be careless of our human nature, whereas Gorz's Traitor, by the effort he has to appropriate every human emotion, reminds us that the human species does not exist.

The error common to those writers whom Sartre refuses to recognize as novelists is that they adopt a position external to their characters. This in effect involves a double error, namely, that the writer fails to understand his own immersion in time as well as that of his characters. These writers treat time as a datum, either as a sociological or a theological assumption. The result is that their art is reduced to the revelation of the spectacle of being and falls into the category of consumption rather than production, or *praxis*. The genuine novelist is obliged to analyse his own historical situation and its effects upon his metaphysical assumptions and literary techniques. This is the task which Sartre undertook in a lengthy essay, *What is Literature?*, where he makes it clear that the novelist's creation of character is an integral factor in the historical process in which man makes himself at the risk of losing himself.

The intention of Sartre's survey of the history of literature is not to separate its future from its past or near-present. Indeed, Sartre is not *surveying* the history of literature in any ordinary sense at all. It is only

---

[1] *Situations*, p. 336.   [2] *Ibid.*, p. 345.

in the light of a literature which is for-itself that its separation from its modality as action identifies it as *having been* a literature of *hexis* and consummatory destruction. The task of literature is to reveal the human situation in order to surpass it towards a community of freedoms. Its own history is internal to the ideal relationship of generosity and freedom which it forges between the writer and the public. In the past literature fell into the category of consumption because it had adopted a metaphysics in which being and having were identical. Thus literature professed to offer through indulgence the fulfilment of being, the appropriation of being through the spectacle of being. By contrast, the literature of *praxis* starts from the metaphysical assumption that being is appropriated only through the act of making itself. The literature of *praxis* is always a literature *en situation*. It inserts itself into the world of gestures and instruments which reveal the world in the act of transforming it.

The late nineteenth century bourgeoisie had employed artists and writers to convince itself that it was capable of useless, gratuitous passions, such as adultery and stamp collecting. For a class which practised honesty out of interest, virtue through unimaginativeness and fidelity from habit, it was satisfying to be told that its daring exceeded that of the seducer or highwayman. Under these conditions the writer, himself formerly a useless passion, became a functionary in producing a *literature of alibis*, titillating the bourgeoisie with a fictional identity of the categories of production and consumption.

Surrealist literature which followed attempted to recreate the identification of literature with consumption radicalized as the pure act of destruction. It embarked upon the destruction of bourgeois subjectivity by pushing its rationality to the limit, in an automated irrationalism which consumes the contours of every object in a radical self-contradiction. In reality, the surrealists merely bracketed the world in order to celebrate its symbolic destruction. Their conception of violence was instantaneous, gratuitous and scandalous, but not such as could undertake a protracted struggle in which the categories of means and ends are essential to the definition of the political situation.

It was the 'forties which altered the pace of history and the ratios of good and evil so as to confront every individual with a situation in which to act was to play one's hand irredeemably in the certainty that destruction and evil were absolute realities. For previous generations evil had been only an appearance, a detour for freedom. Henceforth good and evil were equally absolute because their consequences for collective destruction could no longer be foreseen contemplatively, but required deliberation through action or resistance. Under these conditions the individual lived on the frontier between his own humanity and man's inhumanity to man. In these circumstances, the relativity of things could only be conveyed through a *literature of extreme situations* which involved the reader in the predicament of characters without guarantees. It was no longer possible to create a literature of ordinary situations when each day a man somewhere chose between humiliation and heroism, between the polarities of the human condition.

Finally, in the period of postwar capitalist reconstruction, literature had once again to situate itself relative to the processes of production and consumption. In a context characterized equally by the highest levels of production in history and the most profound sense of alienation it becomes the task of literature to reveal the power of the productive process over the producer, as did Hesiod in an earlier day, and to relate this alienation within the total project whereby man makes history his own history. The writer engaged in such a task must create what Sartre calls *a total literature* which is simultaneously a literary and political activity in which the writer and the reading public communicate man to man, on the model of a socialist society.

The power of nihilation or freedom whereby consciousness becomes aware of what is lacking in its condition is not an act of pure reflection or simple withdrawal. The fundamental project which I am is progressively revealed through an ensemble of real existents which simultaneously separate me from my ends and are structured secondarily as means or obstacles to my purposes. Values come into the world only through the being which carves into the plenitude of being its own lack of being.

We shall use the term *situation* for the contingency of freedom in the *plenum* of being of the world inasmuch as this *datum*, which is there only *in order not to constrain* freedom, is revealed to this freedom only as already *illuminated* by the end which freedom chooses. Thus the *datum* never appears to the for-itself as a brute existent in itself; it is discovered always *as a cause* since it is revealed only in the light of an end which illuminates it. Situation and motivation are really one. The for-itself discovers itself as engaged in being, hemmed in by being, threatened by being; it discovers the state of things which surrounds it as the cause for a reaction of defence or attack. But it can make this discovery only because it freely posits the end in relation to which the state of things is threatening or favourable.[1]

My situation is never reducible to the dead-weight upon me of my body, my place, my past, my environment, my death, my relation to the other. The significance of each of these structures unfolds only within my situation as a practical field in which my decision to act qualifies the facticities of place or environment. It is only in the light of my undertaking that things acquire a coefficient of adversity, that is to say, are designated simultaneously as *data* which have to be assumed by my action and as *possibilities* illuminated by my needs. It is through the exigency which I exist in order to become what I am that nothingness is added to the plenitude of being.

It is because freedom is condemned to be free—i.e., can not choose itself as freedom—that there are things; that is, a plenitude of contingency at the heart of which it is itself contingency and by its surpassing that there can be at once a *choice* and an organization of things in *situation*; and it is the contingency of freedom and the contingency of the in-itself which are expressed *in situation* by the unpredictability and the adversity of the environment. Thus I am absolutely free and absolutely responsible for my situation. But I can never be free except *in situation*.[2]

Thus we are in language as we are in the body; that is, as a vehicle of expression, an excarnation of particular purposes or detotalizations of the total human project. In speech we unveil the world, name its objects, and describe situations in order to transcend them. It is the poet who does not pass beyond words to the practical utilities which they furnish. To the poet these connections are purely magical. He uses words to produce word-objects or images of the world, but not to *express* a certain situation like the writer of a political pamphlet who intends to transform the situation in the light of his description. Every creation of the genuine artist, far from being a finished object opens on to the entire world, calling forth the freedom of his public.

[1] *Being and Nothingness*, pp. 487–488.
[2] *Ibid.*, p. 509.

Each painting, each book, is a recovery of the totality of being. Each of them presents this totality to the freedom of the spectator. For this is quite the final goal of art: to recover this world by giving it to be seen as it is, but as if it had its source in human freedom. But since what the author creates takes on objective reality only in the eyes of the spectator, this recovery is consecrated by the ceremony of the spectacle—and particularly of reading. We are already in a better position to answer the question we raised a while ago: the writer chooses to appeal to the freedom of other men so that, by the reciprocal implications of their demands, they may readapt the totality of being to man and may again enclose the universe within man.[1]

The artist's creation, therefore, appeals to a kingdom of ends for which terror and beauty are never simply natural events but simultaneously an *exigency* and a *gift* to be integrated into the human condition. Whenever the artist is separated from his public, his work loses its quality as an imperative and is reduced to a purely aesthetic object. In turn the artist is forced to substitute the formal relationship between himself and his art for the relationship of commitment and transcendence between the artist and the public. Under these conditions, works of art function not as outlines of the total man, but as treasures whose scarcity is the measure of the absolute poverty of man, whose eternity is the denial of human history.[2]

Together Sartre and Merleau-Ponty were the enemies of 'high-altitude thinking'. But, as Sartre tells the story, the two became estranged by everything they had in common. The thought of Merleau-Ponty was labyrinthine; its anchorage in the body, its passion unity. By contrast, Sartre allows his own thought to appear overlucid, dialectical and, even worse, optimistic in the face of Merleau-Ponty's brooding silence. The events of history forced the two to quarrel over the spontaneity of the proletarian revolution and its organization, the nature of individual and group life, in the course of which they embroiled everything each had ever stood for.

Beneath our intellectual divergences of 1941, so calmly accepted when Husserl alone was the cause, we discovered, astounded, that our conflicts had, at times, stemmed from our childhood, or went back to the elementary differences of our two organisms;

---

[1] *Literature and Existentialism*, pp. 57–58; in the original *Situations* II, pp. 106–107.
[2] 'The Artist and his Conscience', *Situations*, pp. 205–224.

and that at other times, they were between the flesh and the skin; in one of us hypocrisies, complicities, a passion for activism hiding his defeats, and, in the other, retractile emotions and a desperate quietism.[1]

Sartre generously conceded that it was from Merleau-Ponty that he 'learned History' and the testimony to this is his *Critique de la Raison Dialectique*. To some this may suggest the relative inferiority of *Being and Nothingness* to the *Phenomenology of Perception* and the consequent failure of Sartre's identification of the categories of literature and politics. This is the old criticism of Sartrean lucidity that I suggest is unjust to Sartre's phenomenology of action and situation which is the foundation of his novels and plays and his most recent studies of history and social structure. I think my argument for a certain continuity in the approaches of Sartre and Merleau-Ponty, despite their political quarrels, can be seen if we turn now to Merleau-Ponty's phenomenology of what is 'novel' in language and literature.

Merleau-Ponty's approach to the phenomenology of language and action presupposes and illustrates his conceptions of intersubjectivity and rationality and the fundamentals of his philosophy of perception and embodiment. The phenomenological approach to language is ultimately an introduction to the ontology, or to the poetry, of the world. It is a reflection upon our being-in-the-world through embodiment which is the mysterious action of a presence that can be elsewhere. The philosophical puzzles of how we are in the world (ontology) or how the world can be in us (epistemology), which have dictated quite particular analyses of the logic of language and thought, are transcended in the phenomenological conception of embodiment as a corporeal intentiality.

I reach out to my pen when I am ready to write without consciously thematizing either the pen as something to write with or the distance between myself and where the pen lies. My hand is already looking for something to write with and, as it were, scans the desk for a pen or pencil which is there 'somewhere', where it usually is or where I just put it down, so that it too seems to guide my hand in its search. But I can only look for the pen because in some sense I have my hand on it. If writing were painful to me or if I were sensible of having to write to someone I did not care for, or for whom I had only bad

1 *Ibid.*, p. 296.

news, I might 'put off' writing because I do not 'feel' like writing. In this case, my pen there on the desk does not invite me to pick it up except with a painful reminder of my relations with someone else. Thus the structure of the experience of writing is there in my fingers, in the pen and my relations to the person to whom I am writing. It is neither a structure which I 'represent' to myself, which would neglect the knowledge in my fingers, nor is it a simple 'reflex' stimulated by my pen, which would overlook my relations to the person I am writing. The structure of writing is an 'ensemble' in which the elements function only together and whose expressive value for me plays upon my relation to myself and others.

In the same way, speech is a capacity I acquire for communication which arises not just from the expressive values of the words when joined with due respect for logic and syntax but also from my experience of the world, other persons, and the language I inhabit. Linguistics as a science of language treats language as a natural object and logic treats it as an entirely artificial object.[1] The linguistic conception of language presents language as a universe from which man is absent and with him the consequences of time and the disclosure of nature in magic, myth, and poetry. In logic man's power over language which is ignored in linguistics is raised above magic and poetry to the creation of a *mathesis universalis* which sloughs off all historical languages and purifies the word once and for all. The linguistic conception of the relation of language to meaning breaks down for the very reason that a language tells us nothing except about itself.[2] The problems of discrimination, quantification, and predictability, which concern the statistical treatment of language, are independent of the semantic value of the information being processed. From the standpoint of semantics it is words not phonemes which carry meaning. Furthermore, words have meaning on their own account, especially such words as liberty or love, but also as elements in a whole which is not just the phrase or sentence but the entire

[1] Merleau-Ponty's conception of linguistics depends very much upon his own interpretations of Husserl's view on the ontogenesis of speech and his interpolation of a social psychology to complement Saussure's linguistics. Cf. Maurice Lagueux, 'Merleau-Ponty et la linguistique de Saussure', Dialogue, *Canadian Philosophical Review*, vol. IV, No. 3 (1965), pp. 351–364.

[2] For the relations between language, linguistics, logic, and semantics see Mikel Dufrenne, *Language and Philosophy*, translated by Henry B. Veatch with a Foreword by Paul Henle, Bloomington, Indiana University Press, 1963.

'mother' language. To know the meaning of a word is not just a question of an appropriate phonetic motivation. It involves familiarity with an entire universe of meaning in which language and society interpenetrate the lived meaning of words.

Language like culture is often regarded as a tool or an instrument of thought. But then language is a tool which accomplishes far more and is far less logical than we might like it to be. It is full of ambiguity and in general far too luxuriant for the taste of positivist philosophers. As a tool language seems to use us as much as we use it; and in this it is more like the rest of our general culture, which we cannot use without inhabiting it. Ultimately, language like culture defeats any attempt to conceive it as a system capable of revealing the genesis of its own meaning. This is because we *are* the language we are talking about. That is to say, we are the material truth of language through our body, which is a natural language. It is through our body that we can speak of the world because the world in turn speaks to us through the body.

> 'In my book the body lives in and moves through space and is the home of a full human personality. The words I write are adapted to express first one of its functions then another. In *Lestrygonians* the stomach dominates and the rhythm of the episode is that of the peristaltic movement.' 'But the minds, the thoughts of the characters,' I began. 'If they had no body they would have no mind,' said Joyce. 'It's all one. Walking towards his lunch my hero, Leopold Bloom, thinks of his wife, and says to himself, "Molly's legs are out of plumb." At another time of day he might have expressed the same thought without any underthought of food. But I want the reader to understand always through suggestion rather than direct statement.'[1]

Since human perception falls upon a world in which we are enclosed our expression of the world in language and art can never be a simple introduction to the prose of the world apart from its poetry. We express the world through the poetics of our being-in-the world, beginning with the first act of perception which brings into being the perspective of form and ground through which the invisible and ineffable speaks and becomes visible in us. All other cultural gestures are continuous with the first institution of human labour, speech

[1] Frank Budgen, *James Joyce and the Making of Ulysses*, Bloomington, Indiana University Press, 1960, p. 21.

and art through which the world takes root in us. In this sense, we may consider talk, reading, writing, and love as institutions, that is to say, polarizations of the established and the new. We may, for example, distinguish between the institution of *language* as an objective structure studied by linguistics and *speech*, which is the use-value language acquires when turned toward expression and the institution of new meanings.

We start by reading an author, leaning at first upon the common associations of his words until, gradually, the words begin to flow in us and to open us to an original sound which is the writer's voice borrowing from us an understanding that until then we did not know was ours to offer. Yet it comes only from what we ourselves brought to the book, our knowledge of the language, of ourselves, and life's questions which we share with the author. Once we have acquired the author's style of thinking our lives interweave in a presence which is the anticipation of the whole of the author's intention and its simultaneous recovery which continues the understanding.[1] In talking and listening to one another we make an accommodation through language and the body in which we grow old together. We encroach upon one another, borrowing from each other's time, words, and looks what we are looking for in ourselves. In this way our mind and self may be thought of as an institution which we inhabit with others in a system of presences which includes Socrates or Sartre just as much as our friends in the room.

> When I speak or understand, I experience that presence of others in myself or of myself in others which is the stumbling-block of the theory of intersubjectivity. I experience that presence of what is represented which is the stumbling-block of the theory of time, and I finally understand what is meant by Husserl's enigmatic statement, 'Transcendental subjectivity is intersubjectivity.' To the extent that what I say has meaning, I am a different 'other' for myself when I am speaking; and I understand, I no longer know who is speaking and who is listening.[2]

Through language I discover myself and others, in talking, listening, reading, and writing. It is language which makes possible that aesthetic distance between myself and the world through which I can

1 Maurice Merleau-Ponty, 'On the Phenomenology of Language', *Signs*, translated by Richard C. McCleary, Evanston, Northwestern University Press, 1964,
2 *Signs*, p. 97.

speak about the world and the world in turn speak in me. Our thoughts and purposes are embodied in bodily gestures which in the act of expression structure themselves toward habit and spontaneity, and thus we make our world.

Finally, what we may learn from Merleau-Ponty's approach to the phenomenology of language is that expression is always an act of self-improvisation in which we borrow from the world, from others, and from our own past efforts. Language is the child in us which speaks of the world in order to know who he is.

8: Between Montaigne and Machiavelli

Merleau-Ponty's political experience is inseparable from the philosophical reflections in which he sought to express the irreducible ambiguity of thought becoming action and the blindness of action unclarified by critical thought. His meditations are identical with political action because they responded to the political situation of his time. Our politics has failed to acquire a voice of its own in which the call to freedom and intersubjectivity eschews the sterile alternatives of anticommunism and anticapitalism. History it seems has played upon politics the same trick that politics hoped to play upon history. The Right and the Left have failed either to stabilize or to put an end to history. Rather, each has acquired a history which includes the other. Capitalism has its future in socialism, but not by any inevitable path. Socialism, however, has its past in capitalism and is more likely to resemble capitalism than to differ from it, if all that lies between them is a vocabulary of freedom lacking an infrastructure of intersubjectivity. Thus neither the Left nor the Right possesses the truth though neither is false, except as each attempts to stand outside of the other, thereby separating itself from its own history and its anchorage in a common political tradition.

Merleau-Ponty would certainly have merited all the anger, if not the awe, of his political friends and opponents had he simply found a position of political scepticism from which to expose the contradictions of the Right and the Left.[1] He knew well enough that in

[1] Georg Lukács touches the issue most closely in his criticisms of the inadequacy of Merleau-Ponty's existentialist concept of opinion and its dialectical relation to objective social and historical processes. Lukács' conclusion is that Merleau-Ponty's

contemporary politics criticism of the Left is tantamount to support of the Right. Yet he could not accept that criticism of the Right meant unqualified support of the Left. This was not because Merleau-Ponty lacked political will-power or wished to indulge the rationalism of the professional intellectual. He might have chosen silence, but he thought of silence as an originary mode of expression in which meaning is fermented and solicited by the world to which it belongs. It might be mentioned that he had fought beside his fellow men, that he never ceased to argue with them, to write for them, to assume their situation as his own. But this would only add to the enigma of the distance which men felt between Merleau-Ponty and themselves. Moreover, it would be wrong to explain away that distance by an appeal to instances of comradeship. This would be to fail to see that the world and others are present to us through an *aesthetic distance* which permits us to inhabit the world and to encroach upon others without shifting our own ground. It is this very distance that is the presupposition of all secondary structures of physical and social existence. Thus Merleau-Ponty established in himself the wonder that men have for each other but which they mistake for scepticism in those individuals who excel in that wonder.

It is understandable then that Merleau-Ponty's political meditations drew inspiration from Montaigne and Machiavelli and that in reflecting upon them he sought to unravel the ambiguities of scepticism, humanism, and terror in order to clarify that 'astonishing junction between fact and meaning, between my body and myself, myself and others, my thought and my speech, violence and truth' which is the originary ground of social and political life.

I shall attempt to interpret Merleau-Ponty's conception of the ambiguity of politics developed in the essay *Humanism and Terror*[1] by situating that essay between his meditations on Montaigne[2] and

---

existentialism, despite its more concrete approach to politics, ultimately falls into eclecticism and nihilism. Cf. *Existentialisme ou Marxisme?*, Paris, Nagel, 1948, pt 3, chap. 5. My remarks, though not directed at Lukács' criticism, would, I think, answer it as well as give some idea of the rather special sense that Merleau-Ponty gives to the existentialist perspective.

[1] M. Merleau-Ponty, *Humanism and Terror*, An Essay on the Communist Problem, trans. with notes by John O'Neill, Boston, Beacon Press, 1969.

[2] 'Reading Montaigne', in *Signs*, pp. 198–210.

Machiavelli.[1] It is hoped that these reflections illuminate the larger essay in as much as they reveal Merleau-Ponty's conception of political reflection and save it from criticisms of scepticism and non-commitment which I think quite alien to Merleau-Ponty's philosophical thought.

On reading Montaigne it is not enough simply to say of him that he was a sceptic. For scepticism has two aspects. It means that nothing is true, but also that nothing is false. Thus we cannot conclude that scepticism abandons us to an utter relativism of truth. Rather, it opens us to the idea of a totality of truth in which contradiction is a necessary element in our experience of truth. Montaigne's scepticism is rooted in the paradox of *conscious being*, to be constantly involved in the world through perception, politics, or love and yet always at a distance from it without which we would know nothing of it. '*What is taken to be rare about Perseus King of Macedonia— that his mind attached itself to no rank but went wandering through all kinds of life and representing customs to itself which were so vagabond and flighty that it was not known to himself or others what man this was—seems to me more or less to apply to everyone. We are always thinking somewhere else.*'[2] And, as Merleau-Ponty adds, 'it could not possibly be otherwise. To be conscious is, among other things, to be somewhere else.' Thus the sceptic only withdraws from the world, its passions and follies, in order to find himself at grips with the world, having as it were merely slackened the intentional ties between himself and the world in order to comprehend the paradox of his being-in-the-world. Whenever Montaigne speaks of man he refers to him as 'strange', 'monstrous', or 'absurd'. What he has in mind is the paradoxical mixture that we are of mind and body, so that a prince can kill his beloved brother because of a dream he has had.

The variety of human practices produces in Montaigne something more than anthropological curiosity or philosophical scepticism. '*I study myself more than other subjects. It is my metaphysics and my physics.*' Because of the mixture of being that he is, the explanation of man can only be given by himself to himself, through an experience of the problematic nature that he is. Man does not borrow himself from philosophy or from science. He is the treasure upon which the

---

[1] 'A Note on Machiavelli', in *Signs*, pp. 211–213.

[2] The italicized quotations are cited by Merleau-Ponty from Montaigne's *Essays*, Book III.

sciences draw. Nevertheless, man has to make his own fortune and in this the folly of a treasure laid up in a religious heaven is no better, nor for that matter any worse, than the treasures of Eldorado. For the enthusiasm of religion is a mode of our folly and our folly is essential to us.

> When we put not self-satisfied understanding but a consciousness astonished at itself at the core of human existence, we can neither obliterate the dream of an other side of things nor repress the wordless invocation of this beyond.[1]

Montaigne can, however, speak as though we should remain indifferent to the world and in love or politics never allow ourselves to play more than a role. '*We must lend ourselves to others and give ourselves only to ourselves.*' And yet we must adopt the principles of family and state institutions for they are the essential follies of life with others. To attempt to live outside of the state and the family reveals the abstraction of the stoic distinction between what is internal and what is external, between necessity and freedom.

> We cannot always obey if we despise, or despise always if we obey. There are occasions when to obey is to accept and to despise is to refuse, when a life which is in part a double life ceases to be possible, and there is no longer any distinction between exterior and interior. Then we must enter the world's folly, and we need a rule for such a moment.[2]

But this is not a desperate attempt to achieve certainty. It would only be this if we assumed the standpoint of a finished truth toward which we could move from doubt only by a leap. But that would be to exchange our nature for some other existence, whether animal or angel; '*the extinction of a life is the way to a thousand lives*'. If we abandon such a notion then we come back to the ground of opinion, to the fact that there is truth and men have to learn doubt. '*I know what it is to be human better than I know what it is to be animal, mortal or rational.*' Scepticism with respect to the passions only deprives them of value if we assume a total self-possession, whereas we are never wholly ourselves but always interested in the world through the passions which we are. Then we understand the passions as the vehicle by which truth and value are given to us and we see that the critique of the passions is the rejection of false passions

---

[1] *Signs*, p. 203.   [2] *Ibid.*, p. 205.

which do not carry us toward the world and men, but close us in a subjectivity we have not freely chosen.

While it is the evil of public life to associate us with opinions and projects we have not chosen for ourselves, the flight into the self only reveals the self as openness toward the world and men, so that among other things we are for others and their opinion touches the very core of our being.

> The fact of the matter is that true scepticism is movement toward the truth, that the critique of passions is hatred of false passions, and finally, that in *some* circumstances Montaigne recognized outside himself men and things he never dreamed of refusing himself to, because they were like the emblem of his outward freedom, and because in loving them he was himself and regained himself in them as he regained them in himself.[1]

Scepticism and misanthropy whatever the appearances, are misbegotten political virtues for the reason that the essential ambiguity of politics is that its vices derive from what is most valuable to men —the idea of a truth which each intends for all because men do not live side by side like pebbles, but each lives in all. It is the evidence of the vital truths which men hold intersubjectively which provides the infrastructure of social and political life. This is not to say that this prepolitical suffrage ever exists in abstraction from political and social institutions, nor to deny that it is weighted by ideology. Our task is to make it function as the *norm* of political society, to communicate it through criticism, information, and publicity. This is a difficult task and one which demands a philosophy which is free of political responsibilities because it has its own. Such a philosophy can be free and faithful because it does not play at reconstructing politics, passions, and life, but devotes itself to the disclosure of the basic meaning-structures through which we inhabit the world.

Merleau-Ponty's essay on *Humanism and Terror* is an exercise in political philosophy which is true to itself as philosophy because it dwells within the problematic of communism and anticommunism in order to reveal the latent structures of political action, truth, and violence, which are the foundations of all social existence. The starting point of Merleau-Ponty's reflections on the Communist problem, as it is raised by the Moscow Trials, seems to defeat all progress in

[1] *Signs*, p. 207.

the argument and almost ensured that it would win converts from neither side. The argument runs the risk of being dismissed for its hesitation, its noncommitment, or even flatly rejected as an ill-timed invitation to scepticism at a moment when the Third World seems bent upon learning the ideologies of the Right or the Left. And yet it is precisely to the problem of the genesis of political community and the clarification of the historical option which it involves that the essay on humanism and terror addresses itself. It cannot therefore be dismissed as a local tract nor be ignored by those whose hope is for an end of ideology.[1]

'Communism does not invent violence, it finds it established.' Communism has no monopoly on violence. All political regimes are criminal, however liberal the principles to which they subscribe. Liberal societies are compatible with domestic and international exploitation in which their principles of freedom and equality participate as mystifications. The liberal cannot salve his conscience with the myth that violence has been completely legalized in his own society and for that reason he cannot identify terror with communism. But the Communist sympathizer is in no better position. Violence cannot be understood historically or statistically. The death of a single individual is sufficient to condemn an entire regime. 'The anticommunist refuses to see that violence is universal, the exalted sympathizer refuses to see that no one can look violence in the face.'[2] The nature of political action is not contained by the alternatives of the yogi and the commissar, for men are neither entirely interior beings nor wholly the objects of external manipulation. This is not to deny that Rubashov might provide himself with the objectivist arguments of Marxian scientism and historicism. From this point of view the self remains an empty category until the

[1] The following comment upon Arthur Koestler's *Darkness at Noon*, to which *Humanism and Terror* is also a response, seems to be true for both works: 'I fancy that his novel has fallen under a temporary cloud. That is partly because it is political, and because it was inspired by the Moscow Trials the butterflies of criticism imagine that it can be tucked away in the file marked "Topical". It was topical, is topical and always will be topical for in no foreseeable future will the circumstance that gave rise to it be eliminated. It will remain topical just as *Gulliver's Travels* has remained topical for those who have discovered it is not just a children's book.' John Atkins, *Arthur Koestler*, New York, Roy Publishers, 1956, pp. 177–178.

[2] *Humanism and Terror*, p. 2.

party has fulfilled its historical task of providing the economic infrastructure of authentic subjectivity. But this is a position motivated by a conception of consciousness as either everything or nothing. Even if we understand this alternation simply as a political strategy, the question arises: What does Rubashov make of his personal consciousness in the days after the trial when, after publicly saving his past, he is faced with the existential difference between the judgment of universal history and his own self-esteem? To answer this question we must understand something of the relation between political reason and political passions.

'One does not become a revolutionary through science, but out of indignation. Science comes afterwards in order to fill in and determine that empty protestation.'[1] Rubashov and his comrades had started from the evident truth of the value of men and only later learned that in the course of building its economic infrastructure they would have to subject individuals to the violence generated in the distance between the specific circumstances of the revolution and its future. The paradox of the revolutionary is that the recognition of the value of intersubjectivity engages a struggle to the death which reproduces the alienation of the individual between the options of a subjectivism and an objectivism neither of which can reach its proper conclusion. Marxism does not create this dilemma, it merely expresses it. Koestler, on the other hand, poses the problem in such a way that he neglects what is *moral* in the Marxist decision to treat the self solely from outside, from the standpoint of the objective requirements of history. He thereby misses the essential ambiguity of the distinction between the subjective and the objective standpoints. The values of the yogi are not simply the reverse of those of the commissar because each experiences an internal reversal of the values of subjectivism and objectivism whenever either standpoint is assumed as an absolute. We can understand then that, once in prison, Rubashov experiences the value of the self in the depths of its interiority where it opens toward the White Guard in the neighbouring cell *as someone to whom one can talk*.[2] The tapping on the prison walls is the first institution of that communication between men for the sake of which Rubashov had embarked upon his revolutionary career. Between the beginning and the end of his life there is,

1 *Humanism and Terror*, p. 11.
2 *Ibid.*, p. 5.

however, a continuity which is possible only through the contradiction which it embraces.

It is this openness toward its own past and future that prevents political action from ever being unequivocal. Hence the historical responsibility that the revolutionary assumes can never be established as a matter of brute fact. The Trials therefore never go beyond the level of a 'ceremony of language' in which meaning is sensed entirely within the verbal exchanges and not through reference to an external ground of verification.

> The Trials do not go beyond the subjective and never approach what one calls 'true' justice, objective and timeless, *because they bear upon facts which are still open toward the future, which consequently are not yet univocal and only acquire a definitively criminal character when they are viewed from the perspective on the future held by the men in power.*[1]

What the Trials reveal to us is the form and style of the revolutionary. The revolutionary judges what exists in terms of what is to come, he regards the future as more vital than the present to which it owes its birth. From this perspective there can be no subjective honour; we are entirely and solely what we are for others and our relation to them. The revolutionary masters the present in terms of the future, whereas the counter-revolutionary binds the present to the past. The revolutionary shares in an intersubjective conviction of making history—which is, of course, an arbitrary conviction, but with respect to the *future* of which we cannot in principle be certain. However, the evidence of the value of a future society of comrades suffices for a revolutionary decision and its lack of certainty has nothing to do with the individual hesitation that belongs to pre-revolutionary sensibilities. For the revolutionary there exists no margin of indifference; political differences are acts of objective treason. In such circumstances government is terror and humanism[2] is suspended. It is this state of affairs which arouses the greatest offence.

The liberal conscience rejects the barbarism of communism. But

---

[1] *Ibid.*, p. 27.

[2] 'There is no serious humanism except the one which looks for man's effective recognition by his fellow man throughout the world. Consequently, it could not possibly precede the moment when humanity gives itself its means of communication and communion.' *Signs*, p. 222.

this amounts to nothing more than a refusal to give violence its name. Civilization is threatened as much by the nameless violence institutionalized in liberal society as it is by terror exercised openly in the hope of putting an end to the history of violence. In the liberal ideology, justice and politics assume a division of labour between concern for ends and the calculation of means. But this is an abstraction from political reality where conflict is generated in the definition of ends because this activity determines what shall be identified as means. In other words questions of justice are identified in terms of so-called abstract values. In reality, truth and justice are inseparable from the violence of possession and dispossession. This is evident in every revolutionary situation where society cannot be assumed but has yet to emerge from its origins in 'the passional and illegal origins of all legality and reason',[1] where for a time humanism is suspended precisely because it is in genesis.

It is the problem of the genesis of collective life which is the fundamental theme of Merleau-Ponty's reflections upon the ambiguity of humanism and terror in revolutionary societies. But, of course, he is not dealing here with the fiction of a presocial state of nature introduced in order to rationalize revolt or order according to whether the presocial condition of man is pictured as benign or brutish. Indeed, it is just these alternatives which are not open in the state of nature because it is a genetic state in which violence and justice, truth and contradiction are the very matrix from which the option of a specific historical form of society emerges. Marxists themselves lose sight of the essential contingency in the genesis of a revolutionary praxis to the extent that they treat history as an object of knowledge, ignoring their own attempt to *make* history. The Marxist intervention in history inserts into history a norm of inter-subjectivity generated through the very conflict and contingency which a scientific law of history seeks to eliminate.

At the same time Merleau-Ponty does not intend to conclude that history is simply a field of radically contingent action—'this irrationalism is indefensible for the decisive reason that *no one lives it, not even he who professes it.*'[2] That the whole of reality for man is only probable whether in the appearance of things or of the future does not mean that the world lacks a style of physiognomy in its appearance to us. We live in subjective certainties which we intend univer-

[1] *Humanism and Terror*, p. 37.   [2] *Ibid.*, p. 95.

sally and practically and that are in no way illusory unless we posit some apodictic certainty outside the grounds of human experience. 'The future is only probable, but it is not an empty zone in which we can construct gratuitous projects; it is sketched before us like the beginning of the day's end, and its outline is ourselves.'[1] We do not experience uncertainty at the very core of our existence. The centre of our experience is a common world in which we make appraisals, enlist support, and seek to convince our opponents, never doubting the potential permutation of subjective and objective evidence.

While it is true that our perspectives depend upon our motives and values, it is just as true that our values are derived from concrete experience and not drawn from some pre-established sphere. Thus contradiction and conflict do not stem from abstractly opposed principles or perspectives but presuppose a fundamental community of experience which gives meaning to such conflict. 'The dialectic of the subjective and objective is not a simple contradiction which leaves the terms it plays on disjointed; it is rather a testimony to our rootedness in the truth.'[2] This fundamental ambiguity of truth and contradiction, far from being destructive of intersubjectivity, in fact presupposes a community of men as its originary ground. This pre-supposition differs from the liberal assumption of a finished human nature. In terms of the latter it is impossible to understand conflict and error as anything but historical accidents, rather than as elements in a matrix from which truth and community emerge. Marxism differs from liberalism and anarchism[3] in that it can account for violence in history, not in the sense of providing it with excuses but

---

[1] *Ibid.*, p. 95   [2] *Ibid.*, p. 96.

[3] 'Here we are not speaking in favour of an anarchical liberty: if I wish freedom for another person it is inevitable that even this wish will be seen by him as an alien law; and so liberalism turns into violence. One can only blind oneself to this outcome by refusing to reflect upon the relation between the self and others. The anarchist who closes his eyes to this dialectic is nonetheless exposed to its consequences. It is the basic fact on which we have to build freedom. We are not accusing liberalism of being a system of violence, we reproach it with not seeing its own face in violence, with veiling the pact upon which it rests while rejecting as barbarous that other source of freedom—revolutionary freedom—which is the origin of all social pacts. With the assumptions of impersonal Reason and rational Man, and by regarding itself as a natural rather than an historical fact, liberalism assumes universality as a datum whereas the problem is its realization in the dialectic of concrete intersubjectivity.' *Ibid.*, p. 35, n. 11.

in the sense that it situates violence within the ambiguous origins of truth and justice, in the birth of reason from unreason that is the mark of a new society. The notions of truth and freedom arise only in certain cultures and are not historical laws as is pretended in the liberal version of history. Truth and freedom are options of history whose matrix is violence. The option which history opens up for us is ourselves and this option remains irreducibly what it is whether we contemplate it as a spectacle or implement it through action.

The foundations of history and politics are inseparable from the dialectic between man and nature and between man and his fellow men. It is the nature of human consciousness to realize itself in the world and among men and its embodiment is the essential mode of its opening toward the world and to others. The problem of community and coexistence only arises for an embodied consciousness driven by its basic needs into a social division of labour and engaged by its deepest need in a life and death struggle for intersubjective recognition. Embodied consciousness never experiences an original innocence to which any violence would be an irreparable harm; it knows only different kinds of violence. For consciousness finds itself already engaged in the world, in definite situations in which its resources are never merely its own but derive from the exploitation of its position as the husband of this woman, the child of these parents, the master of these slaves. As such the intentions of embodied consciousness already presuppose a common matrix of justice and injustice, truth and deception, out of which they emerge as acts of love, hate, honesty, and deceit. This is the ground presupposed by political discussion and political choice. We never act upon isolated individuals, as the liberal imagines, but always within a community which possesses a common measure of the good and evil it knows. As soon as we have lived we already know what it means for subjects to treat one another as objects, placing into jeopardy the community of subjectivity which is the originary goal of embodied consciousness. None of us reaches manhood outside of this history of the violence we hold for one another. None of us can bear it apart from the attempt within this violence to establish love and communion.

The prospects of humanism are wholly bound up with the *meaning* which Marxism introduces into violence as a polarity within a structure of truth and intersubjectivity against which all other forms of violence are retrograde. But the norm of intersubjectivity is not itself a law of history and its own genesis has no guarantee precisely because it lies in the revelation of man to himself and finds, as it were, its natural limit in man. The attempt to establish harmony within ourselves and with others as an existential truth is not routed by conflict and error, but assumes them as something we can overcome as fellow men.

This last reflection raises once again the question of the relation between truth and community. The problem is that the emergence of truth seems to presuppose a community, and in turn the emergence of a community assumes a concept of truth. The Marxist criticism of the liberal truth lies in the exposition of its lack of correspondence within the objective relations between men in liberal society. The problem of communism is similar, since it has failed so far to make the historical road-repairs which were written into its political charter. Marxism claims to be a truth in the making; it overturns liberal society in order to clear the way for the genesis of a society grounded in authentic intersubjectivity. The birth of Communist society, however, is no less painful than the birth of man himself, and already from the earliest years it is familiar with violence and contradiction.

Merleau-Ponty's thought dwells within the circle of this problem and it seems natural that he should have turned toward Machiavelli whose own meditations embraced the same problematic. 'For he describes that knot of collective life in which pure morality can be cruel and pure politics requires something like a morality.'[1] Had either Montaigne or Machiavelli stood outside of politics in order to contemplate political action, then they might easily have succumbed to the conclusions of scepticism and cynicism. But then they would have broken the circle of being which we inhabit whereas they chose to dwell and to meditate within it. They would not otherwise have provided a model for Merleau-Ponty's reflections upon their experience, which, we suggest, is indirectly his own political experience.

If the cynic is right and humanity essentially an accident, then it is difficult to see what else besides sheer force could uphold collective life. In this mood Machiavelli is obsessed with violence and oppression. But there is a deeper reflection in Machiavelli which discovers something other than sheer force in the phenomenon of conflict and aggression.

[1] *Signs*, p. 211.

While men are trying not to be afraid, they begin to make themselves feared by others; and they transfer to others the aggression that they push back from themselves, as if it were absolutely necessary to offend or be offended.[1]

Human aggression is not simply a conflict of animal or physical forces, but a polarity within a dialectic of intersubjective recognition or alienation. Political power never rests upon naked force but always presumes a ground of opinion and consensus within a margin of potential conflict and violence that is crossed only when this common sense is outraged. 'Relationships between the subject and those in power, like those between the self and others, are cemented at a level deeper than judgment. As long as it is not a matter of the radical challenge of contempt, they survive challenge.'[2] The exercise of power succeeds best as an appeal to freedom rather than as an act of violence which only reinforces itself through the aggression which it arouses. The art of the Prince is to maintain the free consent of his subjects and in this we discover a touchstone for a humanist politics in as much as the people at least seek to avoid oppression if not to aim at anything greater.

The *virtue* of the Prince is a mode of living with others such that their opinion is consulted without being followed slavishly nor merely heard without effect. At such times there is always the possibility that the originary conflict of will and opinion will arise and yet it is only under these conditions that there can be genuine consultation and real leadership. Within such a community the exercise of power is tied to the realm of appearances, for only the Prince can know how the people are and only they know him.

What sometimes transforms softness into cruelty and harshness into value, and overturns the precepts of private life, is that acts of authority intervene in a certain state of opinion which changes their meaning. They awake an echo which is at times immeasurable. They open or close hidden fissures in the block of general consent, and trigger a molecular process which may modify the whole course of events. Or as mirrors set around in a circle transform a slender flame into a fairyland, acts of authority reflected in the constellation of consciousness are transfigured, and the reflections of these reflections create an appearance which is the proper place—the truth, in short—of historical action.[3]

[1] *Signs*, p. 211–212.   [2] *Ibid.*, p. 213.   [3] *Ibid.*, p. 216.

Machiavelli is a difficult thinker because he forces upon us the ambiguity of virtue from which self-styled humanists so often shrink, preferring the history of principles to the history of men. Between Montaigne, Machiavelli, and Marx, on the other hand, there is common effort to consider the nature of history and politics within the boundaries that men set for themselves. That is to say, human action always achieves something more and something less than it envisages and yet political man must assume the consequences. Far from being a fatal flaw in the nature of action this essential ambiguity is what makes human actions neither blindly impulsive nor divinely efficacious. At the same time, the ambiguity of political action is not a justification for the lack of political conviction or fidelity. For what introduces ambiguity into political action is precisely the metamorphoses of truth and justice experienced in putting them into practice without any absolute guarantee that this project will not be attacked, sabotaged, and even undermined from within. It is, in short, the denial of political innocence even at the birth of freedom.

Finally, Merleau-Ponty teaches us the lesson that truth and justice are alien to history and politics in the sense that they can never be completely realized and yet never exist entirely apart from the life and vicissitudes of community and power. The expression of truth and justice is never a solitary confrontation of the philosopher and a truth which he expresses, unless we lose sight of the community to which the philosopher belongs and before whom he expresses the truth. This is not to say that the philosopher expresses the truth solely in accordance with others, any more than for himself alone, or as the voice of a truth in itself in abstraction from himself and others. The enigma of philosophy is that sometimes life has the *same* face for us and for others and before the truth, so that the philosopher is called to share a life whose truth and goodness is evident and he would never think of opposing himself to his fellow men or setting truth against life. And yet the philosopher knows the limits of other men and must refuse them, but with all the more peace that comes from sharing the same world. 'Hence the rebellious gentleness, the thoughtful adherence, the intangible presence that upset those around him.'[1]

To pose the problem of truth and opinion in this way opens

[1] *Eloge de la philosophie et autres essais*, Paris, Gallimard, 1960, p. 41.

memory to what is close to us from the past and lends immediacy to the life and death of Socrates who bore men the same love that he bore towards philosophy. If Socrates had simply denied the gods of the City he would have shown his fellow men nothing more than their daily practice. But Socrates sacrificed to the gods and obeyed the law of the City to his death. Or if Socrates had claimed to believe more than his fellow men he might well have scandalized them; but in either case, whether through excess or revolt, he would not have conveyed his essential irony, which is to have thought religion true but not in the way it understood itself to be true, just as he believed the *polis* to be just but not for reasons of state. Socrates could speak as though he obeyed the laws out of the conservatism of age and the gradualism it calls hope. But his inertia is more truly that of his daimon or the absolute standpoint of an internal truth which admonishes through joining man to his own ignorance. Only by engaging his judges in the example of an obedience which is simultaneously a resistance, in an encounter with a truth which is proved whether they sentence him or acquit him can Socrates introduce into the *polis* the principle of philosophy which transforms the certainty of religion by bringing both religion and philosophy to the same ground. Thus the Socratic irony does not lie in the exploitation of the differences of level between philosophy and religion but in the experience of their reversal. The significance of Socrates' obedience to the laws is that henceforth the *polis* is the guardian of the individual soul; it has become a citadel without walls and hence no longer needs the laws of religion and the state—it needs men.

There is no complacency or self-sufficiency behind the Socratic irony.

The irony of Socrates is a distant but true relation with others. It expresses the fundamental fact that each of us is himself only when there is no escape and yet can recognize himself in the other. It is an attempt to release us together for freedom.[1]

There would be no tragedy in Socrates' stand before the Athenian Assembly if he had not believed that his fellow men could understand him or that no one after him would take a similar stand. Not everyone voted to condemn Socrates; for truth and error, justice and injustice are never whole and have always to be taken up again in every age and by every man.

[1] *Eloge de la philosophie*, p. 47.

PART THREE

On Estrangement and Embodiment

In this section the themes of alienation and embodiment are treated in a specifically Marxist vocabulary. At this stage the essays on Marx are analytic and critical in the conventional sense, attention being given to the unity of Marxist humanism and social science. The argument for the unity of Marx's thought, which has occasioned so much political and intellectual controversy, is in my opinion simultaneously an argument for the complementarity of Hegelian and Marxist thought. This is dealt with as the problem of critical theory in the next section which is the necessary foundation for the following essays on estrangement and mythology in Marx. The *a priori* of Hegelian Marxist thought is the embodiment of human consciousness and the history of its reflexive awareness in the structures of language, work, and politics, governed by the dialectic of domination and recognition. These are the common themes of Marxism and existential phenomenology, although they may be stressed differently, as in the work of Sartre and Maurice Merleau-Ponty.

9: The Concept of Estrangement in the Early and Later Writings of Karl Marx

In his article on 'Alienation and History in Early Marx' L. D. Easton has shown how Marx took over the concept of alienation which he found in Hegel's *Phenomenology of the Spirit*.[1] Apparently, however, when Marx formulated his mature theory of the social structure of capitalism and the laws of its development into socialism by means of a political revolution, Marx chose to neglect a number of critical points he had established in his early study of Hegel. But Mr Easton does not specify any of the intervening mechanisms which are responsible for Marx's lapse of critical attention. It will be the purpose of this essay to sketch two possible theorems by which Marx came to contradict himself. Some further comments will be made upon the need for awareness of the precise application of the attempts by Professors Popper and Hayek, for example, to dispose of Marxian social science on the ground that it is built upon the methodological fallacies of collectivism and historicism. These errors, though absent at first, are described as essential to the final state of Marxian social science in the following remarks of Mr Easton:

> As Marx identified the end of man's alienation with the 'real movement' of history, he came to emphasize its independence

1 *Philosophy and Phenomenological Research*, vol. XXII, no. 2 (December 1961), pp. 193–205; Cf. K. Löwith, 'Man's Self-Alienation in the Early Writings of Marx' *Social Research*, vol. XXI, no. 2 (Summer 1954), pp. 204–230.

from men's actions, likened its laws to those of nature which work with 'iron necessity towards inevitable results', and viewed it as a dialectical relation of classes and entities such as 'proletariat', 'civil society', and 'bourgeoisie'. Within this perspective, especially in terms of achieving class power, 'the State' as such becomes important.[1]

Marx's criticisms of Hegel's philosophical system exposed its structural dependency upon the reification of concepts. Marx argued that Hegel had inverted the relation of logic to ontology. Earlier, Feuerbach had showed the concept of Divinity to be simply a projection of the ethical qualities of human individuals. Similarly, Hegel's dialectical law of the movement of History was exposed by Feuerbach as nothing else than the contradiction of philosophy with itself, namely, denying theology only to restore it later.[2]
In Marx's own words, there is a double error in Hegel:

> The first emerges most clearly in the *Phenomenology*, the Hegelian philosophy's place of origin. When, for instance, wealth, statepower, etc., are understood by Hegel as entities estranged from the *human* being, this only happens in their form as thoughts . . . They are thought-entities, and therefore merely an estrangement of *pure*, i.e., abstract, philosophical thinking. The whole process therefore ends with Absolute Knowledge.[3]

The second error is expressed more briefly within the discussion of Hegel's first mistake:

> It is not the fact that the human being *objectifies himself inhumanly*, in opposition to himself, but the fact that he *objectifies himself* in *distinction* from and in *opposition* to abstract thinking, that is the posited essence of the estrangement and the thing to be superseded.[4]

Hegel, according to Marx, had understood the problem of alienation solely in terms of the separation of the thinking subject from its

---

[1] *Philosophy and Phenomenological Research*, vol. XXII, p. 203.

[2] K. Marx, *Economic and Philosophic Manuscripts of 1844*, Moscow, Foreign Languages Publishing House, Critique of the Hegelian Dialectic and Philosophy as a whole.

[3] *Ibid.*, p. 149; *The Holy Family or Critique of Critical Critique*, Moscow, Foreign Languages Publishing House, 1956, pp. 81–82.

[4] K. Marx, *Economic and Philosophic Manuscripts of 1844*, p. 149.

own experience which it can only express in terms of general concepts. Hegel's *Phenomenology* provides an analysis of epistemological alienation in place of the socio-political alienation which is the ontological source of the separation of man from his essential nature. Hegel's philosophy is nothing else than the philosophical expression of a disintegrated reality.

Are we then to believe that Marx merely substituted for Hegel's *Phenomenology* an economic theory which he then proceeded to develop employing the same conceptual realism and dialectic which he had critically exposed in Hegel?

It is in fact precisely this error which Marx criticized in Proudhon's *La Philosophie de la Misère*,[1] though he acknowledges partial responsibility inasmuch as he was Proudhon's first tutor in Hegelianism.[2] Proudhon's half-assimilated Hegelianism, when applied to economic phenomena, resulted in the description of merely logical antagonisms between economic categories of rich and poor, monopoly and competition, freedom and slavery. Proudhon, according to Marx, misunderstood the relation of economic theory to historical reality and provided a purely ideological account of the basis of economic phenomena.

> Monsieur Proudhon has very well grasped the fact that men produce cloth, linen, silks, and it is a great merit on his part to have grasped this small amount. What he has not grasped is that these men, according to their powers, also produce the *social relations* amid which they prepare cloth and linen. Still less has he understood that men, who fashion their social relations in accordance with their material method of production, also fashion *ideas* and *categories*, that is to say the abstract, ideal expression of these same social relations. Thus the categories are no more eternal than the relations they express. They are historic and transitory products. For M. Proudhon, on the contrary, abstractions and categories are the primordial cause. According to him they, and not men, make history. The *abstraction*, the *category taken as such*, i.e., apart from men and their material activities, is of course immortal, unmoved, unchangeable, it is

1 Marx to P. V. Annenkov, Brussels, 28 December 1846, in K. Marx and F. Engels, *Selected Correspondence 1846–1895*, New York, International Publishers, 1934, pp. 5–18.

2 Marx to Schweitzer, London, 24 January 1865, in *Selected Correspondence*, pp. 169–176.

E

only one form of the being of pure reason; which is only another way of saying that the abstraction as such is abstract. An admirable *tautology!*

Thus, regarded as categories, economic relations for M. Proudhon are eternal formulae without origin or progress.[1]

In the course of his review of Proudhon's work, Marx gives an extremely flexible formulation of the theory of historical materialism which provides the critique of *ideological historiography* in the manner of Hegel and Proudhon. Marx raises the question: 'What is society, whatever its form may be?' He replies that it is 'the product of men's reciprocal activity'. This, however, does not mean that individuals can choose this or that form of society. At a given stage of history men inherit from a previous generation a certain complement of material and cultural production possibilities. This phenomenon is the basis of a certain historical continuity and progression, since each succeeding generation can build upon the accumulated efforts of the past. 'Assume particular stages of development in production, commerce and consumption and you will have a corresponding social order, a corresponding organization of the family and of the ranks and classes, in a word, a corresponding civil society.'[2] Nevertheless, Marx does not at this time posit a one-to-one correlation between the economic substructure and the ideological super-structure. Although he considered the ideological factors dependent variables, Marx was aware that they tended to be lagged variables even possessing a reactive independence which gives to social change a revolutionary character.

It will be necessary to discover how Marx later allowed the theory of historical materialism to harden into the form of a theory of economic, perhaps technological epiphenomenalism. It will be suggested that this effect is in part due to epistemological polemics in which Marx sided with a realist, correspondence theory of knowledge in order to avoid excesses of subjective idealism and the historiography built upon it. The difficulties of the inflexible version of historical materialism are further compounded by the importation of the dialectical formula to express the development of the basic mechanism of social change. In the latter case, what is strictly a methodological decision, namely, the identification of the basic factor

---

[1] Marx to Annenkov, *Selected Correspondence*, pp. 14–15.
[2] *Ibid.* p. 7.

in social change, is confused with the political strategem of backing the proletariat as the ontological medium of social change. The effect of these latter moves in the development of Marx's social theory is to give it the very form of an alienated (estranged) ideology of which he himself had been an early critic.

Where Proudhon had failed, Marx believed himself to have succeeded. Moreover, Marx is ready to acknowledge his own success in terms of its original Hegelian inspiration. Even when critizing Hegel, Marx distilled from the *Phenomenology* an insight which provided a framework for all his later work and which is present even in *Capital*.[1] Marx summarizes his general criticism of Hegel with the recognition of the basic value of the Hegelian inquiry:

> The outstanding thing in Hegel's *Phenomenology* and its final outcome—that is, the dialectic of negativity as the moving and generating principle—is thus first that Hegel conceives the self-genesis of man as a process, conceives objectification as loss of the object, as alienation and as transcendence of this alienation; that he thus grasps the essence of *labour* and comprehends objective man—true, because real man—as the outcome of man's *own labour*.[2]

The perfectly sound intuition in Hegel is that man creates himself in the sense that he reproduces himself biologically and maintains himself through a process of socially organized labour. Just as theoretical concepts may be said to be mental constructs, so the social, political, and economic structure may be said to be the proper expression, product, or externalization of human beings considered as psycho-physical entities.

> *Man* is directly a *natural being*. As a natural being and as living natural being he is on the one hand furnished with *natural powers of life*—he is an *active* natural being. These forces exist in him as tendencies and abilities—as *impulses*. On the other hand, as a natural, corporeal, sensuous, objective being he is a *suffering*, conditioned and limited creature, like animals and plants. That is to say, the *objects* of his impulses exist outside him, as *objects* independent of him; yet these objects are *objects* of his *need*— essential *objects*, indispensable to the manifestation and con-

[1] J. Hippolyte, *Etudes sur Marx et Hegel*, Paris, Rivière, 1955, pp. 95-100; R. Dunayevskaya, *Marxism and Freedom*, New York, Bookman Associates, 1958.
[2] K. Marx, *Economic and Philosophic Manuscripts*, p. 151.

firmation of his essential powers. To say that man is a *corporeal,*
living, sensuous, objective being full of natural vigour is to say
that he has *real, sensuous, objects* as the objects of his being or of
his life, or that he can only *express* his life in real sensuous objects.
To be objective, natural, and sensuous, and at the same time to
have object, nature, and sense outside oneself, or oneself to be
object, nature, and sense for a third party, is one and the same
thing.[1]

As such Marx's formulation does not argue for the primacy of the
socio-economic substructure over the ideological superstructure. The
very phrasing of this last remark is the result of a polemic which
ignores the fact that both spheres involve ideational systems. The
economic process is in fact a subculture within the total social
culture. It may be that the economic system contains the engine of
development which generates cultural possibilities of progress.
Marx asks how it could be otherwise, unless one believes that history
is made by kings and queens, saints and politicians.

There is nothing mysterious, says Marx, in the fact that man,
as a psycho-physical entity, expresses himself through thought-
constructs and cultural objects. The process of *externalization*
(*Entäusserung*) is the natural expression of the kind of being man is.
Marx does not lament the external world, for it is the precondition of
all human effort, the means to human expression. It is when the
products of man's mental and physical energy deny or despoil the
integrity of man's nature that the phenomenon of *estrangement*
(*Entfremdung*) is encountered.

Now the term alienation is frequently used to cover both the
phenomenon of externalization and estrangement. This can only lead
to a misunderstanding of Marx's use of the concept of alienation. It
is clear that the externalization of human behaviour into ideologies,
social institutions, material products is a necessary precondition of the
phenomenon of estrangement, i.e., man being treated, say, as a means
to, rather than the end of, such cultural products. But the reverse is
not true. It is not necessary that the phenonenon of externalization
be accompanied by estrangement. In fact, if this were the case, then
Marx's work becomes unintelligible.[2] Is not the whole purpose of

---

[1] K. Marx, *Economic and Philosophic Manuscripts*, pp. 156–157.

[2] This may surprise those who try to give Marxism a face-lift by making just
such an identification, i.e., revamping Marxism as a *general* critique of social
organization and culture.

Marx's critique of capitalism to show that capitalism, an historically progressive externalization (expression) of human energies attested to by the *Communist Manifesto*, is a necessary step toward the social organization of freedom under socialism or communism? Marx is not the critic of social structure as such. He is the analyst of historical social structures. His criticisms are ethical evaluations of the degree to which social structures realize an ideal of authentic being, i.e., nonestranged or unalienated existence.

Marx did not work out a complete ethical theory of authentic existence.[1] One might say that Marx was attempting to give a sociological interpretation of the regulative principle of Kantian epistemology and the categorical imperative of Kantian ethics. Marx had absorbed through Hegel the Kantian critique of British and Continental empiricism.[2] When Marx objects to the idealist exaggeration of the contribution of consciousness to experience, it is not an anti-epistemological objection; it is a sociological restraint. However, it is the epistemological primacy of consciousness with respect to experience which provides the source of an ethical norm for the relation of individuals to social environment.

Marxian epistemology struggles with the basic postulate of all classical epistemology, namely, the supposition that the world *precedes* our consciousness of it.[3] Marx, particularly in the *Theses on Feuerbach*, understood that the objectivism of classical epistemology overlooks that man is a situated being, that knowledge is in terms of perspective and truth yielded by following out a given systematic orientation.[4] Marx rejected the epistemological solutions of both

[1] V. Venable, *Human Nature: The Marxian View*, New York, A. A. Knopf, 1945, pp. 203–213; R. S. Cohen, 'Contemporary Marxism', *The Review of Metaphysics*, vol. IV, no. 2 (December 1950), pp. 291–310.

[2] F. A. Hayek, *The Counter-Revolution of Science*, Glencoe, Illinois, Free Press, 1952, attempts to dismiss Marxian social science along with the tradition of positivistic scientism since the French Revolution but overlooks that Hegel had in fact provided Marx with a critique of pre-revolutionary positivism which has always been the basis of a critical relation between Marxism and Positivism. Cf. H. Marcuse, *Reason and Revolution*, New York, Humanities Press, 1954, p. 343; F. E. Hartung, 'The Social Function of Positivism', *Philosophy of Science*, vol. IX, no. 4 (1944), pp. 328–341.

[3] Leszek Kolakowski, 'Karl Marx and the Classical Definition of Truth', L. Labedz, *Revisionism*, Essays on the History of Marxist Ideas, New York, F. A. Praeger, 1962, pp. 179–187.

[4] Hannah Arendt, *Between Past and Future*, New York, Viking Press, 1961, has

idealism and materialism. However, he seems to have reacted most violently to the idealist abuse of the constitutive element in thought. The result is that he fell back upon the objectivist view of classical epistemology in its scientific materialist form. The result of this equivocation is very well summarized by E. Knight:

> The philosophy of Marx deviated into scientism because the first concern of most Marxists was to demonstrate how means of production had 'determined' the nature of all other manifestations of social life throughout human history. This was to forget that man can create value not only with his hands, but also with his mind. The economic interpretation of history is proven not by consulting the records, but by turning this thought into matter. The thinker, in other words, is a labourer, except that his product is an event or an institution rather than a commodity. For the objective intellectual, at least in practice, ideas and things run parallel to one another; but the lines can be made to cross, and, indeed, the whole responsibility of the intellectual is to see that they do.[1]

Marx made two attempts to break through the world of alienation (estrangement). In the first, he rejected classical objectivist epistemology and sketched a phenomenology of a world-view based upon the creativeness of authentic personality in the *Economic and Philosophic Manuscripts*. However, this move is submerged by the sociological restraints overemphasized in the polemic with extreme subjective idealism. This is otherwise the only positive path to the formation of a nonestranged world-view, in which the cultural world is

---

criticized the arbitrary nature of certain postulates of political experience. Given the hypothesis of the superiority of the Aryan race, the events at Dachau, Belsen, and elsewhere are perfectly meaningful, necessary experiences. Arendt considers it the basic feature of the totalitarian society that it has the power to establish 'experience' in terms of arbitrary political postulates. But Marx criticized the nature of human experience yielded within the postulates of Classical political economy in similar terms. Arendt's criticism is in effect a natural law criticism of arbitrary political conventions. Marx's standard is humanist. The problem is to give an account of the standard of judgment which avoids the errors of transcendentalism without falling into a form of political and sociological positivism.

[1] E. Knight, *The Objective Society* New York, George Braziller Inc., 1961, pp. 101–102; C. Wright Mills, *The, Sociological Imagination*, New York, Oxford University Press, 1961, chap. VI.

considered a human project and human existence as an *Ecstasis*, as Heidegger for example, has considered it.[1]

The fact is, nonetheless, that Marx appears to have narrowed his broad sketch of a phenomenology of a nonalienated culture into a theory of economic alienation.

The methodological value of Marx's attempted reduction of the general problem of alienation to the specific form of economic exploitation will be examined in the following section of this essay. Critics of Marx's economic theory of history which emerged from his early interest in the phenomenon of alienation argue that Marx constructed a theory in terms of collective entities, 'proletariat', 'bourgeoisie', which evolve, independently of the behaviour of their constituent members, along a historical path determined by successive developments and upheavals in the basic production process. Characterized in this way, Marxian social theory is thought to be clearly in contradiction with its original purpose of analysing the preconditions of social and moral development.

Professors Popper and Hayek have advanced an influential nominalist criticism of Marxian essentialism or conceptual realism. Unfortunately, these critics do not distinguish methodological and normative questions. They argue that to posit theoretical entities of a collective or group nature is both an epistemological error and an indication of a normative devaluation of the individual. Professor Hayek argues that theoretical constructs, other than those of individual psychology, can be considered independent sociological variables only through the failure to distinguish 'those ideas which are *constitutive* of the phenomena we want to explain and the ideas which

---

[1] Our interpretation of Marx's views in the *Philosophical and Economic Manuscripts* is similar to the views of Heidegger on the nature of man: 'Finding himself in the midst of his possibilities, man as human-being is also one who projects (entwirft) them. Interpreting the verb to exist as to-go-out-of-the-self, implies that we are always making *projects*; some are more trivial than others, of course, but nevertheless we could not exist without making some sort of projects all the time. Man as human-being is thus a thrown-projecting being; he is thrown into his possibilities and he always projects them outward. Human-being is always anticipating itself (*sich vorweg sein*); it is never static, but always *ecstatic*.' E. A. Tiryakian, *Sociologism and Existentialism*, New Jersey, 1962, p. 109. However, it is not intended to argue for any general similarity between Marxism and Existentialism. The differences are set out briefly by Adam Schaff's two articles on 'Marxism and Existentialism', *Monthly Review*, vol. XIV, no. 1 (May 1962), pp. 12–18; and *Monthly Review*, vol. XIV, no. 2 (June 1962), pp. 100–111.

we ourselves or the very people whose actions we have to explain may have formed about *these* phenomena and which are not the cause of, but theories, about the social structures'. The analytic error is apparently coupled with a lack of moral courage. The representatives of scientism in the social sciences are 'afraid' to take the ideas of individuals as the data of their theories but instead substitute for them 'popular generalizations' about the reasons for individual behaviour.[1]

Hayek is undoubtedly correct in arguing that theoretical constructs such as the 'whole', 'group', or 'class' cannot causally affect individuals for the reason that the two phenomena are not on the same level of existence.[2] The truth in this argument, however, when asserted together with the truism that the whole is the sum of its parts and inseparable from them, is then employed by Hayek to arrive at the more questionable proposition that explanations of social phenomena must be in terms of individual dispositions.[3]

Hayek's argument concerning the existence of group concepts and laws generally confuses the logical question of descriptive emergence in respect of concepts, which depends upon the criterion of meaning, with the empirical question of the reduction of the laws and theories of the social sciences. Explanation involves the deduction of the explanandum from true premises. Only statements and not concepts can form the premises of a deduction.

Reduction, which is a form of deduction, and thus of explanation, is therefore a matter of laws and theories not of concepts.[4] So-called reduction of concepts is strictly a question of definition. It is possible to define group concepts in terms of descriptive relations between

[1] Hayek confuses the participants' interpretations of their own behaviour, which may provide relevant sociological hypotheses, with the independent legitimate theoretical constructions of the sociologist. Cf. J. Rex, *Key Problems of Sociological Theory*, London, Routledge and Kegan Paul, 1961, p. 37.

[2] E. Gellner, 'Holism versus Individualism in History and Sociology,' P. Gardiner, *Theories of History*, Glencoe, Illinois, Free Press, 1959, pp. 488–503; S. Krupp, *Pattern in Organizational Analysis*, Philadelphia and New York, Chilton Co., 1961, pp. 134–139.

[3] For a critical discussion see T. Abel, 'The Operation called *Verstehen*', *American Journal of Sociology*, vol. LV, no. 3 (November 1948), pp. 211–218.

[4] M. Brodbeck, 'Models, Meanings and Theories', L. Gross (ed.), *Symposium on Sociological Theory*, White Plains, New York, Row Petersen and Co., 1959, pp. 373–403; E. Nagel, *The Structure of Science*, New York, Harcourt, Brace and World, 1961, chap. 2, The Reduction of Theories.

individuals. But this does not permit the prediction of group behaviour from that of its members without empirical composition laws which establish a connection between the conduct of the individuals within the system and the resultant behaviour of the group.[1]

According to Professor Popper, the Marxian conception of history is based upon the mistaken notion that social scientists can plot the historical movements of society in the same way that a physicist can predict planetary motion.[2] The error in this case consists of overlooking that the law-like statements of natural science are stated together with a set of historical statements which indicate the occurrence of certain antecedent conditions.

Scientizing sociologists overlook the dependence of law-like regularities upon the fulfilment of specific antecedent conditions. They more often than not mistake trends for laws. Furthermore, the practical interest which lies behind scientific prediction, also present in the transference of this goal to the social sciences, is said to be defeated by the very social laws on which practical political action might have been based. A kind of historical fatalism replaces the initial pragmatic interest in political action.

When Marx criticized the Hegelian system as an ideological system *par excellence* the substance of his argument was that theoretical constructs are not the sort of entities that can enter into causal relations on the level of historical existence.[3] Marx understood that the Hegelian 'state' is no more a causal factor in history than the concept of 'feudalism'. Moreover, he did not confuse that argument with the more questionable thesis that such theoretical entities as the 'state', 'society', 'capitalism', are spurious methodological constructs. It is the merit of Marxian social science not to have bogged down in the hyperfactualism and poverty of fruitful hypotheses which characterizes positivistic empiricism. Max Weber has pointed to this feature in some remarks which at the same time indicate the pitfalls not only of Marxian theory but of any theoretical structure;

[1] Q. Gibson, *The Logic of Social Inquiry*, London, Routledge Kegan and Paul, 1960, pp. 150–155.

[2] K. R. Popper, *The Poverty of Historicism*, Boston, Beacon Press, 1957.

[3] There is a useful statement of Marx's views in his early writings on essentialism, conceptual realism, the nature of the state, history and the dialectical procedure of Marxian Sociology, in *Cahiers Internationaux de Sociologie*, vol. IV (1948), pp. 3–152; P. Kahn, 'Société et état dans les oeuvres de jéunesse de Marx', *Cahiers Internationaux de Sociologie*, vol. V (1949), pp. 165–175.

. . . all specifically Marxian 'Laws' and developmental constructs
—in so far as they are theoretically sound—are ideal types. The
eminent, indeed unique, *heuristic* significance of these ideal types
when they are used for the assessment of reality is known to
everyone who has ever employed Marxian concepts and hypotheses. Similarly their perniciousness, as soon as they are thought
of as empirically rated or as real (i.e., truly metaphysical) 'effective forces', 'tendencies', etc., is likewise known to those who
have used them.[1]

Just as Marx attacked the errors of methodological collectivism in
its Hegelian form, so he criticized the conception of 'iron' social
laws as it appeared in the analysis of the British classical economists.
In this case Marx, in fact, made the very point which Professor
Popper accuses him of having ignored. Marx pointed out that the
laws of Classical economics only hold within a given social constellation which provides a set of social and psychological middle principles
which restrict the degree of variation in social behaviour, or, in other
words, define regularities or patterns of behaviour for a given society.
Marx's analysis of social laws argues that so-called social laws are
derivative from the overall social orientation which defines a particular society. A society which considers itself governed uniquely by
natural laws is alienated in a manner similar to the individual who
sees himself in the power of an institutional framework which he is
not free to modify. Marx's analysis is intended to show how social
institutions may be manipulated by individuals, modified by a
sociological realism which avoids the naive errors of liberal rationalism.

Professor Popper misunderstands Marx by neglecting the synthesis
of economic deduction and sociological preconditions which characterizes Marxian historical theory. Contrary to what Popper gives us
to understand, Marx in fact argued that there are no absolute social
laws of economics or politics apart from the specification of a set of
relevant sociological middle principles.[2] It is a feature not only of
Marxian economics but of all economics[3] that, in the words of

[1] M. Weber, 'Objectivity in Social Science and Social Policy', trans. E. A.
Shils and H. A. Finch, *The Methodology of the Social Sciences*, Glencoe, Illinois,
Free Press, 1959, p. 103.

[2] A. Löwe, *Economics and Sociology*, London, George Allen and Unwin, 1935; J. S.
Mill, *System of Logic*, London, Longmans, Green and Co., 1906, Bk. VI, chap. 5.

[3] S. Schoeffler, *The Failure of Economics*, Cambridge, Harvard University Press, 1955,
applies Löwe's arguments in a critique of contemporary econometric process models.

A. Löwe, 'determinateness of reasoning' is achieved only through the introduction of certain sociological middle principles:

> Any realistic theory of the modern economic system must start from the general premise that it can no longer deal with a constant structure and with homogeneous processes, but that the economic order under consideration is subject to an evolutionary transformation. Therefore any deductive operation with invariable data is defective from the very outset. Long period analysis cannot dispense with a previous examination of the tendencies of the data themselves, that is to say, the corresponding sociological constellation and its regular changes, and moreover with the examination of the mutual relations of the variations on both sides. Above all this dynamic chain of reciprocal causation between the economic process and its social environment calls for a theoretical system of coordinates which is on the one hand determinate enough to define the course of individual movements, and on the other hand elastic enough to reproduce the regular transformation of the system as a whole. We need not expressly decide henceforth to insert sociological elements into our economic deduction—there was never any substantial statement which was not based on such premises. But we are to render manifest and open to continuous examination and revision those implications which formerly remained latent, and whose modifications were usually neglected.[1]

Oscar Lange has argued that the difference between the explanatory value of 'bourgeois' economics and Marxian economics lies in the ability of the latter to include institutional data which permit it to deal with the evolutionary problems that the static equilibrium systems are obliged to resign to economic history.[2] Bourgeois economics deal only with constant data. Changes in the data are considered exogenous to the logical systems built upon them. The same criticism applies to the so-called dynamic theories which explain economic fluctuations in terms of time lags in the supply adjustments to price changes. The possibility of equilibrium is deduced from the nature of the adjustment mechanism. But changes in the underlying data upon which the adjustment mechanism works

---

[1] A. Löwe, *Economics and Sociology*, pp. 138–139; K. Marx, *Capital*, Chicago C. H. Kerr and Co., 1906, Vol. III, pp. 947–949; 966–968.

[2] O. Lange, 'Marxian Economics and Modern Economic Theory', *Review of Economic Studies*, Vol. 2 (1934–1935), pp. 189–201.

to produce fluctuations cannot be deduced from such theories. By contrast, through the specification of the institutional (class structure) data of the capitalist process changes in the basic data, i.e., the production function, can be deduced and certain laws of development of capitalism can be determined.

Lange also shows that some Marxists are mistaken in attributing the superiority of Marxian economics in dealing with the evolution of capitalism to the labour theory of value. The latter is a static equilibrium theory of value based upon even more restrictive institutional assumptions than the marginal utility theory of equilibrium. Provided only there be free competition, the formal principles of the theory of equilibrium apply equally to any exchange economy whether capitalistic or the ·case that Marx envisaged for the application of the labour theory of value, namely, an economy of small independent producers each owning his own means of production (*einfache Warenproduktion*). The necessity of economic evolution, or, in other words, changes in the production-function, is dependent upon the introduction of specific institutional data which define the capitalist system and distinguish it from simple forms of exchange economy.

We have examined the argument that in his writings Marx fell into the errors of conceptual realism and historical determinism. He himself had criticized these faults in Hegel as the basic ingredients of an alienated ideology. We distinguished two rather different phenomena, namely, estrangement (*Entfremdung*) and externalization (*Entäusserung*), ordinarily covered by the term alienation. Marx does not bewail the necessity of expressing or externalizing experience in terms of general, objective concepts. Thus it was necessary to show that, while Marx criticized Hegelian theory as a form of epistemological alienation, he did not confuse that argument with the legitimate employment of theoretical constructs and generalizations as the basis of a social science. The arguments of Professor Popper and Hayek are simply a positivist and nominalist rejection of the possibility of any social science.[1]

[1] The truly counter-revolutionists of science are the very critics of 'scientism', for example, E. Heimann, *Reason and Faith in Modern Society, Liberalism, Marxism and Democracy*, Middletown, Conn., Wesleyan University Press, 1961, chap. III; L. von Bertalanffy, 'The Psychopathology of Scientism', H. Schoek and J. W. Higgins, *Scientism and Values*, New York, Van Nostrand Co. Inc., 1960, pp. 202–218;

Marx does not shrink from the necessity of interaction with the natural world in order to create medium for the expression of human personality. To Marx the problem of alienation is not *per se* either an epistemological or a technological problem. Alienation is a phenomenon which arises when men are estranged from the products of their mental, physical, and social activity with the result that they fail to realize an ideal of authentic being. According to Marx, conceptual realism, theological transcendentalism, etatism, and sociological theory oriented in terms of a framework of 'iron' social laws are merely manifestations of an existential estrangement which arises within the organization of the means of production.

The core of the problem of alienation (estrangement) as it appears in Marx's more mature theory lies in the legitimacy of Marx's attempt to reduce the examination of all forms of estrangement to the 'basic' phenomenon of economic exploitation or alienation. Daniel Bell argues that by narrowing the general problem of alienation to the specific question of economic alienation Marx closed off a road to a more general and fruitful analysis of the problems of social organization and personality structure.[1]

> The extraordinary thing was that Marx had taken a concept which German philosophy had seen as an ontological fact, and had given it a social content. As ontology, as an ultimate, man could only accept alienation. As a social fact, rooted in a specific system of historical relations, alienation could be overcome by changing the social system. But in narrowing the concept, Marx ran two risks; of falsely identifying the source of alienation only in the private property system; and of introducing a note of

---

F. Machlup, 'The Inferiority Complex of the Social Sciences', ed. M. Sennholz, *On Freedom and Free Enterprise*, Essays in Honor of Ludwig von Mises, New York, Van Nostrand Co. Inc., 1956, pp. 161–172. Cf. the criticisms of Popper's school of thought by E. Knight, *The Objective Society*, Geo. Braziller, Inc., 1962; E. H. Carr, *What is History?*, New York, A. A. Knopf, 1962; A. Macintyre, 'Breaking the Chains of Reason', *Out of Apathy*, London, New Left Books, 1960, pp. 216–222. I have expressed my views on this problem in my introductory essay to *Modes of Individualism and Collectivism*, ed. John O'Neill, London, Heinemann Educational Books, to be published in 1972. This volume presents the whole of the original argument raised by Hayek and Popper and their critics.
[1] D. Bell, 'The Rediscovery of Alienation', *The Journal of Philosophy*, vol. LVI, no. 24 (November 1959), pp. 933–952.

utopianism in the idea that once the private property system was abolished man would immediately be free.[1]

Bell's initial remark that Marx did not conceive alienation as an ontological fact is very well taken. If we accept the distinction between externalization and estrangement previously discussed, then Marx's position is quite clearly that the necessity of objectifying man's natural capacities is not at all problematic. Systematic thought, language, art, work, physical, and cultural objects are all natural expressions of the sort of being man is. This is the substance of Marx's critique of Hegel in *The Economic and Philosophic Manuscripts*. What Marx did wish to argue is that both the process and the products of man's physical and mental activity may escape man's control and, far from being the natural means to the realization of an ethical ideal of authentic, creative being, result in an alienated, estranged condition of man. Marx believed that the basic source of the estrangement of man's freely, creative energies lay in the nature of the sociological and technological organization of work or labour.

In Marx's later writings the theory of alienation is isomorphic with the theory of the class stratification of society. We may distinguish six postulates in Marx's theory of social class.[2]

I. All the cultural manifestations of civil society are ultimately functions of its class structure;

II. Class structure is determined by the structure of production;

III. The social process of production displays a capacity for evolution.

It was part of the purpose of our earlier discussion to show that the above propositions are at least defensible working hypotheses, and as such, basic elements in Marxian social science. The difficulty is that these postulates cannot be separated, in Marxian theory, from the following three:

IV. The class structure is composed of the owners and nonowners of the means of production;

V. By virtue of their position relative to the means of production, the interests of the classes of owners and nonowners are antagonistic;

[1] *The Journal of Philosophy*, vol. LVI, no. 24 (November 1959), p. 939.
[2] J. Schumpeter, *History of Economic Analysis*, New York, Oxford University Press, 1954, p. 439.

VI. The class struggle which results from the antagonism of class interests provides the mechanism, political and economic, which implements the forces of immanent evolution.

Schumpeter remarks that it was an especially 'bold stroke of analytic strategy' to identify capitalism and the phenomenon of social class in terms of ownership in the means of production.[1] But the strategem is in fact perversely Hegelian. The attempt to schematize history in terms of the concept of class struggle between the owners and nonowners of the means of production has only a spurious generality.[2] Not all forms of social conflict are class conflicts. Nor can every form of social change be accounted for in terms of changes in the basis of class power. Furthermore, Marx's assertion that there is a necessary tendency for class conflicts to become increasingly antagonistic until capitalist society is completely split asunder is quite obviously a nonsociological postulate derived from Hegel's dialectic. Finally, the kind of power which derives from legal ownership of the means of production is only a species of the general phenomenon of power and authority relations inherent in *any* social structure. The nature of the connections between specific forms of power arising from the industrial and political system and their interrelations with the social class and stratification patterns of a given society are a matter of empirical not logical connections.

Unfortunately, Marx's perception of the phenomenon of alienation is restricted to the forms of estrangement which appear in capitalist industrial society. According to Marx, such freedom as exists in capitalist society is enjoyed by the owners of the means of production and entails as its logical antithesis the slavery of the proletariat. It is only when the proletariat acquires control over the means of production and the conditions of its work that freedom becomes general and alienation disappears. It should be noticed that the collective ownership of the means of production in socialist society is thought to put an end to two rather different elements in the phenomenon of economic alienation. In the first place, collective

[1] J. Schumpeter, *Capitalism, Socialism and Democracy,* New York, Harper and Brothers, 1950, p. 19; B. Moore, Jr., *Political Power and Social Theory,* Cambridge, Mass., Harvard University Press, 1958, chap. IV.

[2] R. Dahrendorf, *Class and Class Conflict in Industrial Society,* Stanford, California, Stanford University Press, 1959, chap. IV; C. W. Mills, *The Marxists,* New York, Dell Publishing Co., 1962, chap. 6.

ownership is considered a solution to the problem of control over the *product* of labour. In the second place, it is thought to be a remedy for the dehumanization or *depersonalization* which arises from specific role-concentrations within the social and industrial division of labour.[1]

We shall not discuss here the various criticisms of the notion of the worker's control of industry as a practical institution.[2] It is quite clear that a planned economy involves decisions of priority as to the relative expansion of capital-goods and consumer-goods industries, decisions upon saving-investment ratios and the relative growth and rationalization of industrial, agricultural, and service sectors. Such decisions require structured relations of authority which, although perhaps initially related to a technical or professional basis, tend to result in social stratification patterns which are the instrument of a system of differential gratifications. In short, the performance principle of a socialist society would necessarily involve patterns of deferred gratification for the reason that this is a general existential phenomenon.[3] So far from abolishing the asymmetry between individual and social interests, the institutions of collective ownership of the means of production in fact depend upon an extremely rationalized application of the principle of social authority and control.

We have tried to defend the thesis that the externality of social institutions and rule-governed behaviour are not, as such, manifestations of human estrangement. We believe that it is consistent with Marx's own views that social institutions become instruments of estrangement only when they fail to achieve purposes which the participants intended. Estrangement is primarily a phenomenon of the ideological superstructure. For example, the practices required of a successful businessman may conflict with the scruples of a person who wishes at the same time to be a businessman and a member of the Christian Church.[4] In this case, a person may feel estranged by

---

[1] K. Marx, *Economic and Philosophic Manuscripts 1844*, Estranged Labour, pp. 67–83.

[2] D. Bell, *The End of Ideology*, New York, Colliers Books, 1961, chap. XV. 'Two Roads from Marx: The Themes of Alienation and Exploitation and Workers' Control in Socialist Thought'; A. L. Harris, 'Utopian Elements in Marx's Thought', *Ethics*, vol. LV, no. 2 (January 1950), pp. 79–99.

[3] H. Marcuse, *Eros and Civilization*, New York, Vintage Books, 1962, chap. II.

[4] K. Horney, *The Neurotic Personality of Our Time*, New York, W. W. Norton and Company, 1937; M. Birnbach, *Neo-Freudian Social Philosophy*, Stanford, California, Stanford University Press, 1961.

the difficulty of harmonizing the economic means-value system with the end-value system prescribed by his religion. He may in fact find that the ethos of the economic subculture of which he disapproves pervades the general value-system of the Christian life and its institutional structure. In this situation, the individual becomes the focus of an institutional conflict and is burdened with the attempt to rationalize conflicting value-systems. We have in this example a paradigm case of a *socially-induced* neurosis—the state of alienation or estrangement.[1]

This is a condition which has been described from various points of view by Weber, Durkheim, Tönnies, and Mannheim and is a pervasive concern of much sociological journal-literature.[2] Max Weber focused his analysis upon the tension between the charismatic potential of the individual and the necessity of compulsive conformity within role-bound areas, lacking any overall normative structure. Mannheim also called attention to the phenomenon of functional rationalization which induces a flight from responsibility due to the 'expropriation of understanding and intellectual activity'. Durkheim described the state of anomie as a 'disease of the infinite,' that is to say, the confinement of man's impulsive nature within a normative social structure which routinizes and conventionalizes man's needs. Marcuse has analysed the conflict between the freedom of the libidinal subject-object which the human organism desires and the conscription of mind and body as the tools of alienated labour required by the historically conditioned forms of the reality principle, i.e., ἀνάγκη the existential fact of scarcity relationships.[3]

Marx's diagnosis and his prescription for the condition of alienation (estrangement) appears to be less general than the investigations of later writers and his remedy rather more sanguine.[4] These two

1 M. Seeman, 'On the Meaning of Alienation', *American Sociological Review*, vol. XXIV, no. 6 (December 1959), pp. 783–791; J. P. Clark, 'Measuring Alienation within a Social System', *American Sociological Review*, vol. XXIV, no. 6 (December 1959), pp. 849–852; R. C. Tucker, *Philosophy and Myth in Karl Marx*, Cambridge, Cambridge University Press, 1961, pp. 148–149, considers that it was Marx's personal neurosis to have considered social institutions as the predisposing factor in the condition of alienation.

2 S. C. Harris, *A Conceptual Analysis of Alienation*, M.A. Thesis, Columbia University, (1956).

3 H. Marcuse, *Eros and Civilization*, chap. II.

4 D. Braybrooke, 'Diagnosis and Remedy in Marx's Doctrine of Alienation', *Social Research*, vol. XXV no. 3 (Autumn 1958) pp. 325–345.

faults are due, on the one hand, to a defect of analysis and, on the other, to an excess of ethical prescription. Ultimately, Marx appears to have fallen into a form of sociological anarchism. This is the dangerous possibility which derives from understanding alienation as a phenomenon resulting purely and simply from the institutional organization (externalization) of human behaviour. The positive element in Marx's theory of alienation is the ethical ideal of a nonestranged relation between the individual and the artifacts and institutions of his cultural environment.

Mr Braybrooke has observed that the nature of alienation (estrangement) is bound up with the concept of purpose. Marx complained that under capitalism a great number of jobs cannot be identified with any purpose of the worker in any sense beyond being a mere means to survival. That is to say, specific tasks have no intrinsic interest for the labourer nor can they be rationalized as elements of a framework which the worker generally feels to be realizing interests and purposes of his own. Now, we ordinarily speak of a person having a purpose in doing X, or doing X for a purpose, when he performs X in the belief that it is a causal condition of something further, Y, which he values. It is not absolutely necessary that the person can give more than an elliptical account of the causal connection between X and Y. Furthermore, a person may be held responsible for the connections between actions, for example, the result Y of X, if X was done by him on purpose. Though, of course, X may have a number of unforseeable results. In that case it will be a matter of legal or ethical decision as to how far, if at all, an act which at first sight may be said to be 'his' in a descriptive sense is also to be *ascribed* to him as a matter of personal responsibility. Having a 'sense of purpose' in one's work may then be understood as some feeling of responsibility for the causal connection between one's actions within a broadly defined area, for example, working at a plant or teaching in a school rationalized as total activities. A number of other ethical values will contribute to what we call a 'sense of purpose', e.g., to a voluntarily self-sacrificing interest, a willingness to balance short-run and long-run gains, a sense of personal identification with the ultimate values realized by the task or occupation.

Marx appears to have argued that a worker is alienated when he neither understands nor feels any connection between his specific task and the job of which it is part, or the relations between his task, plant, industry, and the overall economy.

We presuppose labour in a form that stamps it as exclusively human. A spider conducts operations that resemble those of a weaver, and a bee puts to shame many an architect in the construction of her cells. But what distinguishes the worst architect from the best of bees is this, that the architect raises his structure in imagination before he erects it in reality. At the end of every labour process, we get a result that already existed in the imagination of the labourer at its commencement. He not only effects a change of form in the material on which he works, but he also realizes a purpose of his own that gives the law to his modus operandi, and to which he must subordinate his will. And this subordination is no mere momentary act. Besides the exertion of the bodily organs, the process demands that, during the whole operation, the workman's will be steadily in consonance with his purpose. This means close attention. The less he is attracted by the nature of the work, and the mode in which it is carried on, and the less, therefore, he enjoys it as something which gives play to his bodily and mental powers, the more close his attention is forced to be.[1]

The expropriation of worker understanding is due to the exclusion of labour from industry control and decision making. Under such conditions, according to Marx, a worker can have no sense of purpose in his labour. The purpose of labour under these conditions is subordinate to physical survival and avoidance of the misery of unemployment. Marx's solution to the problem of alienation or estrangement is based upon a projected abolition of the division of labour and the control of industry by workers as the ingredients of a planned economy which would replace the capitalist production system and competitive market. Marx believed that the tendency of the technological processes of industry to become increasingly complex and consequently to demand more highly skilled, intelligent labour had been dimly recognized by the Factory Act, provisions for workers' education, technical and agricultural schools, *écoles d'enseignement professionnel*. However, the full implications of this phenomenon would, Marx believed, overthrow capitalism in so far as it was tied to an ossified division of labour.

[1] K. Marx, *Capital*, Chicago, C. H. Kerr Co., 1906, vol. I, p. 198.

But if, on the one hand, variation of work at present imposes itself after the manner of an overpowering natural law, and with the blindly destructive action of a natural law that meets with resistance at all points, Modern Industry, on the other hand, through its catastrophies imposes the necessity of recognizing, as a fundamental law of production, variation of work, consequently fitness of the labourer for varied work, consequently the greatest possible development of his varied aptitudes. It becomes a question of life and death for society to adapt the mode of production to the normal functioning of this law. Modern Industry, indeed, compels society, under penalty of death, to replace the detail-worker of to-day, crippled by lifelong repetition of one and the same trivial operation, and thus reduced to the mere fragment of a man, by the fully developed individual, fit for a variety of labours, ready to face any change of production, and to whom the different social functions he performs, are but so many modes of giving free scope to his own natural and acquired powers.

The existence of classes originated in the division of labour, and the division of labour as it has been known up to the present will completely disappear. For mechanical and chemical processes are not enough to bring industrial and agricultural production up to the level we have described; the capacities of the men who make use of these processes must undergo a corresponding development. Just as the peasants and manufacturing workers of the last century changed their whole way of life and became quite different people when they were impressed into big industry, in the same way communal control over production by society as a whole and the resulting new development will both require an entirely different kind of human material. People will no longer be, as they are today, subordinated to a single branch of production, bound to it, exploited by it; they will no longer develop one of their faculties at the expense of all others; they will no longer know only one branch, or one branch of a single branch, of production as a whole. Even industry as it is today is finding such people less and less useful. Industry controlled by society as a whole and operated according to a plan presupposes well-rounded human beings, their faculties developed in balanced fashion, able to see the system of production in its entirety. The form of the division of labour which makes one a peasant, another a cobbler, a third a factory worker, a fourth a stock-market operator has already been undermined by machinery and will completely disappear. Education will enable young people quickly to familiarize themselves with the whole system of production and to pass from one branch of production to another in response to the needs of society or their own inclinations. It will therefore free them from the one-sided character which the present-day division of labour impresses upon every individual. Communist society will in this way make it possible for its members to put their comprehensively developed faculties to full use. But when this happens classes will necessarily disappear.[1]

While one can sympathize with Marx's criticisms of the debilitating and stupifying effects of the more microscopic phrases of work processes and the caste features of the social division of labour, any social reform movement predicated on the basis of the abolition of *all* forms of the division of labour is fantastic. Certainly, the realization of an ideal of authentic personality would require, at the very least, that men be liberated from the most banausic tasks and that they have some sense of choice and worth in their daily work. In addition to the intellectual, moral, and craft abilities demanded by work of a certain level, one might expect from the worker a general understanding of the relation of his occupation to the overall economy and its general welfare implications.

Marx's interest in the phenomenon of estrangement is primarily an ethical interest. Although he attempted an analysis of the structure of alienation (estrangement) in its epistemological, theological, and economic-political forms, Marx did not sufficiently stress the basic structural features of *any* society. Indeed, Engels was forced to remind the anarchists that social life is impossible without structural principles of authority and control.

> . . . a certain authority, no matter how delegated, and, on the other hand, a certain subordination are things which, independent of all social organization, are imposed upon us together with the material conditions under which we produce and make products circulate.

[1] K. Marx, *Capital*, vol. I, pp. 533–534; *The German Ideology*, edited and Introduction by R. Pascal, New York, International Publishers, 1947, Pts I and II, pp. 21–23, 75; F. Engels, *Principles of Communism*, translated by P. M. Sweezy, New York, Monthly Review Pamphlet Series, No. 4, 1952, Question 20. 'What will be the consequences of the ultimate disappearance of private property?'

We have seen, besides, that the material conditions of production and circulation inevitably develop with large-scale industry and large-scale agriculture, and increasingly tend to enlarge the scope of this authority. Hence it is absurd to speak of the principle of authority as being absolutely evil and of the principle of autonomy as being absolutely good. Authority and autonomy are relative things, whose spheres vary with the various phases of the development of society.[1]

The historical urgency of Marx's ethical concept of nonalienated personality fails to transcend his analysis of capitalist society. But man is constantly subject to new forms of historical necessity (ἀνάγκη) which create new dimensions of the moral problem. The test of the vigour of Marxian social science and its ethics is its ability to furnish techniques for dealing with the next stages of capitalism, as well as the problems of socialist societies on the path of industrialization.

[1] K. Marx and F. Engels, *Basic Writings on Politics and Philosophy*, edited by L. S. Feuer, New York, Anchor Books, Doubleday and Co. Inc., 1959, p. 484.

10: Marxism and Mythology

It seems incredible that anyone could read *Capital* and overlook the moral vision which furnishes the driving energy for such a colossal documentation and analysis of the conditions of unauthentic existence in industrial, capitalist society. Yet it is argued that if Marx was a social scientist, as most Marxists claim for him, then he cannot have been a moral philosopher. Indeed, many Marxists themselves have thought that a moral philosophy had no part in scientific socialism. But gradually a certain disenchantment with the political experience of socialism has produced a number of attempts to rejuvenate Marxist metapolitics with fresh interpretations of the original humanism of Marx.[1] The current revolution of the philosophical framework of Marxian thought, however, is seriously prejudiced by the view that Marxian social philosophy is speculative in the worst sense, a view compounded by a method of pseudopsychological explanation. The latter approach has perhaps attracted most attention in Professor R. C. Tucker's treatment of philosophy and myth in Marx,[2] which remains lively enough to provide inspiration for the comparison of Marx's intellectual achievement with that of the drama of St Paul's vision on the road to Damascus.[3]

It would not be difficult to show that Marx's sociological analysis of religion is not on the same level as the phenomenon it treats. Similarly, even if one were to grant the similarity between the

[1] D. Bell, 'The Rediscovery of Alienation', *Journal of Philosophy*, LVI, no. 24 (November 1959), 933–952.

[2] R. C. Tucker, *Philosophy and Myth in Karl Marx*, New York, Cambridge University Press, 1961.

[3] Louis J. Halle, 'Marx's Religious Drama,' *Encounter*, XXV, No. 4 (October 1965), 29–37.

subsequent fate of Marx's writings and the tendency of original religious teachings to become dogmatized in the process of institutionalization, one could easily show the difference between religious teachings, written or unwritten, and Marx's studies in the fields of economics, sociology, and political history. But in practice the characterization of Marxism as a religious phenomenon rarely goes beyond the level of metaphors which are not adequate to the phenomenon of religion itself, let alone Marxian social science. The serious basis of the attempt to denigrate the status of Marxian social science rests ultimately upon an epistemological argument, and it is at this level that it must be engaged.

Tucker assumes that Marxism is not a scientific theory. It is in part a philosophy and in greater part a myth. In so far as it is philosophical, theoretical Marxism is concerned with the ethical problem of good and evil. But, according to Tucker, Marx cannot be classified as a moral philosopher because he fits no obvious category in the history of Western philosophy. Marx is at best a moralist, one concerned with good and evil, but never in terms of a systematic inquiry into the nature of the supreme good considered as *problematic*. Marx is, so we are to believe, a moralist opposed to moral philosophy. Accordingly, Marx can be understood only as a 'moralist of the religious kind'. Such is the nature of the philosophical element in Marxian social theory. But this element is outweighed by the mythical component in Marxism.

Tucker's theory of the nature of myth and, consequently of Marxian social theory, its that 'something by nature interior is apprehended as exterior, that a drama of the inner life of man is experienced and depicted as taking place in the outer world'. By contrast with myth, the attitude of philosophy is to represent external processes as developments of an inner self. This is exemplified in Hegel's introjection of the world-spirit and Marx's critical substitution of a human species-self in place of the Absolute Spirit. But Marx proceeds to mythologize his philosophical intuition by projecting onto the external world his image of the human species-self and by going on to explain the dynamics of self-alienation in terms of supposedly external social forces of alienation.

Whereas philosophy had once arisen against a background of myth, here myth arose against a background of philosophy—the Hegelian philosophy. A phenomenology of spirit, in which the world was consciously represented as a subjective process of realization of a world-self, became first a new phenomenology in which Marx pictured the world as a process of realization of a human species-self. This was done consciously and without mystification, and original Marxism remained fundamentally on the ground of philosophical thought. At a decisive point in it, however, Marx made the transition to the mythic mode of thought. The subjective process of *Entfremdungsgeschichte* was embodied in an image of society.[1]

It should be noticed that this argument allows only two methods of interpreting reality. The philosophical method, allegedly, is to explain outside events in terms of internal (mental) events. Internal events are presumably understood through the method of introspective or philosophical psychology. The procedure of myth is to conceive internal (mental) events in terms of outside events. Tucker seems to consider the status of the external world as essentially mind dependent. However, his use of the concept of myth indicates that the external world cannot be taken as a dumping ground for any and all contents of the mind or psyche. Yet, no criteria are offered for distinguishing which mental events are, in his words, 'by nature interior' and, consequently, not useful for interpreting external events. The view seems to be that reality, more particularly social reality, can be interpreted only in terms of the intentional concepts of individual psychology. The attempt to explain social and individual behaviour in terms of sociological concepts is mistaken for the reason that such concepts can be shown through a nominalist analysis to be figments of the individual imagination, unreal entities projected onto the external world and vainly employed to explain individual behaviour. In turn, the explanation of this sort of conceptual behaviour is, quite simply, that it is pathological.

It is argued that Marx substituted for the Hegelian Absolute Spirit a collective, human species-self, 'alienated man writ large'. So long as Marx saw the world through the jaundiced eyes of alienated *man*, he had the merit of being a philosopher. He would, of course, have benefited from a little nominalist therapy. But, essentially, his subjective view of the world offered the chance of rehabilitation. Apparently, however, Marx regressed at a certain stage of his logical analysis. On the basis of a personal decomposition, Marx proceeded

[1] R. C. Tucker, *Philosophy and Myth in Karl Marx*, p. 219.

to polarize his concept of man into two antagonistic selves, 'the infinitely greedy, despotic, exploiting, vicious, werewolf-self of capital (*Kapitalseele*) on the one hand, and the exploited, enslaved, tormented, rebellious, productive self of labour on the other'.[1] Even at this stage, Marx might have patched up his philosophy with the admission of a more varied psychology of human motivation. But Marx turned away from the possibilities of philosophical psychology into myth—the projection onto the social scene of his own image of a divided, self-alienated man.

This is Marx's myth of the warfare of labour and capital. It is through and through a moralistic myth, a tale of good and evil, a story of struggle between constructive and destructive forces for possession of the world. Its underlying moral theme is the theme of original Marxism: man's division against himself and dehumanization under the despotism of greed, and his final emancipation of himself and his productive activity from this despotism by the seizure of the alienated world of private property. The conflicting subjective forces of creativity and the will to infinite self-aggrandizement are seen and shown as class forces clashing across the battleground of society.[2]

Tucker argues that *Capital* is based upon an entirely mythological psychology of the capitalist and his relation to labour, documented by Marx in terms of a partial selection of economic fact and detail. The question is whether the mythical personality attributed to the capitalist is a figment of Marx's mind or of Tucker's own mind. Marxian social science starts from the premise that there is a legitimate level of sociological generalization and a non-fetishistic employment of group theoretical constructs. Max Weber, while remarking on the danger of assigning causal efficacy to reified concepts, nevertheless concedes the heuristic value of certain of the Marxian categories of sociological analysis.[3] In his early writings, Marx criticized the errors of *conceptual* reification in the Hegelian system.[4]

[1] R. C. Tucker, *Philosophy and Myth in Karl Marx*, pp. 220–221.

[2] *Ibid.*, p. 222.

[3] M. Weber, *The Methodology of the Social Sciences*, Glencoe, Illinois, Free Press, 1949, p. 103.

[4] P. Kahn, 'Société et état dans les œuvres de jeunesse de Marx', *Cahiers internationaux de sociologie*, V (1949), 165–74; M. Rubel, 'Notes on Marx's Conception of Democracy', *New Politics*, I, no. 2 (Winter 1962), 78–90.

Yet is is argued that Marx's mature theory is entirely dominated by a fetishistic or, as Tucker would have it, an alienated conceptualism.

The starting point of Marx's investigation of social phenomena is that individual behaviour, quite apart from the perceptions and intentions of the individuals concerned, is part of a structured or systematic order. It is the task of the social scientist to provide a theoretical interpretation of the phenomenon of social order. From this point of view, Quesnay's *Tableau Economique* is the great landmark of the social sciences.[1] As Marx acknowledged, the basic analytic intuition of the circular flow of economic life—the demonstration of how each economic period becomes the basis of the next, not only technologically but as a stage in a process of social reproduction solved by the exchanges between individual acts of production and consumption—is the permanent achievement of the physiocrats.

> Every child knows that if a country ceased to work, I will not say for a year, but for a few weeks, it would die. Every child knows too that the mass of products corresponding to the different and quantitatively determined masses of the total labour of society. That this necessity of distributing social labour in definite proportions cannot be done away with by the *particular form* of social production, but can only change the *form it assumes*, is self-evident. No natural laws can be done away with. What can change in changing historical circumstances, is the form in which these laws operate. And the form in which this proportional division of labour operates, in a state of society where the interconnection of social labour is manifested in the private exchange of the individual products of labour, is precisely the exchange value of these products.[2]

The Marxian labour theory of value expresses both the quantitative and the qualitative features of the laws determining the distribution of productive effort in a commodity-producing society.[3] In its

---

[1] J. Schumpeter, *Economic Doctrine and Method*, London, Allen & Unwin, 1954, chap. II; Marx to Engels, London, 6 July 1863, *Selected Correspondence 1846–1895*, New York, International Publishers, 1934.

[2] Marx to Kugelmann, London, 11 July 1868, *Selected Correspondence*.

[3] P. M. Sweezy, *The Theory of Capitalist Development*, New York, Monthly Review Press, 1956, chaps. II and III; K. Marx, *Capital*, Chicago, C. H. Kerr, 1906, Vol. III, chap. LI.

quantitative or economic aspect, the labour theory of value is essentially a general equilibrium theory which summarizes the forces integrating (*a*) the exchange ratios between commodities, (*b*) the quantity of each produced, and (*c*) the allocation of the labour force to the various branches of production. Qualitatively, the labour theory of value expresses the exchange relationships between commodities as a social relationship based upon the historical phenomena of the existence (i) of a developed social division of labour, and (ii) private production.

Marx argues that it is not possible to express the workings of the law of value apart from the specification of a set of sociological middle principles. The procedure in *Capital* is to construct a model of simple commodity production, that is, an economy of independent producers each owning his own means of production. The labour theory of value expresses the general equilibrium conditions for this special case.[1] Marx then varies the institutional features of his model of simple commodity production. The ownership of the means of production is concentrated into the hands of a class of capitalists, and labour itself becomes a commodity subject to the laws of exchange value. Marx's conclusion that exchange ratios in the case of capitalist production are ultimately determined according to the labour theory of value is, as is well known, the most controversial feature of *Capital*.[2] Whatever the case, Marx showed that the social order which classical economics took for granted was a violent order created by a process of radical social upheaval and enforced by 'iron laws'. Tucker's account of *Capital* entirely ignores its nature as a piece of economic analysis. However, the economic content of *Capital* cannot be passed over or simply attributed to Marx's casual empiricism.

Tucker deprives himself of an understanding of the analytic achievement of *Capital* because the construct of an economic process or order is, by the standards of methodological individualism, an illusion. Marx's method is to show the operation of the laws of classical economic theory to be dependent upon a particular historical constellation definable in terms of a set of sociological and psycho-

[1] O. Lange, 'Marxian Economics and Modern Economic Theory', *Review of Economic Studies* II (1934–1935), 189–201.

[2] R. L. Meek, *Studies in the Labour Theory of Value*, London, Lawrence & Wishart, 1956.

logical middle principles.[1] It is in the transition from a simple-commodity-producing society to a capitalist mode of production that the psychology of the capitalist is engendered.

Let us consider Marx's general schema of the development of capital and capitalist psychology.

The simple circulation of commodities—selling in order to buy —is a means of carrying out a purpose unconnected with circulation, namely, the appropriation of use-values, the satisfaction of wants. The circulation of money as capital is, on the contrary, an end in itself, for the expansion of value takes place only within this constantly renewed movement. The circulation of capital has therefore no limits. Thus the conscious representative of this movement, the possessor of money becomes a capitalist. His person, or rather his pocket, is the point from which the money starts and to which it returns. The expansion of value, which is the objective basis or main-spring of the circulation M-C-M, becomes his subjective aim, and it is only in so far as the appropriation of ever more and more wealth in the abstract becomes the sole motive of his operations, that he functions as a capitalist, that is, as capital personified and endowed with consciousness and a will. Use-values must therefore never be looked upon as the real aim of the capitalist; neither must the profit on any single transaction. The restless never-ending process of profit-making alone is what he aims at. This boundless greed after riches, this passionate chase after exchange-value, is common to the capitalist and the miser; but while the miser is merely a capitalist gone mad, the capitalist is a rational miser. The never-ending augmentation of exchange-value, which the miser strives after, by seeking to save his money from circulation, is attained by the more acute capitalist, by constantly throwing it afresh into circulation.[2]

Under the sociological conditions of individual ownership of the means of production economic activity is motivated by the desire to satisfy wants. However, where the means of production are the property of a class of capitalists, economic activity is divided into the need of a labouring class to sell itself as a commodity in order to subsist and the imperious drive of the capitalist class to accumulate.

1 A. Löwe, *Economics and Sociology*, London, Allen & Unwin, 1935, pp. 138–139; K. Marx, *Capital*, Vol. III, 947–949, 966–968.
2 K. Marx, *Capital*, I, 169–171.

An economic system of some sort is a functional prerequisite of any society. The capitalist system is simply one historical variant of the economic order. According to Marx, capitalism is defined by specific property relations with respect to the ownership of the means of production. It is the socio-economic system described by the term 'capitalism' which provides a structural focus for behaviour oriented toward acquisition, accumulation, and profit-making. The so-called profit motive is not primarily a psychological disposition. It is a socially acquired goal which is given within the framework of a sociological situation, namely, commercial and industrial capitalism. 'We have to grasp the essential connection between private property, avarice, and the separation of labour, capital, and landed property; between exchange and competition, value and the devaluation of men, monopoly, and competition, etc.; the connection between this whole estrangement and the money system.'[1]

Marx's definition of the sociological situation (capitalism) which provides the matrix for the orientation toward profit concentrates attention upon the property relations or class positions with respect to the means of production. It may be that Marx's definition of capitalism is more relevant to historical rather than analytic features of a capitalist system.[2] Weber's analysis of the prerequisites of the capitalist system stresses the importance of the rationalization of accounting, technology, law, and the permanent enterprise. But neither Marx nor Weber considered the spirit of capitalism to be a basic feature of human nature.[3] The Protestant ethic, 'an unconsciously refined organization for the production of capitalistic individuals' (Weber) provided the economic ethos at a particular juncture of the political and social history of industrial capitalism. The later stage of monopoly capitalism which has given rise to the phenomenon of the affluent society appears to have abandoned the Protestant ethic in favour of a consummatory ethic.[4]

[1] K. Marx, *Economic and Philosophic Manuscripts of 1844*, Moscow, Foreign Languages Press, 1959, p. 68.

[2] R. Dahrendorf, 'A Sociological Critique of Marx', *Class and Class Conflict in Industrial Society*, Stanford, California, Stanford University Press, 1959, chap. IV.

[3] M. Weber, *General Economic History*, trans. F. H. Knight, Glencoe, Illinois, Free Press, 1950, pp. 355–356.

[4] 'The Puritan ethos was not abandoned. It was merely overwhelmed by the massive power of modern merchandising', J. K. Galbraith, *The Affluent Society*, Boston, Houghton Mifflin, 1958, p. 200.

In *Capital* Marx provided a documented critique of the psychology and ethics of capitalism. Marx's method is to demonstrate that the psychological element which appears to be the driving force of capitalism, and is consequently rationalized in terms of the Judaeo-Protestant ethic, is in fact dependent upon a definite historical and sociological constellation defined by the class division of property relations.

But in the course of historical evolution, and precisely through the inevitable fact that within the division of labour social relationships take on an independent existence, there appears a division within the life of each individual, in so far as it is personal and in so far as it is determined by some branch of labour and the conditions pertaining to it. (We do not mean it to be understood from this that, for example, the rentier, the capitalist, etc., cease to be persons; but their personality is conditioned and determined by quite definite class relationships, and the division appears only in their opposition to another class and, for themselves, only when they go bankrupt.)[1]

Individual psychology is the dependent variable in the definition of a sociological situation, such as the nineteenth-century family, or capitalism. The functional design of these latter sociological systems acts selectively upon the motivation of the individual members so that their behaviour, whatever its individual significance, though there will be considerable endemic convergence, contributes to the maintenance of these institutional systems as such. Thus Marx demonstrated, for example, that in a commodity-producing society, despite independent and unco-ordinated decisions about production and sales, there results not a chaos but an order which is expressed in the operation of the law of value.

Since these [individual capitalists] meet one another only as owners of commodities, and every one seeks to sell his commodity as dearly as possible (being apparently guided in the regulation of his production by his own arbitrary will), the internal law enforces itself merely by means of their competition, by their mutual pressure upon each other, by means of which the various deviations are balanced. Only as an internal law, and from the point of view of the individual agents as a blind law,

[1] K. Marx, *The German Ideology*, New York, International Publishers, 1947, Parts I and III, p. 76.

does the law of value exert its influence here and maintain the social equilibrium of production in the turmoil of its accidental fluctuations.[1]

In any society there is an economic order. But under capitalism, the social equilibrium of production is maintained through the working of a 'blind' law. However, with certain changes in the relations of production and ownership of the means of production (the socio-economic aspect of socialism) the 'blind' operation of the law of value would be replaced by the principles of rational economic planning.[2] The latter is a principle ingredient in the ethical formula of socialism. Thus, Marx is not saying that the functional autonomy of social institutions is an ethical imperative. Quite the contrary, the social framework of individual action should in fact be subject to the conscious control of its members. The difficulty for Marx was to express the ethical requirement that social institutions not obstruct the goal of achieving an authentic individual existence without falling into the errors of naive rationalism and the contractual formula of psychologistic individualism.[3] In practice, Marx often preferred to give greater stress to the institutional determinants of individual behaviour rather than express himself in the psychologistic style of liberalism. He did so because his intuition of the ethical problem is deeper than that of bourgeois individualists.

The division between the personal and the class individual, the accidental nature of the conditions of life for the individual, appears only with the emergence of class, which is itself a product of the bourgeoisie. This accidental character is only engendered and developed by competition and the struggle of individuals among themselves. Thus, in imagination individuals seem freer under the dominance of the bourgeoisie than before, they are less free, because they are more subjected to the violence of things.[4]

Tucker prefers to read *Capital* as an allegorical tale of good and evil in which all the metaphors are drawn from economic theory and twisted into an insane theology.

[1] K. Marx, *Capital*, III, 1026.
[2] *Ibid.*, I, 90–91.
[3] K. Marx and F. Engels, *The Holy Family or Critique of Critical Critique*, Moscow, Foreign Languages Publishing House, 1956, pp. 162–163.
[4] K. Marx, *The German Ideology*, p. 77.

This [capital] is an economic concept in name only. The word comes from Adam Smith and the political economists; the idea, from Hegel and the world of German philosophy. Marx's *Kapital* is just as much a citizen of this world as, for example, Schopenhauer's *Wille* or Nietzsche's *Wille zur Macht*, with which it has obvious affinities. But the immediate affiliation of the idea is Hegelian. The *absolute Bereicherungstrieb* is a translation in economic terms of the drive to infinite self-enrichment that Hegel ascribes to spirit, which is insatiably greedy to appropriate all things cognitively as 'property of the ego' and thus to assert its power over them. The Hegelian dialectic of aggrandizement, whereby spirit is driven to infinitize itself in terms of knowledge, reappears in Marx's mature thought as dialectic of the self-expansion of capital—a movement of self-infinitizing in terms of money.[1]

When one considers Tucker's interpretation of German idealist philosophy since Kant, one can only feel that he has fallen victim to his own mixture of myth and metaphor.[2] His summary of German idealism as a self-infinitizing movement is meant to describe the phylogenesis of Marx's own neurotic conception that man is motivated by a drive for infinite self-aggrandizement in terms of wealth. German philosophy between Kant and Hegel is read in terms of the Faust theme. Now Marx considered that the romantic projections of the irreducible self concept of the Kantian epistemology are part of a neurotic literature not, as Tucker argues, because they conflict with the conceptions of biblical literature but because they lack an adequate sociological content.[3] Tucker seems to be willing to recognize that there is a certain moral advance in Feuerbach's view that man's business is not to deify himself but simply to reappropriate the full potential of his human nature, once the problem of God has become a dead issue. Tucker argues, further, that this is the position of original Marxism, with the difference that Marx considered Feuerbach's critical cognitive act an inadequate solution to the problem of alienation. But in the *Theses on Feuerbach*, Marx states his own argument

---

1 Tucker, *op. cit.*, pp. 213–214.
2 On the relation of German idealist philosophy to Protestant theology, see P. Asveld, *La Pensée réligieuse du jeune Hegel: Liberté et aliénation*, Louvain, Publications Universitaires de Louvain, 1953; G. M. M. Cottier, *L'Athéisme du jeune Marx: ses origines Hégéliennes*, Paris, J. Vrin, 1959.
3 K. Marx, *The German Ideology*, pp. 32, 50–51.

that the problem of alienation is a sociological problem which requires practical political intervention for its treatment.

Tucker's view is that Marx and Feuerbach were on the right track, so long as they considered the phenomenon of alienation as a self problem. It was Marx who mythologized the psychological results when he projected the internal conflicts of his own alienated self onto the social scene. What constitutes the shift from original Marxism to mature Marxism is the sociological projection of an original intuition of psychological conflict. Moreover, Marx himself suspected that the phenomenon of alienation might be due more to man's 'own infamy' than to the complex of class and property relationships in the production process. Apparently, Marx later struggled to suppress the psychological interpretation of capitalism by introducing as a principle of interpretation the maxim that the individual psychic structure is patterned upon the structure of external social relations. In the later writings, the so-called profit motive or acquisitive instinct is to be considered an element in the definition of a specific socio-economic situation, namely, competitive capitalist accumulation. But Tucker argues that Marx in fact contradicted himself on this very point. In the *Economic and Philosophic Manuscripts of 1844* Marx had argued that the driving force, the *ethic*, of bourgeois political economy is greed and the war between the greedy, namely, competition. In his later writings, Marx's position changed to the view that competition, as a market phenomenon, cannot be explained in terms of psychological motives. On the contrary, the existence of acquisitive behaviour, which may be explained teleologically by a variety of ad hoc purposes, is structurally dependent upon its function in maintaining the market situation. The fact of the matter here is that Marx was well aware[1] of the capitalist ethos which Weber later described in

---

[1] Marx's version of the Protestant ethic has largely passed unnoticed, and so we may be justified in reproducing it here. 'Thus, from the viewpoint of this enlightened political economy which has discovered the *subjective* essence of wealth within the framework of private property, the partisans of the monetary system and the mercantilist system, who consider private property as a *purely objective* being for man, are *fetishists and Catholics*. Engels is right, therefore, in calling Adam Smith the *Luther of political economy*. Just as Luther recognized *religion* and *faith* as the essence of the real *world*, and for that reason took up a position against Catholic paganism; just as he annulled *external* religiosity while making religiosity the *inner* essence of man; just as he negated the distinction between priest and layman because he transferred the priest into the heart of the layman; so wealth external

his *Protestant Ethic and the Spirit of Capitalism*. Moreover, while they may have disagreed as to the short run, Marx and Weber agree that, in the long run, the Protestant ethic is the dependent variable in the relationship with capitalism. But Tucker's view is that Marx must have been uncomfortably aware that the entire structure of *Capital* was dependent upon the postulate of infinite greed as the driving force of capitalist production. Tucker then comments upon what is in fact his own brain-child as follows: 'To suggest that this [the postulate of infinite greed] could be derived from the competitive mechanism itself was a way of minimizing the total dependence of the system upon a highly questionable postulate, and at the same time of reinforcing the postulate.'[1] But this rather doubtful psychological postulate of Marxism was deduced, it should be remembered, from Tucker's analysis of German idealism which we have discussed above.

We now consider the argument that the genuine philosophical element in Marxism is the moral concern with the phenomenon of self-alienation. Marx, we are to believe, located the source of self-alienation in a self-infinitizing movement, which he named *Kapital*

---

to man and independent of him (and thus only to be acquired and conserved from outside) is annulled. That is to say, its *external* and *mindless objectivity* is annulled by the fact that private property is incorporated in man himself, and man himself is recognized as its essence. But as a result, man himself is brought into the sphere of private property . . . just as, with Luther, he is brought into the sphere of religion. Under the guise of recognizing man, political economy, whose principle is labour, carries to its logical conclusion the denial of man. Man himself is no longer in a condition of external tension with the external substance of private property; he has himself become the tension-ridden being of private property. What was previously a phenomenon of *being external to oneself*, a real external manifestation of man, has now become the act of objectification, of alienation. This political economy seems at first, therefore, to recognize man with his independence, his personal activity, etc. It incorporates private property in the very essence of man, and it is no longer, therefore, conditioned by the local or national characteristics of private property regarded as existing outside itself. It manifests a cosmopolitan, universal activity which is destructive of every limit and every bond, and substitutes itself as the *only* policy, the *only* universality, the *only* limit and the *only* bond. But in its further development it is obliged to discard this hypocrisy and to show itself in all its cynicism'. *Economic and Philosophical Manuscripts*, in *Karl Marx, Early Writings*, trans. and ed. T. B. Bottomore, London, Watts & Co., 1963, pp. 147–148.

[1] Tucker, *op. cit.*, p. 217 n.

but which in the Judaeo-Christian tradition is ordinarily called the sin of pride. Marx's mistake was to believe that man's disease of the infinite is a fact either of religion or economics. The disintegration of the self as a result of taking either God or Henry Ford as one's ego ideal is certainly in individual cases a matter for the psychiatrist. Tucker argues that even where considerable numbers of people break down under similar illusions this never becomes more than a statistical phenomenon of individual psychology.[1] The evil lies within ourselves. It is never a social problem. To imagine otherwise, as Marx did, is to create a political myth.

It is frequently asserted that historical materialism lacks an adequate psychological theory.[2] It is argued, for example, that in order to escape psychologism Marx regressed to conceptual fetishism, using economic theory rather than philosophy or theology to foist a new alienated ideology upon the world.[3] Marx, however, was aware for critical purposes of the nominalist position that it is individuals who act and not institutions, social trends, or laws that 'act' upon individuals. Indeed, this was the principle Marx employed to attack the conceptual realism which characterized idealist historiography. 'It is not "history" which uses men as a means of achieving—as if it were an individual person—*its* own ends. History is *nothing* but the activity of men in pursuit of their ends.'[4] At the same time,

---

[1] Tucker, *op. cit.* pp. 239–240.

[2] 'The Marxist theory of motivation developed within this framework [historical materialism] has two components. The first emphasizes the role of purely external pressures on individuals: force, fraud and compulsion. The second begins with a concept of class interests', N. Birnbaum, 'Conflicting Interpretations of the Rise of Capitalism: Marx and Weber', *British Journal of Sociology*, IV (June 1953), p. 130. Birnbaum's argument that Weber supplies the psychological analysis of the rationalization of economic life which Marx simply attributed to the 'immanent laws of capitalist development' overlooks that Marx in fact derived the Protestant or bourgeois ethic from the literature of the classical economists, as we have pointed out above.

[3] L. D. Easton, 'Alienation and History in Early Marx', *Philosophy and Phenomenological Research*, XXII, no. 2 (December 1961), 193–205. Marx's critique of psychologism is recognized by one of his most hostile critics as Marx's major contribution to social science (see K. R. Popper, 'The Autonomy of Sociology', *The Open Society and Its Enemies*, New York, Harper & Row, 1963, Vol. II, chap. XIV).

[4] K. Marx, *Selected Writings in Sociology and Philosophy*, trans. and ed. T. B. Bottomore and M. Rubel, London, Watts & Co., 1956, p. 63.

Marx did not advance a psychologistic explanation of social phenomena in terms of a contractual or rationalistic means–end model.

It would be naïve, of course, to underestimate the difficulty raised for the social sciences, Marxian or not, by the question of the nature of the mechanism of interaction between the sociological and psychological aspects of behaviour.[1] Nevertheless, there are two notable attempts to account for individual psychology in Marxian terms.[2] In his early writings, Erich Fromm attempted to explain the mechanism by which the individual introjects the sociological determinants of behaviour. The individual libidinal structure is shaped by influences in the family which is in turn located in the social class structure which shapes its economic life chances.[3] In a complementary way, Herbert Marcuse has emphasized the nature of work as the medium through which the individual introjects the performance principle, that is, the dominant reality principle.[4] Any form of society requires a modification of the instinctual expression of individuals in view of the basic necessity of work and the social division of labour involved in any working society. However, according to Marcuse, the specific social institutions, laws, and property rights that embody the basic reality principle introduce additional controls which result in 'surplus repression' in order to preserve the interests of a class with a property right, so to speak, in the social structure. Marxian psychology stresses the importance of the individual's psychological history and the changing institutional contexts within which the individual develops. It is especially concerned with the defence of the argument that there are *socially induced* neuroses, largely described by the concept of alienation.

Now, if there are individual maladies whose source lies in the nature

1 'So far no Marxist theoretician has yet detailed the crucial psychological and institutional nexuses which show how the "personifications" or masks of class role are donned by the individual as self-identity', D. Bell, *The End of Ideology*, New York, Collier Books, 1961, p. 426. For an attempt to treat these 'transmission belts', see P. A. Baran, *Marxism and Psychoanalysis*, 'Monthly Review Pamphlet series', no. 13, New York, Monthly Review Press, 1960, pp. 50–52.

2 More justly, one should include Sartre's attempts to add to Marxian anthropology the method of existential psychoanalysis (Jean-Paul Sartre, *Search for a Method*, trans. Hazel E. Barnes, New York, Alfred A. Knopf, Inc., 1963).

3 M. Birnbach, *Neo-Freudian Social Philosophy*, Stanford University Press, 1961, pp. 77–82.

4 H. Marcuse, *Eros and Civilization*, New York, Random House, 1962, p. 34.

of the prevailing social institutions, for example, the nature of the work process, it follows that treatment of the condition will involve not only individual therapy but institutional reform. While there is no logical connection between a given methodological strategy and certain moral and political orientations, in practice the two do influence each other.[1] Tucker, for example, rejects the view that there are sociological causes of neurosis on the ground that to posit sociological entities is simply to indulge in the projection of the components of an alienated psyche. The alienated individual suffers from a myth-making neurosis which induces him to believe that there are entities outside his self-system which influence his behaviour. As a result, there arises the completely illusory view that the condition of alienation can be treated by means of a political revolution. The truth is, as Tucker will have it, that alienation is a personal problem and its solution lies in an ethical conquest of the self.

> It is essentially a work of self-clarification and *self-changing*. Its tools are the power of understanding, the urge to be free, and the willingness to be merely human. Its dialectic is a Socratic dialectic of 'Know thyself'. The 'revolution' or real change of self that emerges in and through this movement of emancipation is, likewise, a moral revolution. The change of 'circumstances' with which it coincides is a change of the self's character, meaning the habitual circumstances within the self that have been shaped by alienated living and stand in the way of its freedom, the inner autocracy or coercive system. Such a revolution within the self cannot occur or start in a violent catastrophic episode. It is the outcome of a gradual process, and *is* this process taken as a whole. Alternatively, it is the merely theoretical point of culmination of the whole slow growth of inward freedom and repossession of the productive powers of the self which takes place in the movement and by the labour of self-liberation.[2]

The passage just quoted is remarkable for the way in which Tucker introjects the external world by identifying 'circumstances'—why between quotes?—with 'habitual circumstances within the self'. On

---

[1] It has been suggested that Fromm's nominalist usage (*The Sane Society*, New York, Holt, Rinehart & Winston, 1955, pp. 72, 78, 273) provides support for his theory of radical change (J. H. Schaar, *Escape from Authority*, New York, Basic Books, 1961, pp. 166–168).

[2] Tucker, *op. cit.*, pp. 240–241.

this basis, Tucker then advances the view that by revolution we may no longer mean a violent change[1]—presumably, he disapproves of shock therapy—but only a 'theoretical point of culmination of the whole slow growth of inward freedom'.

Tucker's argument is that Marx's contribution to the social sciences is to be understood in the light of the dynamics of his neurosis. Marx's relatively valuable philosophical achievement derives from his early moral intuition of authentic individual existence. Marx's later investigations in the social sciences are simply a function of a myth-making neurosis engendered by his own circumstance of self-aliena-tion. The manner in which Tucker's thesis fails to deal with the *structure*[2] of Marx's philosophical and sociological thought is illus-trated in the paradoxical result it produces even when expanded somewhat. A. J. Gregor, for example, accepts Tucker's distinction between original and mature Marxism but attempts to salvage its over-all humanism by emphasizing its dependence upon Feuerbach's critique of idealism.[3] At the same time, Gregor argues that the year in which Marx wrote *The German Ideology*, 1845, is precisely the year in which Marx settled with his philosophical conscience in an 'entirely *empirical* manner'.[4] According to Gregor, Marx, prior to *The German Ideology*, at first argued that the phenomenon of alienation is an ontological datum, a logical and causal condition of economic and political alienation. But Marx finally saw that this was simply an argument in the idealist mode. Thus he reversed it and got the empirical formula that it is the division of labour and private pro-perty which are the cause of alienation. But this argument carries us to the embarrassing conclusion that once private property and the

[1] On Marx's use of the term 'revolution' see L. S. Feuer, 'John Stuart Mill and Marxian Socialism', *Journal of the History of Ideas*, X, no. 2 (April 1949), 297–303.

[2] For a statement emphasizing the unity of Marx's thought in terms of the Hegelian frame of reference, see R. Dunayevskaya, *Marxism and Freedom*, New York, Bookman Associates, 1957, Part III, and J. Hyppolite, *Etudes sur Marx et Hegel*, Paris, Riviére, 1955, pp. 95–100.

[3] A. J. Gregor, 'Philosophy and the Young Karl Marx', *Studies on the Left*, II, no. 3 (1962), 95–102; cf. L. Feuer, 'What Is Alienation? The Career of a Concept', *New Politics*, I, no. 3 (Spring 1962), 116–134.

[4] A. J. Gregor, 'Erich Fromm and the Young Karl Marx', *Studies on the Left*, III, no. 1 (1962), 85–92. The theory of the two Marxes is shared also by L. Kreiger, 'Marx and Engels as Historians', *Journal of the History of Ideas*, XIV, No. 3 (June 1953), 381–402; G. Gurvitch, 'La Sociologie du jeune Marx', *La Vocation actuelle de la sociologie*, Paris, Presses Universitaires de France, 1950, pp. 568–602.

social division of labour are abolished the phenomenon of alienation
will disappear. Gregor sees that this 'almost romantic normative
ideal' is a problem in the study of the mature Marx.

Elsewhere,[1] we have argued for the distinction between the phenomena of externalization and estrangement, or alienation, which are
originally covered by the single term 'alienation'. Marx did not lament
the necessity of creating socioeconomic institutions or objectifying
human behaviour (externalization). Here Gregor's reading of the
Economic and Philosophical Manuscripts seems to be at fault, and even
to contradict his better understanding when discussing the relation
of Marx to Feuerbach. What Marx said in relation to Hegel is that
estrangement is not an epistemological problem, nor, as Feuerbach
thought, a theological product. Estrangement, but not, of course,
externalization, is a socioeconomic phenomenon. Now Marx's
stratagem of identifying the (undifferentiated) phenomenon of
alienation with economic exploitation and the class structure of
capitalism has suggested a definitional resolution of the problem which
the political history of socialism has yet to provide. The significance
of the contemporary discussion of the philosophical structure of
Marx's thought lies in the attempt to recover its foundations in the
phenomenology of the Western mind. This is not an abstract en-
deavour, of course, any more than the Hegelian legacy upon which
Marx drew in the first place. It is an essay in the clarification of the
cultural presuppositions of the institutions and mentality of Western
man. Certainly, there is myth and drama in the Marxian heritage—
not, however, the guilt of Oedipus, as the Freudians would have it,
but the compassionate rebellion of Prometheus.

[1] J. O'Neill, 'The Concept of Estrangement in the Early and Later Writings of
Karl Marx', *Journal of Philosophy and Phenomenological Research*, XXV, no. 1 (September 1964), 64–84. Chap. 9 above.

11: Embodiment and History in Hegel and Marx

The rediscovery of the concept of alienation by Marxists in search of a framework for the interpretation and critique of socialist reality has been challenged as an attempt to refurbish a speculative Hegelian notion which Marx abandoned for the more precise concept of exploitation. The 'historical Marx', that is to say, Marx of the *Communist Manifesto* and *Capital*, whom Marxists themselves have given to history, is now to be forsaken for a history made out of the revolutionary event of Marx's discovery of alienation in the property system and the utopian suggestion that the collectivization of property would end alienation and the prehistory of man.[1] These events might be taken to indicate that here at any rate Marx's critique of Hegel appears to have backfired and that Hegel's original concept of alienation as an ontological experience is the more general concept that Marxists now need for the understanding of the unhappy socialist consciousness.

I think it can be argued that what is usually set forth as Marx's redefinition of the Hegelian concept of alienation is nothing else than a progression to be found in *The Phenomenology of Mind*. If this is indeed so, then the 'existentialist' version of Hegel's concept of alienation is not wholly true to Hegel's account of the relation between the individual and society and cannot be employed to revise Marx. The attempt to correct late Marx with early Marx appears to be a correction in favour of Hegel only if Hegel himself is corrected in terms of a reading of the early phenomenological

[1] J. O'Neill, 'Alienation, Class Struggle and Marxian Anti-Politics,' *Review of Metaphysics*, XVII, No. 3 (March 1964), 462–471.

description of the 'Unhappy Consciousness'. But if this discussion is followed through to the historical description of self-estrangement and culture then it becomes clear that in Hegel the experience of alienation is neither individual nor social in origin but the historical mediation of society and the individual through the process of work as self-expression or culture (*Bildung*) in which alienation is ultimately suspended. Now I admit that this more complete account of Hegel's concept of alienation is closer to that of Marx than perhaps Marx himself understood in the *Economic and Philosophical Manuscripts 1844*. But if we must consider Marx's philosophical and economic thought as a unity,[1] as I think we must, then our Hegelian friends must do the same for Hegel. We may then proceed in agreement, as Marx was fond of saying to Engels.

I am dealing with the convergence between Hegel and Marx and I want to show that the 'existentialist' version of this phenomenon is not properly grounded in either Hegel or Marx. The consequences of this may be seen in Sartre's struggle in the *Critique de la raison dialectique* to unite the ontological alienation involved in the dialectic of recognition of the other with a concept of intersubjectivity as the necessary ground of political action and organization.

The ultimate goal of self-consciousness is to recover the unity of the self and the world which it discovers abstractly in the unity of the mind and its objects. The recovery of the world is mediated by desire which reveals the world as my praxis. But this is still only abstractly a world until my interests are recognized by the other. The dialectic of recognition appears as a life and death struggle because of desire which binds consciousness to the world of things and simultaneously reveals its transcendence as the negation of things and the Other. But the categories of subject and object, negation, self, other and recognition are not a priori categories of experience. They arise in the course of the self-interpretation by consciousness of its modes of lived experience which involve consciousness in a dialectic between intentionality and an irreducible ontological difference which generates the world and the recognition of the Other. For if consciousness did not encounter the resistance of things and others, it could only know things perceptually and others by analogy

---

[1] J. O'Neill, 'The Concept of Estrangement in the Early and Later Writings of Karl Marx,' *Philosophy and Phenomenological Research*, XXV (September 1964), 64–84. Chap. 9 above.

and it would have no organic or social life. But this means that consciousness can never be satisfied in a desire for objects and the Other. For in this it would only consume itself whereas it needs a common world in which things and others reflect consciousness back upon itself. 'Selfconsciousness, which is absolutely for itself, and characterizes its object directly as negative, or is primarily desire, will really, therefore, find through experience this object's independence.'[1] Desire then is not the actuality of self-consciousness but only its potentiality for actualizing itself in a common world and intersubjectivity. Hence the struggle to the death which originates in desire is exteriorized in the relation to objects established between the Master and the Slave which preserves their independence in the form of a living dependency. 'In this experience self-consciousness becomes aware that life is as essential to it as pure self-consciousness.'[2]

With respect (fear) for life that is born from the struggle to the death there is initiated a further dialectic in which the Slave's apprenticeship to things makes possible the practical observation of the laws of their operation. Though he works for another, the Slave learns to work with objects whose independence now submits to his production though not to his consumption. By the same token the Master's independence of things mediated by the Slave becomes his dependence upon the Slave's cultivation.

> Labour, on the other hand, is desire restrained and checked, evanescence delayed and postponed; in other words, labour shapes and fashions the thing. The negative relation to the object passes into the form of the object, into something that is permanent and remains; because it is just for the labourer that the object has independence.[3]

Thus from the recognition of the value of life and the fear of death, expressed in submission to things for the sake of life, the experience of domination and servitude opens up the cycle of culture as the objective mediation of self-expression and the world. It is through work that the world is revealed as conscious *praxis*, as a field of individual interests which are in turn opened to the interests of others and hence to a common measure of good and evil. As a field of practical intentions the world is the element of consciousness, its

1 *The Phenomenology of Mind*, translated by J. B. Baillie, London, Allen & Unwin, 1910, p. 210.

2 *Ibid.*, p. 234. 3 *Ibid.*, p. 238.

'original nature' which the activity of consciousness moulds to its purposes. Hegel is quite explicit that there is no room for the experience of estrangement in the act whereby the self externalizes itself in the world of objects. It is the very nature of consciousness to act to externalize itself in the deed, or work.

> The act is something simply determinate, universal, to be grasped as an abstract, distinctive whole; it is murder, theft, a benefit, a deed of bravery, and so on, and what it *is* can be *said* of it. It *is* such and such, and its being is not merely a symbol, it is the fact itself. It *is* this, and the individual human being *is* what the *act is*. In the simple fact that the act *is*, the individual is for others what he really is and with a certain general nature, and ceases to be merely something that is 'meant' or 'presumed' to be this or that. No doubt he is not put there in the form of mind; but when it is a question of his being *qua* being, and the twofold being of bodily shape and act are pitted against one another, each claiming to be his true reality, the deed *alone* is to be affirmed as his genuine being—not his figure or shape, which would express what he 'means' to convey by his acts, or what any one might 'conjecture' he merely could do. In the same way, on the other hand, when his performance and his inner possibility, capacity, or intention are opposed, the former *alone* is to be regarded as his true reality, even if he deceives himself on the point, and, after he has turned from his action into himself, means to be something else in his 'inner mind' than what he is in the act. Individuality, which commits itself to the objective element, when it passes over into a deed no doubt puts itself to the risk of being altered and perverted. But what settles the character of the act is just this—whether the deed is a real thing that holds together, or whether it is merely a pretended or 'supposed' performance, which is in itself null and void and passes away. Objectification does not alter the act itself; it merely shows what the deed *is*, i.e., whether it *is* or whether it is *nothing*.[1]

Only if we abstract the moments of purpose, means, and object can we speak of the transcendence of consciousness over its accomplished deeds or works. But apart from the process of work, consciousness would remain an empty project and its freedom a pure negativity without a world. It is in the process of work that con-

---

[1] *The Phenomenology of Mind*, pp. 349–350.

sciousness experiences the identity of freedom and nature. The externalization of consciousness is a natural experience through which an objective culture and history is created which in turn gives shape to the individual who acquires through it his essential or generic humanity.

It is often remarked that Hegel spiritualized action where Marx materialized it. Marx himself believed this to be the substance of his critique of Hegel. But I think there is some evidence for the argument that Hegel and Marx are engaged in a similar critique of alienation as estrangement from action as expression; and thus there is a continuity between Hegel's *The Phenomenology of Mind* and Marx's *Economic and Philosophical Manuscripts*.

In his remarks on physiognomy Hegel argues that the externalization of consciousness is not contingently related to its purpose but is essential to consciousness as embodied being. Thus the human hand and human speech are essential organs of conscious expression and it is by means of them that we establish a common world of artifacts and meanings. It is through the body that we give to our immediate surroundings 'a general human shape and form, or at least the general character of a climate, of a portion of the world', just as we find regions of the world characterized by different customs and culture. It is through the expressive organs of the hand and speech that we realize a unity of purpose and object which conveys our presence in the world and to others. The human body is thus the expressive instrument of spirit and not its simple objective alienation; it is the instrument whereby there can be culture and history which in turn shape human sensibility, thought, and perception.

> For if the organs in general proved to be incapable of being taken as expressions of the inner for the reason that in them the action is present as a process, while the action as a deed or (finished) act is merely external, and inner and outer in this way fall apart and are or can be alien to one another, the organ must, in view of the peculiarity now considered, be again taken as also a middle term for both. . . .[1]

Thus self-consciousness is not estranged by its natural being, for the human body is an expressive organ through which meaning is

[1] *Ibid.*, p. 343.

embodied in speech and the work of human hands which together articulate the nature of man.

> That the hand, however, must exhibit and reveal the inherent nature of individuality as regards its fate, is easily seen from the fact that after the organ of speech it is the hand most of all by which a man actualizes and manifests himself. It is the animated artificer of his fortune; we may say of the hand it is what a man does, for in it as the effective organ of his fulfilment he is there present as the animating soul; and since he is ultimately and originally his own fate, the hand will thus express this innate inherent nature.[1]

The expression of the human spirit is not the abstract confrontation of a pure interiority with a simple exteriority but the reciprocation of intentionality, gesture, and the deed through which joy, sorrow, and nobility delineate their own meaning in the eyes, the voice, and the hands of man.

The growth of human culture is the growth of human sensibility. So long as culture is dependent upon the class domination of Resources or Wealth, then the judgment of Good is identified with the Power to command wealth and Bad with the wealth that always threatens to be lacking but for power over it. But the universalization of culture implicit in the expressive activity of work is progressively made explicit in the power of the spoken word to express the intellectual, political, and economic ideal of action as self-expression, of which the supreme prerevolutionary expression is Diderot's *Neveu de Rameau*. The liberal identification of self-expression with the organization of society as a system of needs results in a hybrid political economy. And it is the critique of political economy begun in Hegel which provides the bridge to Marx. The nub of Hegel's critique of liberal society is that it rests upon a confusion of a law discovered in the workings of the passions, the invisible law of the market, with law in the ethical sense of a law embraced by rational self-consciousness. This distinction is the basis for Hegel's transition to his philosophy of the State which Karl Löwith, for example, considers as an apparent dialectical transition within liberal society, or rather only its 'suspension through the ideal of the *polis*'.[2] We

[1] *The Phenomenology of Mind*, p. 343.

[2] Karl Löwith, *From Hegel to Nietzsche*, translated by David E. Green, New York, Holt, Rinehart, and Winston, 1964, p. 242.

might then understand Hegel's critique of liberal society not as a recommendation that the 'State' supersede 'Society', but that the liberal subordination of law to an empirical law of the passions as a criterion for the organization of society be superseded in favour of a society organized about a conception of law based on the sublime need of self-consciousness to achieve self-expression in its objects and activities.

Whatever the nature of the differences between *The Phenomenology of Mind* and the *Philosophy of Right*, it is perhaps fateful that Marx began his critique of Hegel with an attack on the Hegelian conception of the State. Marx attacks the Hegelian State as a cultural universal on the ground that it only abstractly mediates the separation between the private interests of the bourgeoisie, summarized in the doctrine of Natural Rights, and the nature of Man supposedly outlined in the doctrine of Rights. 'Here man is far from being conceived as a member of a general class; rather the life of this class itself, society, is conceived as a framework external to the individuals, a restriction upon their original independence. The only bond holding them together is . . . need and private interest.'[1] Marx concludes that bourgeois society cannot be transcended politically, for the state rests upon and is nothing else than the legitimation of an individualistic society. The critique of bourgeois society can only be grounded in a re-examination of the process through which the totality of human life and expression is reduced to a set of needs defined by the impoverishment of labour.

It is not necessary to trace Marx's economic and historical analysis of the institutional preconditions of alienation.[2] This is the aspect of Marx's work which, though not lacking in Hegel, separates Marx from Hegel. The differences, however, seem smaller once attention is given to Marx's conception of the universal nature of work and the human world and sensibility which is its product. I have tried to show earlier that Hegel did not regard man as pure self-consciousness. His treatment of consciousness as embodied being in which the organs of hand and speech are the naturally expressive and creative agencies of a human world should at least modify the criticism that Hegel's concept of alienation confused the two pro-

---

[1] *Ibid.*, p. 245.
[2] J. O'Neill, 'Marxism and Mythology', *Ethics*, LXXVII, no. 1 (October 1966), pp. 38–49.

cesses of externalization and estrangement. Insofar as Hegel's conception of Man is that of an embodied consciousness, then I think Hegel could well have concurred with the anthropological concept that Marx thought he was opposing to Hegel in the following remark.

> To say that man is a corporeal, living, real, sensuous, objective being full of natural vigour is to say that he has real, sensuous objects as the objects of his being or of his life, or that he can only express his life in real, sensuous objects. To be objective, natural, and sensuous, and at the same time to have object, nature, and sense outside oneself, or oneself to be object, nature, and sense for a third part, is one and the same thing.[1]

Finally, there are several aspects of Marx's concept of alienation among which there is, I think, a central notion where again Marx and Hegel share a common conception of action as self-expression. For Marx alienation is a fact of political economy not of phenomenology. That is to say, in the first place, under capitalism man is estranged from the product of his work which in turn estranges him from his own nature as a sensuous and social being. Under such conditions the meaning of work becomes merely a means of subsistence for the satisfaction of purely animal needs and loses its nature as a human need which is to work creatively even in the absence of physical needs. Man and Nature are thus involved in a cultural matrix in which the natural history of man is interwoven with the humanization of natural history.

> Only through the objectively unfolded richness of man's essential being is the richness of subjective human sensibility (a musical ear, an eye for beauty of form—in short, senses capable of human gratifications, senses confirming themselves as essential powers of man) either cultivated or brought into being. For not only the five senses but also the so-called mental senses—the practical senses (will, love, etc.)—in a word, human sense— the humanness of the senses—comes to be by virtue of its object, by virtue of humanized nature. The forming of the five senses is a labour of the entire history of the world down to the present.[2]

The evolution of human nature proceeds in terms of the interaction between man and nature and the technology and social relations

[1] *Economic and Philosophical Manuscripts of 1844*, Moscow, Foreign Languages Publishing House, 1956, p. 156.

[2] *Economic and Philosophical Manuscripts*, p. 108.

of production which mediate that process. In this sense the potentiality of human nature may be regarded as a function of the means and relations of production.

> Because of this simple fact that every succeeding generation finds itself in possession of the productive forces won by the previous generation which serve it as the raw material for new production, a connection arises in human history, a history of humanity takes shape which has become all the more a history of humanity since the productive forces of man and therefore his social relations have been extended. Hence it necessarily follows: the social history of men is never anything but the history of their individual development, whether they are conscious of it or not.[1]

Thus, I think, it is possible to conclude that neither Hegel nor Marx separated Nature from History and that both regarded world history as a history of culture in which human needs furnish a primary structure open to a multiplicity of cultural forms which in turn shape the existential character of need but directed toward the truly human needs of creativity and sociality.

[1] Marx to Annenkov, Brussels, 28 December 1846, *Selected Correspondence, 1846–1895*, translated by Dora Torr, London, Lawrence and Wishart Ltd., 1934, p. 7.

PART FOUR

On Reflexive Sociology

A number of the preceding essays have been predominantly critical in tone, even though I have tried to preface them with a positive intention. In this section I try to express the foundations of my thought on the nature of social and political experience. Again, the discussion is predominantly critical, in particular of Gouldner, Habermas and Althusser. However, this would be a casual conclusion in view of my attempts to make sense of the problematic of criticism and of the perspectives of knowledge and language. Worst of all, it would be to forget my teachers, among whom I count all those whose arguments have provoked my own thoughts. There can, of course, be no last word here. What is needed, is a thoroughly direct approach to the problems of a social ontology, and this I have attempted in my forthcoming book *Making Sense Together*.

12: How is Society Possible?

I am going to take Simmel's question 'How is Society Possible?',[1] and by twisting its Kantian formulation into the mode of Husserlian phenomenology, interpret the question in the form, 'How is Society *made* possible?'. That is to say, I want to show that by shifting Simmel's question away from the search for invariant categories or forms of social reality, we may propose that the real nature of the question is to take members' own practices as the rule of the social construction of reality. Before proceeding, I should clarify briefly the relationship between the proposal here and the traditional concerns of the sociology of knowledge. Recently, there has been a development of the foundations of the sociology of knowledge which otherwise seemed to be drying up by reason of the very success of its classical sources, Marx, Freud, Nietzsche, Durkheim, Weber, Scheler, Dilthey, and Mannheim. In 1959 Kurt Wolff raised the question of the nature of the existential truth underlying the sociology of knowledge and sociological theory.[2]

Meantime the exploration of Alfred Schutz's writings[3] on the

[1] Georg Simmel, 'How is Society Possible?', translated by Kurt H. Wolff, *Essays on Sociology, Philosophy and Aesthetics*, by Georg Simmel *et al.*, edited by Kurt H. Wolff, New York, Harper and Row, 1965, pp. 337–356.

[2] Kurt H. Wolff, 'The Sociology of Knowledge and Sociological Theory', *Symposium on Sociological Theory*, edited by Llewellyn Gross, New York, Harper and Row, 1959, pp. 567–602.

[3] Alfred Schutz, *The Phenomenology of the Social World*, translated by George Walsh and Frederick Lehnert, Evanston, Northwestern University Press, 1967; *Collected Papers* I: The Problem of Social Reality, edited by Maurice Natanson, The Hague, Martinus Nijhoff, 1962; *Collected Papers* II: Studies in Social Theory, edited by Arvid Brodersen, The Hague, Martinus Nijhoff, 1964; *Collected Papers* III: Studies in Phenomenological Philosophy, edited by Ilse Schutz, The Hague, Martinus

phenomenology of the social world and commonsense knowledge of social structures, courses of action, and motivation, has led to a sociology of practical reasoning which contributes fresh theoretical and empirical dimensions to the concerns of the sociology of knowledge.[1] Peter Berger has argued that the sociology of knowledge must now be concerned with the basic processes of the social construction of reality in order to correct the intellectualist bias of its classical origins.

> The theoretical foundations of reality, whether they be scientific or philosophical or even mythological, do not exhaust what is 'real' for the members of a society. Since this is so, the sociology of knowledge must first of all concern itself with what people 'know' as 'reality' in their everyday, non- or pretheoretical lives. In other words, commonsense 'knowledge' rather than 'ideas' must be the central focus for the sociology of knowledge. It is precisely this 'knowledge' that constitutes the fabric of meanings without which no society could exist.[2]

I want, then, to follow out Berger's prescription by taking Simmel's apparently intellectualist formulation of the problem of the social construction of reality and showing the ways in which it can be understood as an everyday practical accomplishment which continuously solves its own contingencies in ways that are not a concern for existentialist absurdities.

In what follows I shall expand upon Simmel's three 'sociological apriorities', drawing upon Schutz's notion of typification[3] and Goffman's concept of 'face'.[4] My purpose is to connect the cognitive and expressive 'motivations' or 'knowing' through which individuals

---

Nijhoff, 1966; *Reflections on the Problem of Relevance*, edited, annotated, and with an Introduction by Richard M. Zaner, New Haven and London, Yale University Press, 1970.

[1] Harold Garfinkel, *Studies in Ethnomethodology*, Englewood Cliffs, N.J., Prentice-Hall, 1967; Aaron V. Cicourel, *The Social Organization of Juvenile Justice*, New York, John Wiley and Sons Inc., 1968; Bukart Holzner, *Reality Construction in Society*, Cambridge, Mass., Schenkman Publishing Company, Inc., 1968; Peter L. Berger and Thomas Luckmann, *The Social Construction of Reality*—A treatise in the Sociology of Knowledge, New York, Doubleday and Company, Inc., 1967.

[2] *The Social Construction of Reality*, p. 15.

[3] *Collected Papers* II, Studies in Social Theory, pp. 229–238.

[4] Erving Goffman, *Interaction Ritual*, Essays on Face-to-Face Behavior, New York, Doubleday Anchor Books, 1967.

organize their standing as competent members in any common enterprise, and in ways that are presupposed in any empirical pattern of motivation or ideology that usually furnishes the subject of analysis in the sociology of knowledge.

First A Priori

Each of Simmel's three sociological apriorities is intended to elucidate the fundamental axiom that we inhabit a common world in which the presence of the other is not simply an alien perspective whose relation to myself is always problematic. The task which Simmel undertakes is the clarification of my relation to the other *as an exemplar of the same social system*.[1] The wider context of the first antinomy is the relationship between the generalized other and the philosophical problem of universals and particulars. In *Mind, Self, and Society*, Mead raises the problem of universals in terms of a theory of abstraction based upon taking the roles of the generalized other and the 'specific other'. Apart from the generalized other there could be no universality in human experience and consequently nothing to correspond to the emergence of a self, which is properly a social and not an individual status. Alternatively, where the individual is adopted as a starting point, as in *The Philosophy of the Act*, then the status of the generalized other, that is to say, its constitution by the individual is a problem which remains unresolved.

Simmel's discussion of the generalized other proceeds in terms of a remarkable anticipation of Schutz's notion of typification processes in the structure of self, other, and specific world relations.

> We see the other not simply as an individual but as a colleague or comrade or fellow party member—in short, as a cohabitant of the same specific world. And this inevitable, quite automatic, assumption is one of the means by which one's personality and reality assume, in the imagination of the other, the quality and form required by sociability.[2]

At the same time, Simmel argues as though the need to employ self-typifications as well as role and course-of-action typifications were not the constitutive foundation of social reality but arose from

[1] Maurice Natanson, *The Social Dynamics of George H. Mead*, Washington, D.C. Public Affairs Press, 1956, pp. 64–68.
[2] *Essays on Sociology, Philosophy and Aesthetics*, p. 344.

our inability ever to penetrate to the ideal core either of ourselves or of others. Thus typification is merely a compensation for the inadequacy of our knowledge and imagination in respect of one another. It is at best a veil which we throw over our mutual ignorance.

The distortions derive from all these *a priori*, operative categories: from the individual's type as a man, from the idea of his perfection, and from the general society to which he belongs. Beyond all of these, there is, as a heuristic principle of knowledge, the idea of his real, unconditionally individual nature.[1]

It is not my purpose merely to point out Simmel's equivocal conception of the constitutive role of typifications in the construction of social reality. Here in this first antinomy of the particularity and generalization of the other I think it quite possible to understand Simmel's argument in terms of a range of typifications from face-to-face to increasingly anonymous situations in which the repertoire of tasks, relevances, gestures, language, and context varies as something that can be assumed in common but *without any radical break between what can be taken for granted and what becomes problematic*. This is not to say that we cannot be mistaken about one another or about ourselves. But it means that we do not presume ourselves in error and that we only encounter error and deceit in the same world upon which we rely to correct for them. Thus ordinary vision is not simply a compensation for the blind spot in our field of vision, and no one would think of arguing that perfect vision can never be achieved unless this blind spot were removed. Similarly, the phenomenon of typification rather than being a substitute for knowledge of particulars is the only way they can be given to us at all.

The practice of life urges us to make the picture of a man only from the real pieces that we empirically know of him, but it is precisely the practice of life which is based on those modifications and supplementations, on the transformation of the given fragments into the generality of a type and into the completeness of the ideal personality.[2]

At this point it would be necessary to undertake a constitutive phenomenology of meaning and understanding in order to clarify the foundations of Simmel's first *a priori*. It would then be possible

[1] *Essays on Sociology, Philosophy and Aesthetics*, p. 345.
[2] *Ibid.*, p. 344.

to show how the processes of typification resolve the antinomy of subjective and objective understanding according to a variety of social contexts.[1] Here it may suffice to indicate the place of such an analysis and its natural fit with the structure of Simmel's sociological apriorities.

Second A Priori

Each of Simmel's sociological antinomies may be related to the expressive as well as the cognitive dimensions of the self and social reality. Schutz's analysis of subjective meaning in face-to-face situations and increasingly anonymous social situations may be referred to in the case of the first *a priori*. In the case of the second antinomy of social commitment and social withdrawal what we can know of the self and the other is a question of the 'presentation'[2] of the self to others who support the self in a certain 'face'. Simmel's emphasis is not so much upon the 'reality' problem suggested by the stage metaphor.[3] Although he sometimes suggests it, Simmel's argument is effectively directed against the notion that the individual is not really present in his social roles or that he can literally enter or exit from the social scene.

> Rather, the fact that in certain respects the individual is not an element of society constitutes the positive condition for the possibility that in other respects he is: the way in which he is sociated is determined or codetermined by the way in which he is not.[4]

Our experience of social reality would be something quite different from what it is if we were to assume that those we encounter are neither more nor less than what they find scope for in a specific social role. We are not to suppose that people lead double lives, far less many lives. Rather, people lead their lives along a continuum which ranges from the maximal degree of social commitment as evinced, for example, by the bureaucrat or priest, to a minimal degree

---

1 *The Phenomenology of the Social World*, pp. 176–207.

2 Erving Goffman, *The Presentation of Self in Everyday Life*, New York, Doubleday Anchor Books, 1959.

3 John O'Neill, 'Self Prescription and Social Machiavellianism', Proceedings of the XXII Congress of the International Institute of Sociology, Rome, 15–21 September 1969.

4 *Essays on Sociology, Philosophy and Aesthetics*, p. 345.

of such commitment, or alternatively a maximal degree of social withdrawal as in the case of the lover or hermit. This, of course, does not mean that the *same man* cannot be both a bureaucrat and a lover, nor, for example, that a period of relative social withdrawal may not be a prerequisite for maximal social commitment as in the training of elites or charismatic figures, or in the allowances made to lovers whose intentions are ultimately honourable before a congregation.[1]

Simmel very carefully distinguishes the sense in which certain types such as the stranger, the enemy, and the pauper may be said to be outside of society. This usage depends upon the degree to which individuals are deprived of typical chances to operate the normal stock of knowledge, symbolic means, and resources available to the average member of the society in question.[2] At both the expressive and cognitive level we encounter the phenomena of maximal social withdrawal and maximal social commitment as dimensions respectively of individual freedom and transcendent social determinism. Here, however, Simmel points out that the postures of loneliness, solipsism, rebellion, and alienation require social support from others who must adapt their behaviour accordingly to respect the boundaries of subculture and milieu, locale or scene, in which these attitudes are cultivated.

> The essence and deepest significance of the specific sociological *a priori* which is founded on this phenomenon is this: The 'within' and the 'without' between individual and society are not two unrelated definitions but define together the fully homogeneous position of man as a social animal.[3]

The transubstantiation of the profane to the sacred is an ecological transition effected by beings whose hands are the same in prayer as in work and for whom both work and prayer are never-ending tasks.

Knowledge, Truth, and Falsehood in Human Relations.[4]

Yet, just as our apprehension of external nature, along with illusions and inadequacies, nevertheless attains the truth required

---

[1] Philip E. Slater, 'On Social Regression', *American Sociological Review*, vol. 28, no. 3 (June 1963), pp. 339–364.

[2] Alfred Schutz, 'The Stranger', *Collected Papers* II, pp. 91–105.

[3] *Essays on Sociology, Philosophy and Aesthetics*, p. 350.

[4] *The Sociology of Georg Simmel*, translated, edited, and with an Introduction by Kurt H. Wolff, Glencoe, The Free Press, 1950, pt IV.

for the life and progress of our species, so everybody knows, by and large correctly, the other person with whom he has to deal, so that interaction and relation become possible.[1]

Before taking up Simmel's third antinomy, or *a priori* of symbiosis, it may be useful to try to convey more of the sense of the cognitive and expressive bases of intersubjectivity contained in Simmel's first two apriorities of typification and presentation. The value of this may be to counter the likely objection that Simmel's social phenomenology is based upon a naive realism which confounds the subjective and objective approaches to conduct. At the same time, it is necessary to give some account of error and deception which does not open the door to misanthropy and scientism.

It is the starting assumption of every social relationship that each of us knows with whom he is interacting. This involves the typification of each partner's actions, motives, and situation. There is, however, no necessity that these typifications be accessible in a perfectly reciprocal way in order to sustain social interaction. All the same, person and action typifications are corrigible through experience. But what is not true is that we withhold our trust in others until we have certain grounds for it. Socially speaking, seduction precedes both deduction and induction as the basis of our experience with others. Thus in the ordinary course of life we take others at face-value and expect to be sustained in the face which we ourselves project. It follows that at least in primary institutions the focus of social interaction is the expressive communication between self and other. We must then regard language, gesture, task, motive, and situation as resources for expressive social bonding which is itself the precontractual basis of all other covenants. The primary task of sociability, as Hegel might have put it, is to solve the dialectic of recognition or intersubjectivity.[2] And this is something which each of us achieves in the face of the other, according to his lights and just deserts.

With an instinct automatically preventing us from doing otherwise, we show nobody the course of our psychic processes in their

[1] *Ibid.*, p. 307.
[2] G. W. F. Hegel, *The Phenomenology of Mind*, translated, with an Introduction and Notes by J. B. Baillie, London, George Allen and Unwin Ltd., 1910, pp. 228–40. This is not to ignore the problems of intersubjectivity in dyads, families, and groups as analysed by Freud and Sartre.

purely causal reality and—from the standpoints of logic, objectivity, and meaningfulness—complete incoherence and irrationality. Always, we show only a section of them, stylized by selection and arrangement. We simply cannot imagine any interaction or social relation or society which are *not* based on this teleologically determined non-knowledge of one another. This intrinsic, *a priori*, and (as it were) absolute presupposition includes all relative differences which are familiar to us under the concepts of sincere revelations and mendacious concealments.[1]

From the standpoint of sociability, truth, and falsehood, knowledge and ignorance are practicalities in which any member of a social group may ordinarily be expected to be versed under pain of risking his status as a fellow. Where a commonsense awareness of the practical typifications and self-presentations is lacking, either on occasion or in some more serious way, a member's sense of social reality may be questioned, apologies, excuses, or explanations demanded which in turn touch upon the member's continued identity in the group. Now Simmel's fundamental insight into the nature of social interaction lies in his demonstration that ordinary social interaction presupposes the *a prioris of knowledge and ignorance as practicalities* which any social agent can articulate without explicit rule, according to the needs of specific social enterprises. In other words, the way in which society is possible is never anything else than a practical task which commonsense rationality and sentiment solves continuously,[2] or, as Simmel would say, 'teleologically'.

Third A Priori
Simmel's third antinomy is concerned with society experienced alternately as a deterministic environment or force (*milieu*) and as our very element or beneficient shell (*ambiance*).[3] This antinomy is essential to the dialectic of individual and social consciousness which are not separate entities but simply vital dimensions of our human

---

[1] *The Sociology of Georg Simmel*, p. 312.

[2] For an experimental confirmation of this basic postulate of constitutive social phenomenology, see Harold Garfinkel, 'Studies of the Routine Grounds of Everyday Activities', *Social Problems*, vol. II, no. 3 (Winter 1964), pp. 225–250.

[3] Leo Spitzer, '*Milieu and Ambiance*: An Essay in Historical Semantics', *Philosophy and Phenomenological Research*, vol. III (1942–1943), pp. 1–42 and 169–218.

awareness and biography.[1] There are times when we experience ourselves as the simplest element in the vast swarm of social life. This
experience of society as a transcendent and determinant force is not
fundamentally an experience of alienation even though the metaphors of organicism and machinery used to convey the experience
may be given this interpretation. There is a commonsense experience
of the world and society as that which precedes us and survives us in
which the simple sense of tradition and posterity is cultivated. So
far from being an alien experience social transcendence provides us
with a sense of the social world as somehow fashioned to our wants
and needs, shaped to the scheme of our practices and relevances. If
the social world is larger than us it is in the way that a child finds
his home richer than himself in meeting all his needs. In this sense
we experience social transcendence in the daily borrowings of our
lives and in the symbiosis of gift and need which is the presupposition
of all exchange and organization.

Yet it is also the case that we experience the great anonymity of
society and the social division of labour as something in which we
are called to find a place through our own peculiar vocation. Indeed,
as Durkheim has shown, it is the modern development of the social
division of labour which creates the moral space in which vocation
and personality flourish. Simmel, as well as Durkheim and Weber,
remarks on the crisis of trust which arises with the volume of exchange and abstract communication in a modern society. Yet, here
again, we may remark that the sense of individual vocation is not
necessarily anomic. It may, for example, be perfectly synchronous
with the symbiosis of social life. This may be seen from the original
Christian conception of charisma[2] in which the varieties of gifts, of
tongues, of healing, of liberality, and of teaching, are conceived as
operations of the same spirit and the same God in us and exercised
within the same unity as the temporal and Christian body politic.

Each of Simmel's *a priori*'s, or, as we may call them, the *a prioris
of typification, presentation, and symbiosis*, are constituent features of
individual and social existence. They circumscribe the cognitive and
expressive operations of social bonding but are prior to all empirical
patterns of motivation. As such they furnish members' commonsense knowledge of social structures and motivation in ways that

---

[1] See chap. 1.
[2] *I Corinthians*, ii, 4–31.

make the question, 'How is Society Possible?', not at all a question about the 'idea' of society, but an appeal for the elucidation of the everyday ways in which we know one another and the contours of the situations in which we find ourselves.

13: The Hobbesian Problem in Marx and Parsons

The problem of order is as much a question about the human nature of social reality as an inquiry into the nature of moral and political order. The consideration of the structure and logic of social order involves us in the imputation of some concepts of human nature and truth. The legitimation of any state implies a notion of some repository of truth and the conditions of access to it. In turn, any conception of the nature and scope of true human knowledge has direct consequences for the nature of social action and participation. Political action involves the coordination of means towards the goals of life as determined by the needs and values of a given social structure. But the conditions of political action are never merely factual givens, just as their realization is never a simple end in itself. The conditions of political action are always immanent to the principles of legitimation which arch the goals of social life. Thus it may be argued what has been called the Hobbesian problem of order is also tied to the nature of the ultimate legitimacy of the formal and substantive modes of rationality and action, or the *Weberian problem*, as well as the institutional relations between the sentimental and rational bases of social order, which constitutes the *Durkheimian problem*. The metatheoretical concerns of Hobbes, Marx, Durkheim, and Weber are so finely interwoven with their analytic concepts and empirical generalizations that extreme care should be exercised in trying to separate their theories of human nature from their conceptions of sociological and political analysis. The pattern of these concerns cannot be discerned in purely analytical terms. It also requires an historical approach to the sociological tradition itself as an emergent feature of industrial optimism and its subversive and disenchanted alternations.

What is unique in the work of Parsons is the profundity of his grasp of the whole intellectual tradition in which the Hobbesian problem of order arises. For this reason, I am inclined to regard *The Structure of Social Action* as in many ways the greatest of Talcott Parsons' works. For it is both a major work of social and political philosophy in the great tradition of utilitarianism with which it struggles as well as the embryo of the general analytic theory of action to which we owe the major theoretical and empirical synthesis of the social sciences. I am not myself a Parsonian. This itself may be painfully obvious to those who are Parsonians from the kind of emphasis I have chosen to put on *The Structure of Social Action*. All the same, there it is, I regard Parsons as one of the great social philosophers in the sentimental tradition[1] of Adam Smith, Burke, McLuhan, and Goffman.

Parsons is so much at home in the western intellectual tradition from Hobbes to Freud, that even when he attempts a fresh theoretical synthesis or brings some further empirical domain within the Parsonian framework it is always with a sense of the whole intellectual tradition from which sociology emerges and claims its 'analytical' autonomy. For this very reason, it is necessary to recognize that the Parsonian conception of sociology, particularly the sublimity of that conception, rests very much on the way Parsons reads the classics from which he constructed *The Structure of Social Action* and the general theory of action. Since much has already been said to one side and another about Parsons' views on the social system and its sub-systems of action,[2] along with the contributions in the present volume, perhaps I may be permitted an exercise of a somewhat different nature. I cannot claim any greater merit for my approach and, indeed, its only value may be to call attention to considerations that others will articulate more clearly. I am going to examine the Hobbesian problem in some detail and, with a look at Hegel and Marx, consider what Parsons calls the

[1] By 'sentimental tradition' I refer to the concern with the relation between the rational and sentimental bases of social order raised by the market reorientation of motivation, for example, in Adam Smith's *Theory of Moral Sentiments*, as well as the political contractarian interpretation of motives, for example, in Edmund Burke's *Reflections on the French Revolution*. McLuhan and Goffman extrapolate these concerns into the cool media of bureaucracy, electric technology, and their motory and sensorial codes.

[2] M Black (ed.), *Social Theories of Talcott Parsons*, New Jersey, Prentice Hall, 1961.

Durkheimian and Weberian problems.[1] However, instead of regarding these problems solely as stages in the development of the general analytic theory of action, I am going to treat them in the framework of an historical–philosophical essay on the problem of rationality.[2] The perspective I am adopting is to be found, I believe, in Marx, Durkheim, and Weber in their concern with the *meaning* or value of western rationality which seems to them to undermine its own presuppositions in the sentimental or precontractual order of human relations and patterns of motivation, raising questions about the relative value of formal and substantive rationality.[3] This is, then, as Parsons would say, an essay in residual categories, or the points where the theory of rational action becomes conscious of its limitations.

Rationality and the Problem of Order

The problem of the relationship between the nature of western rationality and the social order is a question with which historicism is deeply concerned. However, Parsons restricts his discussions of historicism to its methodological features: the institutional critique of generalizations and the holistic arguments against methodological individualism within historicism itself.[4] But this account ignores the

1 *Sociological Theory and Modern Society*, New York, The Free Press, 1967, pp. 117–118. For the statement of the reasons why Parsons regards Marx and Tocqueville as outsiders with respect to the core development of sociological theory see his Introduction to the Paperback Edition, *The Structure of Social Action*, Vol. I, New York, The Free Press, 1968.

2 Edmund Husserl, 'Philosophy and the Crisis of European Man', in *Phenomenology and the Crisis of Philosophy*, translated with Notes and an Introduction by Quentin Lauer, New York, Harper Torchbooks, 1965. For an approach to the problem of rationality in terms of a constitutive phenomenology of routine social structures, see Alfred Schutz, 'The Problem of Rationality in the Social World', *Collected Papers* II: Studies in Social Theory, ed. Arvid Broderson, The Hague, Martinus Nijhoff, 1964; and the contributions to a social phenomenology of practical reasoning in Harold Garfinkel, *Studies in Ethnomethodology*, New Jersey, Prentice Hall, 1967; as well as Alan F. Blum, 'The Corpus of Knowledge as a Normative Order: Intellectual Critiques of the Social Order of Knowledge and the Commonsense Features of Bodies of Knowledge', *Theoretical Sociology*, Perspectives and Developments, edited by John C. McKinney and Edward A. Tiryakian, New York, Appleton-Century-Crofts, 1970, pp. 319–336.

3 Karl Mannheim, *Man and Society in an Age of Reconstruction*, Studies in Modern Social Structure, London, Routledge and Kegan Paul, 1966, p. 58.

4 For a discussion of the Marxian position, as I understand it, on the issues of holism and individualism, see chap. 9.

historicist phenomenology of knowledge and rationality which is the very foundation of the method of *verstehen*. It seems to me that the problem of the relation between the physical and social sciences when discussed solely in terms of the unity of scientific method, an important theme in *The Structure of Social Action*, rests upon an abstract or inadequately historical concept of rationality. It is this observation which I consider to be at the heart of the phenomenology of Hegel, Marx, Durkheim, and Weber.

Parsons' own methodology invites us to weave together the historical and empirical contexts in which the theoretical problem of rationality arises. It is this existential connection between theory and practice which underlies the ideal-type method which Parsons adopts from Weber and Marx. The method of ideal-type understanding represents, of course, a radical break with the common assumption of rationalists and empiricists on the identity of actor and observer points of view on social conduct. The assumption of this identity was basic to the positivist conception of scientific research and the utilitarian ethic which adopted the paradigm of rationality as a code for moral as well as scientific conduct.

The significance of Marx and Weber is that between them they raised the idealist question, if you will, Nietzsche's question, of the intrinsic meaning of accumulation and rationalization apart from its purely practical and technical significance.

Consequently, 'will to truth' does *not* mean 'I will not let myself be deceived' but—there is no choice—'I will not deceive, not even myself': *and with this we are on the ground of morality*. For one should ask oneself carefully: 'Why don't you want to deceive?' especially if it should appear—and it certainly does appear—that life depends on appearance; I mean, on error, simulation, deception, self-deception; and when life has, as a matter of fact, always shown itself to be on the side of the most uncrupulous *polytropoi*. Such an intent, charitably interpreted, could perhaps be a quixotism, a little enthusiastic impudence; but it could also be something worse, namely, a destructive principle, hostile to life. 'Will to truth'—that might be a concealed will to death. Thus the question 'Why science?' leads back to the moral problem, 'For what end any morality at all', if life, nature, and history are 'not moral?' . . . But one will have gathered what I am driving at, namely, that it always remains a *metaphysical faith* upon which our faith in science rests—that even we devotees of knowledge today, we godless ones and antimetaphysicians, still take *our* fire from the flame which a thousand of years old has kindled: that Christian faith, which was also Plato's faith, that God is truth, that truth is divine . . .[1]

How shall we understand the pursuit of cultural and economic values in the absence of any self-imposed or socially imposed limit which would make the acquisition of these values a meaningful end rather than a self-expanding and socially alienating process? This is the crux of the Durkheimian and Weberian problems. German idealism and historicism were just as much concerned with the ordered disorder or anomie of industrial society as with the nature of historical 'laws'. This is the intuitive focus of their comparative studies of western philosophy, social sciences, and social structure and it is from that standpoint that we can best understand the Marxian and Weberian ideal-type conceptions of capitalism. The model of economic rationality is not simply a construction of the social scientist's understanding. It also reflects the shift from a social structure in which power was based on status to a social structure in which all statuses are ascribed on the basis of economic power. In short, the ideal-type of capitalism is, as Hegel might put it, the truth of subjectivity as it experiences itself under the conditions of liberal society in which the bonds of traditional sentimentality are broken in favour of a vast machinery of individual rights, exchange, and private property. In the Marxian and Weberian use of the ideal-type there is never any question of the reduction of social facts to technological factors. The latter are only introduced as middle principles whose meta-economic meaning is the self transvaluation of human experience through the market as a Faustian generator of wants and needs and the problem of death. This is the context of the Weberian problem to which we shall return.

The idealist critique of positivist methodology and its conception of physical and social reality may be seen as a response to a reversal within the positivist theory of action itself. As Parsons sketches it, the positivist theory of action is internally unstable and results in a switch from a 'radical rationalist' positivism to a 'radical anti-

[1] *The Gay Science:* Book V, *The Portable Nietzsche*, selected and translated, with an Introduction, Prefaces, and Notes by Walter Kaufmann, New York, The Viking Press, 1954, pp. 449–450.

intellectualistic' positivism.[1] I believe this oscillation is a constant in the whole tradition of thought with which Parsons is dealing, from Hobbes to Freud, and that it even affects the Parsonian theory of action.[2] The early optimism of seventeenth- and eighteenth-century rationalism which inspired the positivism of classical utilitarianism had gradually turned by the late nineteenth century to the fatalisms of heredity and environment, the rationalizations of a social order threatened by the spectre of its own violence in the opposing rhetorics of class struggle, Superman and the mythology of oedipal revolt.

Positivist methodology is predisposed to the notion of social reality as an external constraint of the same sort as physical reality. But the assumption of the eternality of social reality prejudices the question of the relation between individual action and social order, despite the mediations of internalization or socialization processes, in the direction of constraint in terms of the social system values of functional hierarchy, technical rationality, and pattern maintenance. Parsons approaches the structure of the positivist theory of action primarily as a problem in the conceptual analysis of the social act. The result is that although he is not unaware of the historical crisis which is the empirical context of the problem of the subjective meaning of order and rationality, in the end he settles for a 'rational optimism'.[3] This perspective seriously affects Parsons' reading of the intellectual tradition to which Hobbes, Marx, Durkheim, Weber, and Freud all belong, for they were all concerned with the subjective meaning of action as a problem of meaningful freedom and order not to be settled as a derivative of the values of technical rationality.

But it is not my purpose here to quarrel with Parsons' conceptual or behavioralist analysis of the unit social act. I am interested in tracing the historical and philosophical background to the Parsonian conception of the normative orientation of social action,[4] which I think offers a more substantial basis to the ideological controversies

[1] Talcott Parsons, *The Structure of Social Action*, A Study in Social Theory with Special Reference to a Group of Recent European Writers, New York, The Free Press of Glencoe, 1964; chap. II, The Theory of Action.

[2] John Finley Scott, 'The Changing Foundations of the Parsonian Action Scheme', *American Sociological Review*, XXVIII, no. 5 (October 1963), pp. 716–735.

[3] Edward A. Tiryakian, 'Existential Phenomenology and the Sociological Tradition', *American Sociological Review*, XXX, no. 5 (October 1965), p. 684.

[4] Harold Kaplan, 'The Parsonian Image of Social Structure and its Relevance for Political Science', *The Journal of Politics*, XXX (November 1968), pp. 885–909.

around the Parsonian assumptions of rational optimism and consensus, and the place accorded to conflict and strain.

I want now to take a close look at the problem of order as Hobbes confronted it, paying particular attention to the problematic nature of the Hobbesian concept of knowledge and rationality. Medieval ontology was profoundly individualist and may be regarded as the ultimate source of the natural rights and social contractarian principles which established the double standard of equality before God and equality in hope which underlay the secular doctrines of liberty, authority, and obligation.[1] The seventeenth-century discussion of the nature of social and political conduct represents a fusion of a *normative* law of nature with a deterministic theory of the *conditions* of action based upon the model of mechanical physics.[2] It is assumed that the ends of action are essentially random and that rationality consists solely in the efficient pursuit of whatever ends man proposes to himself. As Hobbes saw it, the basic problem of rational egoism is to command the services and recognition of other men. Where men are so equal in nature that they can entertain 'equality of hope' there is nothing to prevent them from resorting to fraud and violence in the pursuit of their ends. In short, Hobbes raised very clearly the question of the need to set limits to violence in a social order predicated upon the principle of rational egoism.

The fiction of a social contract fails to save the question raised by Hobbes since, as Marx later pointed out, the costs of keeping promises can be shifted onto a class which lacks the freedom to contract and thus Hobbes's 'state of war' comes to rest upon a 'class war'. Thus the problem of order is ultimately a problem of power which could not be solved within the liberal utilitarian tradition. But, as Parsons remarks, theoretical difficulties are often patched in practice and in this case Locke's postulate of the natural identity of interests matched the early experience of liberal individualism better perhaps than Hobbes's more consistent fears. Thus the problem of recognition came to rest in the doctrine of the natural identity of interests until Marx

1 Otto Von Gierke, *The Development of Political Theory*, translated by Bernard Freyd, New York, Howard Fertig, 1966.

2 The tendency to deduce normative propositions from factual propositions is not just an instance of the naturalistic fallacy, as might be argued nowadays. It can be understood in the light of certain sociological preconceptions assumed in Hobbes' analysis. C. B. Macpherson, *The Political Theory of Possessive Individualism, Hobbes to Locke*, Oxford, The Clarendon Press, 1962.

demonstrated that the system of social exchange and division of labour under capitalist conditions produces a class which recognizes itself only in the conditions of its own dehumanization.

The Hobbesian problem should also be considered in the context of the challenge to knowledge raised by the collapse of the feudal community. The question raised for political knowledge by the loss of a natural basis for community was whether it was possible to construct a community out of the principles of individualism and rational egoism. It had always appeared from the standpoint of medieval community that chaos could be the only result of slipping the divine anchor and leaving the passions to a free play. Indeed, this was the fearful prospect of Renaissance and Reformation freedom, especially once it had found in the market an infinite field for the expansion of desire and the accumulation of power. At the same time, this sudden and terrible expansion of moral and political freedom was being translated into an orderly system of economic exchanges which in turn rested upon the growth of mathematical and physical knowledge and its applications to technology and commerce. But there is a subtle and profound change between the ancient and medieval conception of order and the Hobbesian concept of order. It is a change which stems from the shift in concept of truth and knowledge which occurs between ancient and modern philosophy.[1]

Modern rationality and its institutional organization rests upon the axiological assumption of man's domination of nature which radicalizes the subject–object split and propels knowledge towards quantification and the creation of a moral and political arithmetic. It is natural that the scientific aspirations of sociology should lead to similar assumptions. But prior to the question of whether sociological laws have the same kind of universality as physical laws and thereby guarantee the scientific status of sociology is the phenomenon of the ambiguity in the moral and physical sense of the concept of law upon which the drama of western civilization is founded. Socrates it will be remembered turned away from the study of physical nature in favour of the study of human nature. In this manner Socrates raised the question of the unity of human knowledge as a *praxis* whose values are revealed in the effects upon the soul of the kinds of knowledge pursued in a given social order. With the Renaissance discovery of the experimental method the dramatic affinity of

[1] Michael Oakeshott, Introduction to *Leviathan*, Oxford, Basil Blackwell, 1946.

western knowledge for power was unleashed, unfettered by the moral universals of the ancient and medieval world. Yet to Erasmus the Baconian equation of knowledge and power appeared to be a pagan reversal rather than the intensification of the inherent logic and axiology of western knowledge. 'Never forget,' he remarked, 'that "dominion", "imperial authority", "kingdom", "majesty", "power", are all pagan terms not Christian. The ruling power of a Christian state consists only of administration, kindness, and protection.'[1] Erasmus' comment is a reflection of the crisis of community to be found in the political and religious controversies of the late sixteenth and early seventeenth centuries. In the face of the collapse of church unity and the rise of individual conscience the normative grounds of community could no longer be presumed upon and yet it became clear that any particular covenant or contract was nothing more than, in Milton's words, 'the forced and outward union of cold, and neutral, and inwardly divided minds'. Hobbes's concept of philosophy as the pursuit of clear and precise discourse on the model of geometry dictates his aim of bringing peace and order into civil life by a set of political definitions founded on sovereign authority which would put an end to the anarchy of values and opinions.

> For I doubt not, but if it had been a thing contrary to any man's right of dominion, or to the interest of men that have dominion, *that the three angles of a triangle, should be equal to two angles of a square*; that doctrine should have been, if not disputed, yet by the burning of all books of geometry, suppressed, as far as he whom it concerned was able.[2]

Henceforth rationality is never a substantive concept based on the 'nature of things'. The task of reason is confined to providing conclusions 'about the names of things'. Ultimately, it is Hobbes's conception of philosophical knowledge and science which governs his treatment of the problem of order. What has happened is that the standard of rationality furnished by Hobbes's science of politics is totally divorced from the traditional sentiments and usages of reason.

[1] Quoted by Erich Hula in his Comment on Hans Jonas, 'The Practical Uses of Theory', in Maurice Natanson (ed.), *Philosophy of the Social Sciences: A Reader*, New York, Random House, 1963, p. 151.
[2] *Leviathan*, pt I, chap. 11, p. 68.

This dilemma faced by Hobbes was partly owing to a failure to realize what other apostles of 'scientific' politics have not yet seen, that one of the basic reasons for the unsurpassed progress of science was that scientific discourse, unlike political discourse, had rejected not only the common vocabulary of everyday life, but also the modes of thought familiar to the common understanding.[1]

In the end Hobbes failed to solve the problem of order in anything but an external fashion. Hobbes's citizens live in a mutual and common fear which corrodes their private lives and leaves society dependent upon the sovereign whose power can never be anything but the exercise of fiat because the civil order itself lacks any sense of community or constituency.

Hobbes's positivist concept of law and his doctrine of the state as *causa sui* is the strict derivation of his empiricist rejection of the rationalist conception of law as the embodiment of a rational principle open to speculative reason, such as we find in Hegel's *Philosophy of Right*. The rule, *autoritas, non veritas facit legem*, means that only sovereign sanction can impose truth and rationality upon the political community. The Hegelian position is that the appeal of law is based upon its *a priori* rationality grounded in the nature of being itself. To this Marx adds that the rational foundations of law and order can only be grounded in a rational society in which submission to law is an act of freedom and not just a means to material rights and property. This argument is essential to Marx's conception of the nature of organic solidarity and should not be overlooked in the discussion of the Durkheimian problem to which we now turn.

The Rational and Sentimental Bases of Order: Marx and the Durkheimian Problem

Hobbes's doctrine of political sovereignty raised in its sharpest form the problem of the relation between utilitarian rationality and the sentimental or non-rational bases of political community. However, an intellectual tradition does not live by logic alone. Hobbes's fearful Erastianism did not suit the liberal temper which settled for the more sentimental metaphysics of the natural identity of interests. In this case, Parsons remarks that the development of the theory of

[1] Sheldon S. Wolin, *Politics and Vision*, Continuity and Innovation in Western Political Thought, Boston, Little, Brown and Company, 1960, p. 261.

social action was better served by Locke's utilitarianism than Hobbes's logic, even if less respectably.

For, in so far as the basic action schema is employed for analytical purposes, the fact that economic action is actually empirically important must inevitably raise the question of the adequacy of the utilitarian version of the theory of action, if the contention is right that it cannot without extraneous assumptions, account for the element of order in social relationships necessary to make this possible. Indeed, the central problem may be stated thus: How is it possible, still making use of the general action schema, to solve the Hobbesian problem of order and yet not make use of such an objectionable metaphysical prop as the doctrine of the natural identity of interests?[1]

The utilitarian theory of action oscillates between two conceptions of the rational pursuit of means to given ends. To the extent that rationality is conceived as a social exchange process coinciding with the identity of interests of the partners to it, it is necessary to assume a social order in which violence and fraud are restrained. On the other hand, where rationality is conceived as a process of satisfying intrinsically conflicting interests, some measure of consensus or rules of the game have to be assumed if anarchy is to be avoided. This is what Parsons calls the Durkheimian problem. Now I think that this problem involves a conflict between the patterns of 'substantive' rationality and 'formal' or technical rationality and is not simply a question of the analytic differentiation of the normative and non-normative elements in the general theory of action. I also think this view is closer than Parsons' interpretation of Durkheim and Marx. Parsons sees clearly enough that the reason why the utilitarian theory of action is theoretically and politically indeterminate is that it cannot solve the problems of *class* interests. In the context of the increasing inequality of property and power the postulate of the natural identity of individual interests becomes a sheer illusion. Now this is not simply a Marxist reduction of the relation between economy and politics,[2] since in any case such a move at least presupposes an

[1] *The Structure of Social Action*, p. 102.

[2] For an exhaustive documentation of Marx's views on the relation between the state, law, and economy, which should make it quite clear that Marx's position is not reductionist see, Stanley W. Moore, *The Critique of Capitalist Democracy*, An Introduction to the Theory of the State in Marx, Engels, and Lenin, New York, Paine-Whitman Publishers, 1957.

awareness of the analytic distinction between polity and economy. Parsons argues nevertheless that Marx failed to make the distinction between economic and political interests because his theory of class interests and its rhetoric of class polarization and revolution required the identification of these two levels of action.

> The Durkheimian problem raised the question of the long-standing ambiguity in Marxian theory about the status of normative order, notably at the legal level, with respect to the distinction between 'material' base and the superstructure. Marx's inclination to work at a rather low level of analytical abstraction, reinforced by his historicism, tended to locate this element of normative order in the 'relations of production', which constitute the core of the interest structure of capitalism itself. Durkheim's analysis, however, showed that the crucial institution of contract, as he called it, was analytically distinct from the interests of contracting parties and varied independently of them.[1]

I think it can be shown that Marx was quite aware of the analytic distinction between the institution of contract, or the rule of property, as he would call it, and the class interests which it serves. Indeed, Marx, no less than Durkheim or Weber, pointed out that the universality or normative status of the rule of property is essential to the transition from feudal to bourgeois society. However, this does not require the rule of property or contract to vary independently of the general social structure in which it functions. What Durkheim and Marx, as well as Weber,[2] were concerned to argue was that the normative systems of technical rationality, expressed in the doctrines of rights, property, and contract, itself generates counter-norms of substantive rationality based on the values of participation, self-expression and the common ownership of property.

---

[1] *Sociological Theory and Modern Society*, p. 115.

[2] 'If it is nevertheless said that the economic and the legal order are intimately related to one another, the latter is understood, not in the legal, but in the sociological sense, i.e., as being *empirically* valid. In this context 'legal order' thus assumes a totally different meaning. It refers, not to a set of norms of logically demonstrable correctness, but rather to a complex of actual determinants (*Bestimmungsgründe*) of actual human conduct.' *Max Weber on Law in Economy and Society*, translated by Max Rheinstein and Edward Shils, Cambridge, Massachusetts, Harvard University Press, 1966, p. 12.

Parsons' own reduction of the Durkheimian problem to the analytic distinctions between economy, law, and polity misses the central concern in Durkheim, Marx, and Weber over the historically specific contexts of the interaction of law and economy. In particular, it avoids the problem of the way in which legal rationality undermines the traditional, sentimental bonds of association in favour of market 'freedoms' or property rights, and, ultimately, the heartless laws, or meaningless ways of bureaucracy. Again, the Durkheimian and Weberian problems cannot be kept separate if we are to understand the relationships between the ultimate principles of legitimacy or political authority, the state, the class, and property systems and the problem of the subjective meaning of individual action within these contexts. Marx and Durkheim criticized the utilitarian theory of action, not merely to elaborate the argument for the analytic levels of individual and societal action, but as part of a metatheoretical concern with the meaningfulness of individual behaviour in different kinds of society, that is to say, with the substantive bases of the legitimacy of social and political order.[1]

It is the tension between these historical patterns of rationality which underlies the ideal-typical contrarieties of mechanical and organic solidarity or *Gemeinschaft* and *Gesellschaft*. The latter are not, properly speaking, societal polarities so much as pattern alternatives of value orientation in any society and consequently expressive of the problem of integration rather than contrary solutions to it. Understood in this way, the ideal-type contrast between substantive and technical rationality represents a tension within the self-understanding of western rationality which cuts across the resort either to optimism or despair.

Parsons 'dehumanizes'[2] the Durkheimian problem by treating it as a question of the analytic distinction between the state and economy whereas it is part of the larger problem of anomie and alienation. Durkheim was concerned with the way in which organic solidarity is predisposed to anomie because the relationship between law and economy in modern society is such that the state can hardly hope to

1 For an attempt to relate the principle of authority to the substantive values of the organic, sensible, and libidinal levels of the polity, see chap. 6.

2 John Horton, 'The Dehumanization of Anomie and Alienation: A Problem in the Ideology of Sociology', *British Journal of Sociology*, XV, no. 4 (December 1964), pp. 283–300.

contain the social forces which make for the infinitude of wants, class conflict, and the anomic division of labour. Durkheim attacked these problems in terms of the need to ground social solidarity in a transcendental bond which would provide a sense of meaning deeper than the regulative norms of mechanical and organic solidarity. Marx's notion of alienation furnishes a criterion in individual expression and social relations of an ultimate but immanent principle of social solidarity. His conception of the basis of a just social order differs from Durkheim's because Durkheim's failure to propose any scheme for the reform of the economic system left him with an ultimately Hobbesian concept of human nature faced with an external political constraint.

An adequate discussion of the issues here involves some consideration of the idealist critique of utilitarianism contained in Hegel's *Phenomenology of Mind* and the *Philosophy of Right*. Parsons' treatment of idealism deals only with the historicist and methodological arguments against utilitarian atomism and empiricism. But the Hegelian discussion is essential for the critique of the utilitarian conception of rationality and randomness of ends which are the complementary assumptions of utilitarian atomism and empiricism. There is further reason for considering Hegel because Marx was thoroughly familiar with the Hegelian critique of the utilitarian conception of civil society and the state and adopted it as the model of his own theory of the relation between state and society.[1]

Hegel regarded history as a process which unfolds through a number of living ideologies, such as the Enlightenment, Utilitarianism, and the Absolute Liberty of the French Revolution. Each of these ideologies is correlated with a definite cultural and social reality through which the nature of human rationality and freedom is progressively revealed. Once the Enlightenment had won its struggle with religious superstition the question arose as to the nature of the philosophical truth which the Enlightenment was to set in its place. The truth of the Enlightenment is Utilitarianism which makes everything subject to its usefulness for man but is unable to solve the dilemma of man's utility to other men; this raises the problem of exploitation which could not be solved within the utilitarian

[1] Jean Hyppolite, *Studies on Marx and Hegel*, translated, with an Introduction, Notes, and Bibliography by John O'Neill, London, Heinemann Educational Books, 1969.

tradition.[1] Marx seizes upon this dilemma in utilitarianism in a passage characteristic of his own development of Hegelian insights:

> Hegel has already proved in his *Phänomenologie* how this theory of mutual exploitation, which Bentham expounded *ad nauseam*, could already at the beginning of the present century have been considered a phase of the previous one. Look at his chapter on 'The Struggle of Enlightenment with Superstition', where the theory of usefulness is depicted as the final result of enlightenment. The apparent stupidity of merging all the manifold relationships of people in the *one* relation of usefulness, this apparently metaphysical abstraction arises from the fact that, in modern bourgeois society, all relations are subordinated in practice to the one abstract monetary–commercial relation. This theory came to the fore with Hobbes and Locke, at the same time as the first and second revolutions, those first battles by which the bourgeoisie won political power.[2]

Once the Physiocrats had demonstrated the nature of the economic process as a circular flow, all that remained to complete classical political economy was to give an account of individual attitudes and motivations within that economic framework. This was Bentham's contribution, although, as Marx observes, the theory of utility could not have the generality it claimed because it ignored its own institutional assumptions. For a time, the utilitarian theory of the natural identity of interests had some empirical basis in the facts of the social division of labour and exchange. It was not until Marx adapted Locke's labour theory of value to demonstrate that it contained the working principles of the exploitation of formally free labour that the sociological framework of classical economics was shattered. The point here is that utility is subject to appropriation in the form of

---

[1] 'As everything is useful for man, man is likewise useful too, and his characteristic function consists in making himself a member of the human herd, of use for the common good, and serviceable to all. The extent to which he looks after his own interests is the measure with which he must also serve the purposes of others, and so far as he serves their turn, he is taking care of himself: the one hand washes the other. But wherever he finds himself there he is in his right place: he makes use of others and is himself made use of.' G. W. F. Hegel, *The Phenomenology of Mind*, translated with an Introduction and Notes by Sir James Baillie, London, George Allen and Unwin, 1910, pp. 579–580.

[2] Karl Marx and Friedrich Engels, *The German Ideology*, Moscow, Progress Publishers, 1964, pp. 448–449.

capital which is then able to command the services of others to their disadvantage whatever the circumstances of a formally free contract. Hence the attempt to base the social and political order upon the postulate of the natural identity of interests is broken once and for all.

Marx's labour theory of value expresses both the quantitative and the qualitative features of the laws determining the distribution of productive effort in a commodity-producing society.[1] In its quantitative or economic aspect, the labour theory of value is essentially a general equilibrium theory which summarizes the forces integrating (*a*) the exchange ratios between commodities, (*b*) the quantity of each produced, and (*c*) the allocation of the labour force to the various branches of production. Qualitatively, the labour theory of value expresses the exchange relationships between commodities as a social relationship based upon the historical phenomena of the existence (i) of a developed social division of labour, and (ii) private production. Marx argues that it is not possible to express the workings of the law of value apart from the specification of a set of sociological middle principles. The procedure in *Capital* is to construct a model of simple commodity production, that is, an economy of independent producers each owning his own means of production. The labour theory of value expresses the general equilibrium conditions for this special case.[2] Marx then varies the institutional features of his model of simple commodity production. The ownership of the means of production is concentrated into the hands of a class of capitalists, and labour itself becomes a commodity subject to the laws of exchange value.

Between them Hegel and Marx developed a thorough critique of the social and political foundations of utilitarian economics. Classical liberalism depended upon the protection of a sphere in which the values of personal integrity, property, and contract could be realized as the expression of market society. But, as Hegel showed in the *Philosophy of Right*, in a society conceived solely as a field for market behaviour, economic laws cannot provide the only framework of law,

[1] P. M. Sweezy, *The Theory of Capitalist Development*, New York, Monthly Review Press, 1956, chaps. II and III; K. Marx, *Capital*, Chicago, C. H. Kerr, 1906, vol. III, chapter II.

[2] O. Lange, 'Marxian Economics and Modern Economic Theory', *Review of Economic Studies*, II (1934–1935), pp. 189–201.

if personality, property, and contract are to be preserved as anything more than instruments of market freedom. The political principles of liberal utilitarianism can only be preserved by a system of civil laws based on the principle of rational understanding which differentiates them from the laws of the market.[1] In other words, Hegel argues that the utilitarian concept of society based upon economic laws pre-supposes a rational concept of law, which is the basis of civil society (*bürgerliche Gesellschaft*). The laws of economic society and civil society are in turn distinct from the State which is the highest stage of the realization of the ethical will.

Marx's critique of the liberal bourgeois concept of the state, society, and individual rights is substantially the same as Hegel's. The difference is that Marx's argument also proceeds in terms of a destructive critique of Hegel's own concept of the state and its bureaucratic rationality which in many ways anticipates Max Weber.[2]

If power is taken as the basis of right, as Hobbes, etc., do, then right, law, etc., are merely the symptom, the expression of *other* relations upon which State power rests. The material life of individuals which by no means depends merely on their 'will', their mode of production and form of intercourse, which mutu-ally determine each other—this is the real basis of the State and remains so at all stages at which division of labour and private property are still necessary, quite independently of the *will* of individuals. These actual relations are in no way created by the state power; on the contrary they are the power creating it. The individuals who rule in these conditions, besides having to constitute their power in the form of the *State*, have to give their will, which is determined by these definite conditions, a universal expression as the will of the State, as law—an expres-sion whose content is always determined by the relations of this class, as the civil and criminal law demonstrates in the clearest way.[3]

Marx's argument concerning the relation between state and society is not primarily a reductionist theory of politics so much as an argu-

[1] Hegel's *Philosophy of Right*, translated with Notes by T. M. Knox, Oxford, The Clarendon Press, 1942, Third Part, Sub-Section 2, Civil Society.

[2] Henri Lefebvre, *The Sociology of Marx*, translated by Norbert Guterman, New York, Pantheon Books, 1968; chap. 5, Political Sociology: Theory of the State.

[3] *The German Ideology*, p. 357.

ment over the nature of society. The utilitarian conception of society, i.e., of civil society (*bürgerliche Gesellschaft*), is characterized by a separation of the state and society which reduces the enforcement of law to the preservation of property and the personal rights in its acquisition and alienation.[1] The utilitarian conception of society enforces a radical dualism between private and public man which is the basis for all other forms of individual and social alienation.

> Political man is only the abstract, artificial individual, the individual as an allegorical, moral person . . . All emancipation leads back to the human world, to human relationships, to men themselves. Political emancipation is the reduction of man, on the one side, to the egoistic, independent individual, on the other side to the citizen, to the moral person.[2]

Marx's distinction between political and human emancipation turns upon the difference between the utilitarian conception of civil society and Marx's rationalist conception of society whose laws would not appear to the individual as an external constraint simply, not merely as the framework of his own appetites.

> Not until the real, individual man is identical with the citizen, and has become a generic being in his empirical life, in his individual work, in his individual relationships, not until man has recognized and organized his own capacities as social capacities so that the social energies are no longer divided by the political power, not until then will human emancipation be achieved.[3]

By shifting the emphasis from political to human emancipation Marx's theory of the state goes beyond Hegel's political realism and its conception of personality as the subject of civil rights and economy. In Hegel's view it is only in the context of civil society that man feels he has rights as a person and is in so far prepared to assert his equality.

> In [abstract] right, what we had before us was the person; in the sphere of morality, the subject; in the family, the family-member; in civil society as a whole, the burgher of *bourgeois*.

[1] Mitchell Franklin, 'On Hegel's Theory of Alienation and its Historic Force', *Tulane Studies in Philosophy*, vol. IX, 1960, pp. 50–100.
[2] Henri Lefebvre, *The Sociology of Marx*, p. 133.
[3] *Ibid.*

Here at the standpoint of needs . . . what we have before us is the composite idea which we call *man*. Thus this is the first time, and indeed properly the only time, to speak of *man* in this sense.[1]

Marx argues that Hegel's definition of man as the subject of material needs and rights is a reflection of the spiritual division between man's public and private morality in bourgeois civil society. It is important to understand that Marx did not question the brilliance of Hegel's conception of bourgeois civil society but only his presentation of it as an essential structure of state–society relations.[2]

It is not the recognition of the Durkheimian problem which divides Marx and Durkheim so much as their different responses to it. The critical analysis of utilitarianism undertaken by Hegel, Marx, and Durkheim all pointed to the problem of discovering a basis for the legitimation of the norms which liberal economic freedom presupposed but continuously undermined short of an arbitrary appeal to coercion, or the metaphysical postulate of a natural identity of interests. Marx concluded that this contradiction or instability in the utilitarian pattern of means/end rationality was the critical basis for an attack upon it by the social forces working towards the institutionalization of a pattern of substantive rationality, based upon participation and the abolition of private property. Durkheim's vision of the consequences of the instability of the normative pattern of organic solidarity was not different from Marx's but his response was more like Hegel's divinization of the rational state as the highest realization of ultimate common values. Durkheim's solution has also to be understood, as I have argued throughout, in terms of the theory of knowledge with which he and others opposed the individualistic conception of rationality developed in the classical epistemologies of Locke, Kant, Mill, and Spencer. Durkheim's critique of utilitarianism involved a reassertion of the sacred origins of truth and social institutions which it had been the task of individualist nominalism, utilitarianism, and secularization to progressively deny. The clincher in Durkheim's argument is his demonstration that modern individualism

[1] Hegel, *Philosophy of Right*, para. 190.

[2] For the problems underlying Marx's final aesthetic or ethical conception of the relations between men in society, see, Eugene Kamenka, *The Ethical Foundations of Marxism*, New York, Frederick A. Praeger, 1962, pt I, 4: 'The "Truly Human" Society'; and pt III, 2: 'Ethics and the "Truly Human" Society'.

so far from creating industrial society presupposes its differentiation of the socio-psychic space which creates the concepts of personality and autonomy. By the same token, Durkheim was aware that he had not changed the nature of his problem: he had only described its 'field'. The Durkheimian or Hobbesian problem of the integration of knowledge, moral authority, and personality still remained to be solved under the conditions of organic solidarity. More precisely, Durkheim leaves it unclear whether religion is the idealization of society as it is to be found with both what is good and evil in it or whether religion is the vehicle solely of the idealism which social life may inspire in individuals.

I remarked earlier that Parsons dehumanizes the Durkheimian problem by reducing it to a question of the analytic status of the polity and economy rather than taking the problem in the broad sense of the meaning of life in a modern industrial society. Now that is not entirely the case and I should now consider how Parsons in fact treats the larger question. Parsons also discusses the Durkheimian problem as a problem of the structural location of the motivational aspects of social commitment. A modern industrial economy can only function provided 'A positive obligation to enter into the general allocative system',[1] is institutionalized in the existence of a market, money, and mobile, alienable factors of production, including labour.

> The division of labour brings freedom from ascriptive ties regarding the utilization of consumable goods and services and the factors of production themselves. The structural location of organic solidarity thus concerns the dual problem of how the processes by which the potentially conflicting interests that have been generated can be reconciled without disruptive conflict (this leads, of course, into the Hobbesian problem), and of how the societal interest in efficient production can be protected and promoted.[2]

The commitment to the 'generalization' of resources and factors of production through their release from ascriptive and kinship ties is a commitment to the values of technical effectiveness and legal-

---

[1] 'Durkheim's Contribution to the Theory of Integration of Social Systems', *Sociological Theory and Modern Society*, p. 16.
[2] *Sociological Theory and Modern Society*, pp. 14–15.

rationality which rests upon non-rational values. In the context of a modern industrial economy based upon technological and legal rationality the Hobbesian problem becomes a cybernetic problem of the interchange of generalized symbolic media of money and value-commitments.[1] The task of the polity is to translate the generalized commitment which it receives from the value-system into 'effectiveness', i.e., collective action in the public interest. The 'factor' interchange between the polity and the value system raises the question of the nature of the ultimate legitimacy principles, that is to say, not just their congruent or conflicting tendencies but also the relations between the component of rational and non-rational values which determines political commitment or alienation. The problem of the ultimate legitimacy of the social and political order is a question of meaningful values which is broader than the pattern-variable subordination of expressive values to technical-rational organization.

Parsons is well aware that Durkheim's argument is that *anomie* is not the experience of an alien institutional order. It is a problem of the meaningfulness of the actor's goals and situational chances which under conditions of institutionalized scarcity leads to non-normative but subjectively meaningful responses of revolt, ritualization, and alienation. From Hobbes to Durkheim the problem of order and solidarity has not changed except for the escalation-effect of the shift to civil society, under the conditions of the capitalist property system, upon the psychology of individual wants and desires. As the nineteenth century wore on, the attack on economic rationalism from the standpoint of its consequences for social solidarity was joined by romantic conservatives, utopian socialists, Marxists, and even Fascists. It is also the background of Freud's work in social and political anthropology. 'In *Group Psychology and the Analysis of the Ego*, Freud adumbrated the distinction between two archetypes of social psychology: the individual psychology which is the primal horde belonged to the father alone, and the group psychology of the sons, or brothers. Fatherhood and brotherhood are the archetypes brooding in the background of such sociological abstractions as Durkheim's mechanical and organic solidarity, or Gierke's *Herrschaft* and *Genossenschaft*, the imperial and fraternal principles, which dialectically combine to weave the changing fabric of western social corporate

[1] Talcott Parsons, 'On the Concept of Value-Commitments', *Politics and Social Structure*, New York, The Free Press, 1969, chap. 16.

bodies. It is the specific gift of psychoanalysis to see behind these sociological abstractions the human face; and their name is "fatherhood and brotherhood".'[1] Regarded in this way, the principal of the identity of interests must be seen as furnishing a counter-norm of substantive rationality variously grounded in the family, fraternity, class, or utopian community, depending upon the context chosen for the abolition of property and the subordination of sentimental to technical rationality.

These are ideological thickets which Parsons is always anxious to avoid. Yet he chooses an extremely vulnerable strategy in his attempt to 'generalize' the problems involved. As Parsons sees it, the 'fashionable' concern with alienation and the problem of identity is a problem of locating oneself in the social system. This problem has cognitive and affective dimensions which it is the task of the theory of social control or commitment to understand. I do not wish to quarrel with Parsons' account of identity as a precipitate of subsystem social interaction processes linked with codes of generalization at the social system level. In this he has made a significant theoretical integration of Durkheim and Freud. But at the same time he has sacrificed the founders' concern with the problems of instability, conflict, and alienation involved in these processes. Parsons regards instability as a 'reasonable' feature of the modern social system and its model personality type. He classifies critical reponses to its risks in terms of two types of 'irrational' responses (i) a security 'demand' which minimizes risk at the expense of creativity, and (ii) a 'utopian' orientation which ignores the constraints on creative success for the sake of blind commitment.[2]

In essence, this represents the Mertonian version of Durkheim's conception of anomie. Durkheim's argument, unlike that of Merton and Parsons, does not leave unquestioned the nature of the ultimate values of the society which result in a range of anomic responses on the part of the individuals. His point is precisely that it is because individuals are committed to the norm of institutionalized discontent as well as to norms of equality and justice that there exists an endemic strain towards social disorganization and class struggle.

[1] Norman O. Brown, *Love's Body*, New York, Random House, 1966, p. 9.
[2] Talcott Parsons, 'The Problem of Identity in the General Theory of Action', *The Self in Social Interaction*, edited by Chad Gordon and Kenneth J. Gergen, New York, John Wiley and Sons, Inc., 1968, pp. 11–23.

'Just as ancient peoples needed, above all, a common faith to live by, so we need justice, and we can be sure that this need will become even more exacting if, as every fact presages, the conditions dominating social evolution remain the same.'[1]

Parsons is quite aware that the value-system like other media is subject to hot and cold alternations, or, as he prefers, to the inflation and deflation of commitments.[2] Thus the norm of institutionalized discontent is the source of an inflationary tendency in the value-system of the capitalist social order (complex society) which attempts to cool itself through a variety of deflationary commitments ranging from fundamentalism to socialism and yippie love cults. The 'liquidity' problem of the modern value system arises not only because of its own tendency to undermine depositors' trust but because moral innovators threaten to cause 'runs' on its 'commitment banking' system. These are basically neo-Keynesian metaphors which reflect the way in which Parsons responds to the moral challenge that faces the American social and economic order. Their effect is to lose the sense of squalor that infects, for example, Galbraith's concerns for the quality as well as the 'effectiveness' of affluence. A proper discussion of this context of the Hobbesian problem would require an analysis of the way in which the relative disposition of the public and private sectors of the capitalist economy shapes the contours of the generalized pattern of social values, and leaves life 'nasty, short, and brutish' even today in America's own cities and countryside, not to speak of her colonies.[3] It might then be possible to relate these structural features of the social and economic order to the levels of surplus repression and repressive desublimation through which the 'commitment banking' system seeks to control the psychic economy of its card-carrying creditors. We need only refer to Marcuse's development of the Marxian and Freudian interpretations of the mechanism of civilized discontents.

This aside, it might be observed that once again Parsons' attempt to achieve generality through high levels of abstraction results only in a sublimation of the problem, in this case by means of a money

---

1 *The Social Division of Labor*, p. 388.
2 *Politics and Social Structure*, pp. 463–467.
3 See chap. 3; Paul A. Baran and Paul M. Sweezy, *Monopoly Capital: An Essay on the American Economic and Social Order*, New York and London, Monthly Review Press, 1966.

metaphor which enables him to speak in apparently value-free terms about the phenomena of value conflict, moral innovation, and alienation. Alternatively, in the face of these questions Parsons settles his analytical conscience by passing the torch to the 'theory of cultural systems', inasmuch as shifts in value patterns fall to the anthropologist's care. This move, as well as Parsons' return to the use of economic conceptualizations of the problem of order and legitimacy, seems to me to contradict his own sense of the autonomy of sociological abstraction in favour of his old desire for a general theory of action.[1] Here I think Weber is a better guide. What we can understand from Weber is that the *sociological ethic* requires of us the study of the problems of power and authority without any hope for a 'scientific' politics beyond what reasonable men may hope for in the conflict of values.[2]

Rationality and Meaning: Marx and the Weberian Problem
At several points in the discussion we have suggested that the problem of order has to be seen in the context of the nature of western rationality and its tendency to destroy the non-rational foundations upon which it rests. Thus Hobbes's science of politics divorces itself from commonsense opinion which is the traditional fabric of political experience. Hobbes's nominalist precision only introduces order into opinion by veiling its own inability to deal with the problem of recognition and mutuality in the doctrine or fiat of an ultimately divine sovereignty. The tendency of scientistic rationality to undermine the non-rational bases of trust and recognition is the focus of what Parsons calls the Durkheimian and Weberian problems. Parsons, however, frames the problem solely in terms of the analytic differentiation of the normative and institutional conditions of

---

[1] 'Problems of order, as distinguished from those of the categories of "interests" that define the primary subject-matter of economics and political science, thus constitute the core of sociological concern; normative order also forms the basis of sociology's intimate interdependence with the theory of cultural systems.' Talcott Parsons, 'Max Weber 1864–1964', *American Sociological Review*, XXX, no. 2 (April 1965), p. 174.

[2] Guenther Roth, 'Political Critiques of Max Weber', *American Sociological Review*, XXX, no. 2 (April 1965), pp. 213–223; but especially Maurice Merleau-Ponty's essay on Weber's ethic, 'The Crisis of the Understanding', *The Primacy of Perception*, and Other Essays, edited by James M. Edie, Evanston, Northwestern University Press, 1964.

social action. I have argued that in this way Parsons gives us rather special readings of Durkheim, Marx, and, as I believe, of Weber's conception of rationality. Indeed, Parsons' viewpoint by and large misses the subjective context in which the Hobbesian problem of order arises.

Classical utilitarian thought from the time of Hobbes, through Locke, Marx, and Durkheim, cannot be understood apart from the sense of constitutional, class, and industrial crises in which the doctrine of the natural identity of interests, however logically objectionable, provided a metaphysical prop without which the drama of modern individualism and market rationality might not have been staged. As the famework of market society, class, and property gradually evolved, the shift from the sentimental ties of kinship to the rational social division of labour figures as the articulation of modern self-consciousness.

The problem of order is an historical as well as a sociological problem. It is the problem of the origins and teleology of civilization. It is important not to overlook that this is the way the question of order appeared to Marx, Durkheim, and Weber and, of course, to Freud. The other line through which this question comes into modern consciousness is Nietzsche, Dilthey, Burckhardt, Husserl.[1] In this aspect the problem of order is the riddle of history, namely, the problem of man's estrangement through civilization lay in the need to set restraints to the infinitude of wants. Durkheim, attempted to draw a distinction between individuality and personality in order to cope with the ways in which society at once aggravates and ennobles individual aspirations. Moreover, Durkheim was aware that these problems were wider than the limits of law and the bonds of solidarity. He sensed that they had their origins in the ambivalence of modern knowledge, including perhaps sociology despite his hopes of it as a social remedy.[2] Marx argued that the forces which divide man against himself derive from the class division of property which is prior to the problems of specialization and division of labour. But the deep question is what is the meaning of the surplus repression or

---

[1] Reinhard Bendix, 'Max Weber and Jacob Burckhardt', *American Sociological Review*, XXX, no. 2 (April 1965), pp. 176–184.

[2] Reinhard Bendix, 'The Age of Ideology: Persistent and Changing', *Ideology and Discontent*, edited by David E. Apter, New York, The Free Press of Glencoe, 1966, chap. VIII.

value set upon value-accumulation which provides the driving force, the glory and the misery of modern civilization.

I have tried earlier in this essay to sketch the history of western knowledge and its affinity for power. Admittedly, this is a rough sketch and lacks an adequate consideration of the theological, political, and historical-psychoanalytic features of the problem.[1] Since not everything can be attempted at once, I shall have to confine myself to expanding the earlier discussion in terms of a treatment of the ascetic bases of modern rationalism first brought to attention by Weber, but also, as I shall show, a feature of Marx's understanding of the problem.

The understanding of western rationality demands a structural analysis of the dialectic between man's fundamental historical and social nature and the alternations of freedom and determinism. It is necessary to start from the institutional matrix in which specific norms of action shaped and were in turn shaped by a particular conception of human nature. With the rise of capitalism man's rational nature was increasingly understood in terms of an instrumental orientation toward the domination of physical nature. At the same time, this instrumental orientation toward nature involved an expressive as well as cognitive reorientation toward the perception of self, society, and the elements of nature. The essence of this shift is grasped by Hegel and Marx in their conception of human freedom as 'man making himself'. Between Hegel's *Phenomenology of Mind* and Marx's *Communist Manifesto* the 'world' has become the immanent term of human thought and activity which sustains the alternation of freedom and determinism. The significance of Marx's critique of the ideological relations of philosophical thought is to bring human ideas into a permanently efficacious present, shaped by and giving shape to the processes through which a society endures and changes. Thus the weight of the past, articulated in the social division of labour and the ideological superstructure of past religions and philosophies, is not just the residue of historicism or relativism. It is the

---

[1] *The Protestant Ethic and Modernization*, A Comparative View, edited by S. N. Eisenstadt, New York, Basic Books, 1968, provides considerable historical and comparative materials but makes no mention of the psychoanalytic interpretations in Herbert Marcuse, *Eros and Civilization*, Boston, Beacon Press, 1955; Norman O. Brown, *Life Against Death*, The Psychoanalytical Meaning of History, New York, Vintage Books, 1959.

phenomenological reality of truth as the product of social life and the creation of *homo faber*.[1]

With the benefit of Hegel, Marx grasped the internal logic of knowledge and action in modern society. Furthermore, with the advantage of a more detailed knowledge of the nature of capitalist institutions, Marx was able to show that the logical connection between man's technological domination of nature and the complete integration of man's individual and social experience lay outside of the conception of utilitarian rationality. Marx's analysis of capitalist society is directed primarily at the connections between social norms and economic systems. Marx, no less than Weber, makes very clear the ascetic basis of capitalist rationality and its conditioned motivation to the accumulation of value. Parsons, however, holds to the criticism that Marx failed to go beyond the utilitarian assumption of the givenness of wants and their essentially materialistic bias. 'The crucial point is that Weber's analysis, the core of which is the Protestant ethic thesis, bridged the theoretical gap between "want" in the economic–psychological sense and "cultural patterns" in the idealistic senses. To put it simply and radically, Weber's solution was that, once cultural patterns of meaning have been internalized in the personality of an individual, they define the situation for the structuring of motives.'[2]

In drawing attention to Marx's argument my intention is not simply to question whether Marx understood the Weberian problem. It is ultimately to argue with the Parsonian view of the orientation toward increasing rationality[3] which I think overlooks Weber's own questions about the meaning of rationality and the concern with alienation which brings him closer to Marx.[4] In a remarkable passage

---

[1] Hannah Arendt, *The Human Condition*, Chicago, University of Chicago Press, 1958; Kurt H. Wolff, 'On the Significance of Hannah Arendt's *The Human Condition* for Sociology', *Inquiry*, IV, no. 2 (Summer 1951), pp. 67–106.

[2] *Sociological Theory and Modern Society*, p. 184.

[3] *The Structure of Social Action*, p. 752.

[4] Strictly speaking Parsons does note these concerns of Weber, as in the following passage, but in my opinion he has not drawn upon them in the same way that he developed the analytical and comparative aspects of Weber's work. 'Weber takes the fundamental position that, *regardless of the particular content of the normative order*, a major element of discrepancy is inevitable. And the more highly rationalized an order, the greater the tension, the greater the exposure of major elements of a population to experiences which are frustrating in the very specific sense, not

from the *Economic and Philosophical Manuscripts*, Marx explains how political economy develops against the background of the alienation of labour and property from their anchorages in use-values. The emancipation of labour is the precondition of the substitution of exchange values for use-values which leads to the subordination of all fixed forms of life and property to the accumulation and expansion of wealth. In their endlessly reproducible forms, as the prices of capital and labour-power, private property, and labour alienate human needs in favour of market wants. Marx concludes that modern individualism acquires its impulse through the subjectivization of the bases of feudal community which simultaneously supplies the motivational orientation toward market behaviour. The Physiocrats identified all wealth with land and cultivation, leaving feudal property intact but shifting the essential definition of land to its economic function and thereby exposing feudal property to the later attacks on ground-rent. The objective nature of wealth was also in part shifted to its subjective basis in labour, in as much as agriculture was regarded as the source of the productivity of land. Finally, industrial labour emerged as the most general principle of productivity, the factors of production, land, labour, and capital, being nothing else than moments in the dialectic of labour's self-alienation.

> Thus, from the viewpoint of this enlightened political economy which has discovered the *subjective* essence of wealth within the framework of private property, the partisans of the monetary system and the mercantilist system, who consider private property as a *purely objective* being for man, are *fetishists* and *Catholics*. Engels is right, therefore, in calling Adam Smith the *Luther of political economy*. Just as Luther recognized *religion* and *faith* as the essence of the real *world*, and for that reason took up a position against Catholic paganism; just as he annulled *external* religiosity while making religiosity the *inner* essence of man; just as he negated the distinction between priest and layman because he transferred the priest into the heart of the layman; so wealth external to man and independent of him (and thus only

---

merely in the sense that things happen and contravene their "interests", but that things happen which are "meaningless" in the sense that they *ought* not to happen.' Max Weber, *The Sociology of Religion*, Translated by Ephraim Fischoff, Introduction by Talcott Parsons, Boston, Beacon Press, 1963, p. xlvii. But see the Review Article of this work by Benjamin Nelson, *American Sociological Review*, XXX, no. 4 (August 1965), pp. 595–599.

to be acquired and conserved from outside) is annulled. That is to say, its *external* and *mindless* objectivity is annulled by the fact that private property is incorporated in man himself, and man himself is recognized as its essence. But as a result, man himself is brought into the sphere of private property, just as, with Luther, he is brought into the sphere of religion. Under the guise of recognizing man, political economy, whose principle is labour, carries to its logical conclusion the denial of man. Man himself is no longer in a condition of external tension with the external substance of private property; he has himself become the tension-ridden being of private property. What was previously a phenomenon of *being external to oneself*, a real external manifestation of man, has now become the act of objectification, of alienation. This political economy seems at first, therefore, to recognize man with his independence, his personal activity, etc. It incorporates private property in the very essence of man, and it is no longer, therefore, conditioned by the local or national *characteristics of private property* regarded as existing outside itself. It manifests a cosmopolitan, universal activity which is destructive of every limit and every bond, and substitutes itself as the *only* policy, the *only* universality, the *only* limit and the *only* bond.[1]

Marx and Weber raised a common question. They asked what is the human value of a specific mode of social organization, namely capitalism: what is its *raison d'être;* what is the sense in its universality? Admittedly, Weber may have gone further in the comparative study of the conditions of the emergence of the normative and institutional bases of capitalism. But each took the same view with regard to the major task of understanding the historically unique phenomenon of the rational domination of nature and the accumulation of values in the determination of conduct or action in capitalist society. We need to understand the 'vocation' of western science and rationality. Modern science is chained to progress through invention and discovery. Every scientific finding asks to be surpassed in the light of accumulated knowledge. Each scientist resigns himself to making only a partial and fleeting contribution to a task that is conceived as limitless. 'And with this we come to inquire into the meaning of science. For, after all, it is not self-evident that something subordinate

[1] Karl Marx, *Early Writings*, translated and edited by T. B. Bottomore, London, C. A. Watts and Company, 1963, pp. 147-148.

to such a law is sensible and meaningful in itself. Why does one engage in doing something that in reality never comes, and never can come to an end.'[1]

Weber compares the question of the meaning of science which he himself raises to Tolstoi's question about the meaning of death in modern civilization.[2] Civilized man has broken with nature. Cultural values have replaced use-values and the cycle of life familiar to the peasant and feudal lord has exploded into a self-infinitizing progression in the accumulation of cultural values. The peasant could encounter the totality of meaning ordained for him in the feudal order and die at peace with his station in life because his daily life was congruent with the whole of his life. But modern man, in virtue of being pitted against an ever-expanding universe of ideas, problems, and values, though he can be weary of life always encounters death as meaningless; for death robs him of infinity. 'And because death is meaningless, civilized life as such is meaningless; by its very "progressiveness" it gives death the imprint of meaninglessness.'[3] For want of a science of ends which might illuminate the ideal of western rationality and its affinity for power and accumulation Weber turned to the notions of the 'calling' and the 'ethic of responsibility'. It is implicit in the Weberian use of the ideal-type method that the growth of rationality in science, politics, and economics is only a meaningful way of representing western experience so long as we choose to understand it *in its own terms (verstehen)*. But as soon as we consider western rationality from the standpoint of comparative history it loses its self-evidence. That is to say, the increasing rationality of modern technology and of the sciences developed on the model of functional rationality remains a self-styled enigma. For this reason Weber's pessimism is surely no worse than Parsons' optimistic generalization of the 'law of increasing rationality'.[4]

Although Parsons is aware that Weber's conception of the process

1 'Science as a Vocation', *From Max Weber: Essays in Sociology*, translated, edited, and with an Introduction by H. Gerth and C. Wright Mills, New York, Oxford University Press, 1958, p. 138.

2 Leo Tolstoi, *The Death of Ivan Ilyich*, Bradda Books Ltd., Letchworth, Herts., 1966; Barney G. Glaser and Anselm L. Strauss, *Time for Dying*, Chicago, Aldine Publishing Company, 1968; David Sudnow, *Passing On*, New Jersey, Prentice Hall.

3 *From Max Weber*, p. 140.

4 *The Structure of Social Action*, p. 752.

of rationality involved judgments about its substantive meaningfulness and its potential for alienation, he nevertheless relegates these
considerations to factors which affect merely the *rate* of the process of
rationalization but hardly its direction. Again, Parsons presumes that
the question of the value-relevance (*Wertbeziehung*) of rationality is
merely a question about the integrative function of the cultural
norm of functional rationality with respect to the adaptive sub-
systems of empirical knowledge and thus raises no other questions
outside those of the 'strains' in the institutionalization and differentiation of the sciences.[1]

The pattern of rationality (the subordination of particularistic–
ascriptive values to the values of universalism and achievement)
characterizes the major institutions, businesses, schools, factories, and
hospitals of modern society. Weber reminds us that rationality becomes an 'iron cage' as soon as it segregates itself from non-rational
values and behaviour. Weber had a sense of the volatile and vital
forces of history which make it possible for the human spirit to go
underground or to come out of the desert, the jungle, or the mountains
to wage war in the arid lands of bureaucracy and rationality.

> No one knows who will live in this cage in the future, or
> whether at the end of this tremendous development entirely new
> prophets will arise, or there will be a great rebirth of old ideas
> and ideals, or, if neither, mechanized petrification, embellished
> with a sort of convulsive importance. For of the last stage of
> this cultural development, it might well be truly said: 'Specialists
> without spirit, sensualists without heart; this nullity imagines
> that it has attained a level of civilization never before attained.'[2]

Whether due to its own electric technology or to the inherent primitivism of Left pot and politics, the urban industrial landscape is
now ablaze with tribal costumes, wigs, dance, and music. Weber's
prophets have forsaken the cage and the birds of paradise are on the
wing in New York City, Chicago, Los Angeles, Liverpool—and in
Canada they flock in strawberry fields.

The confrontation of reason with its own non-rational sources is a
necessary exercise which forces upon us the justification of the limits

[1] 'An Approach to the Sociology of Knowledge', in *Sociological Theory and Modern
Society*, pp. 139–165.

[2] Max Weber, *The Protestant Ethic and the Spirit of Capitalism*, translated by Talcott
Parsons, New York, Charles Scribner's 1958, p. 182.

of reason and non-reason which brings the artist to the edge of his own sanity and sets the scientist on the margins of his own culture. The Hobbesian problem demands nothing less. In Marx, Durkheim, and Weber sociology has been fortunate in the rare combination of a poetic and scientific sense of the limits of the reality we inhabit. Today the Hobbesian problem is as much as ever a motive to creative sociologies of action, talk, death, revolt, accommodation, and numerous other practicalities. Meantime Parsonian structural-functionalism strains to accommodate conflict, change, and more radical empiricism. Yet there are few who would want to forsake the theoretical legacy which Parsons has preserved and consolidated for sociology. There is enough of the artist in Parsons that he had to shape the sociological tradition in his own style, with magnificent insights here and blindnesses there—but never without vision. Nowadays it is said that Parsons has no followers. That is a conceit of critics.

14: Reflexive Sociology or the Advent of Alvin W. Gouldner

The state of sociology should, in keeping with its own genus, lack a Hamlet or, for that matter, a ghost. And yet things continue so to rot and stink there that someone has to play Hamlet to the Parsonian ghost, and who better than Alvin W. Gouldner to set the play? It is surely evidence of the sad state of sociological thought in America that Gouldner's *The Coming Crisis of Western Sociology* should unashamedly advertise itself as a work of 'magisterial' scholarship when it hardly does more than tell a tale of conventional troubles in its land.[1]

Before any understanding of Gouldner's enterprise is possible, it is necessary to free oneself from the machinery which it has devised to pulverize all criticism once a youthful act of faith has been wrung from its readers. From the very start Gouldner senses that he may be hoist by his own petard, such is the paradox of the sociology of sociology. Gouldner's opening tactic, therefore, is to attempt to understand the theoretical apathy of the New Left with whom he might be identified were it not for his remorse over his own earlier invention of these half-beasts. The paperback and drugstore success of sociology appears to have boomeranged in the face of its expositors. Students now suspect anything so amenable to commodity fetishism as post-war American sociology, fat with its convention displays of embourgoisement, where it does not insultingly ape the dress and hairstyles of gentler peoples. Radical sentiment, for want of a fitting theoretical framework, is likely to declare the irrelevance of all

[1] Alvin W. Gouldner, *The Coming Crisis of Western Sociology*, London, Heinemann Educational Books, 1971.

theory and to do little more in support of its own know-nothingism than note the way the life-style of successful purveyors of sociological theory as popular culture revolts radical sensibilities. But the radical students need to know that in sociology nothing succeeds like success. They will never make it in the city on Marx, Mao, and the Frankfurt school of critical sociology or ethnomethodology; and though there's Alice's Restaurant between them they will be driven back into 'the most vulgar currents of American culture: to its small-town, Babbitlike anti-intellectualism and know-nothingism'.

Just as affluent society at large has trouble in recognizing its tribalized offspring gathering in strawberry fields, so too academic sociology is incredulous of its own youthful and unsocialized Sociology Liberation Movement. The birth of such radical offspring appears to Gouldner as one of the 'internal contradictions' of academic sociology, as surely it must, unless he sees that its children fear to be blown to bits in the great American holocaust, to see their own offspring asphyxiated or genetically twisted by what is euphemistically called the American Way of Life, and did not have to wait for academic sociology to tell them about the world they inhabit. All the same, Gouldner is of the belief that sociological understanding can foster its radical offspring. But to do so sociology must achieve a critical sense which avoids opportunism of the sort that comes from living *off* sociology rather than *for* it. The sociological critic is neither a sniper nor a codifier. He is a man with a deep sense of what is great in the sociological tradition and of what is urgent about its present political and academic contexts.

That Gouldner entertains a noble conception of the sociological critic is not to be denied. Yet there is an underlying impatience in his introductory attempt to achieve theoretical perspective. It is clear that he does not believe that the New Left has anything to teach sociology for he attempts nothing like a sociological analysis of the New Left beyond taking at face value certain of its arguments on the irrelevance of theory but nothing of its political experiences. Such primitivism can only be remedied once the radicals learn how to wield the mighty pen that will slay the task master of American sociological theory. And though they have not read Parsons, Gouldner can rely like so many other critics upon giving his audience the impression that they did once, but stopped just where Gouldner comes in to make their troubles light. However, I shall not consider the play within the play, namely, Part Two on The Words of Talcott Parsons, since it does not advance the main action and has been attempted by others of us for what it is worth.[1]

Gouldner's critical bravado requires that with this passing nod to his New Left contemporaries, so different from C. Wright Mills' understanding 'Letter to the New Left', he move circuitously upon his Parsonian prey, clearing first some of the historical undergrowth that might afford him cover.[2] With just a pause to check that Marxism is still in the cage where it has always been, the first demon to be encountered on this long journey is complacency, or the comfortable separation of ourselves from other men.[3] Complacency is a special temptation in the sociological priesthood since it violates the sociologist's concern with all men by leaving out of that concern the practice of sociology itself. It should be noted that Gouldner is not concerned strictly speaking with the theories or methods of sociology but with its priestly assumptions about human nature and society, which he calls its 'domain assumptions'. Again, with respect to such assumptions, Gouldner is not concerned to argue that they are either unavoidable or logically tied features of sociology, but only that as beliefs it is prudent to assume they affect the practice of sociology. But what is the effect of such distinctions? Surely, in a work of the scope that Gouldner sets himself some concern with the philosophical assumptions of the sociology of sociology is in order if we are not to be led to give more credence to Gouldner's readings than they deserve as conventional sociological argument? For we should not be deceived about the profundity of Gouldner's claims. He merely observes that before anyone is a sociologist he is a member of a society whose ways he is ordinarily not given to inspect. Whatever his motivation for doing so later on, as a sociologist, it is more likely that he will question social institutions and practices that are remote from those in which he himself spends most of his time, but which could be made equally strange in a more general sociology. Anyone familiar

---

[1] C. Wright Mills, *The Sociological Imagination*, New York, Oxford University Press, 1959; Daniel Foss, 'The World View of Talcott Parsons', in Stein, Maurice, and Vidich (eds.), *Sociology on Trial*, Englewood Cliffs, Prentice Hall, Inc, 1968; J. O'Neill, 'The Hobbesian Problems in Marx and Parsons'.

[2] C. Wright Mills, 'Letter to the New Left' in P. Lond (ed.), *The New Left*, Boston, Porter Sargent, 1970.

[3] See chap. 1.

with contemporary sociology would recognize behind this plain reading of mine the work of Schutz and Garfinkel.[1] The philosophical understanding of these commonplaces is, of course, more than an exercise in platitudes.[2]

But Gouldner is not concerned with the deep structure of social science knowledge in the way that philosophers of science, or phenomenologists and ethnomethodologists treat it. He is writing for the sociological profession and this is enough to dictate a methodology that they will understand. The substance of it is that within the larger framework of social and personal reality we construct 'role realities'. In particular, there arises a contradiction between these reality domains which is consequential for the development of sociology. Thus, as sociologists we postulate the functional autonomy of society and culture, although personally and at least since the Enlightenment we believe that society ought not to be independent of individual and political sentiments. This contradiction is aggravated by high science methodologies which put social causes beyond the layman's grasp, at the same time confusing the sociologist about the purity and objectivity of his own motives for their analysis. Sociological autonomy and liberal conformism replace the original motive of sociological authenticity.

The structural development of sociology, which Gouldner traces historically through its four phases of Sociological Positivism, Marxism, Classical Sociology, and Parsonian Structural-Functionalism, turns upon the way sociologists have responded to the problem of order endemic to the utilitarian culture which is the matrix of the modern social sciences. Here it is natural to compare Gouldner's historical sociology with the classical analytic history of the same problematic focus in Parsons' *The Structure of Social Action*. The collapse of the feudal order consequent upon the development of the market economy and the abandonment of man by the Protestant *deus*

---

[1] Alfred Schutz, *Collected Papers*, I, II, III, The Hague, Martinus Nijhoff, 1962; Harold Garfinkel, *Studies in Ethnomethodology*, Englewood Cliffs, Prentice Hall, 1967; we might also mention Thomas S. Kuhn, *The Structure of Scientific Revolutions*, Chicago, University of Chicago Press, 1962.

[2] It involves some understanding of the phenomenology of Husserl and Schutz, at the very least. My own attempt to deal with the platitude of our social being is contained in my *Making Sense Together*, forthcoming, London, Heinemann Educational Books.

absconditus left open the generation of a moral and social order. This is the dilemma which inspired Hobbes's nasty vision no less than the benign adjustments of Adam Smith's invisible hand or Locke's principle of the identity of interests which Marx's doctrine of class struggle in turn withered away as the nineteenth century wore on. In a society dominated by the market the social construction of reality is systematically ambiguous, shifting and subject to definition through naked power at the expense of moral authority. Classical utilitarianism is the simple expression of these dilemmas which it seeks to repress through the reduction of rationality to a calculation of means in a system of ends which are enigmatic to reason so conceived.

Gouldner rightly points out that the problematic nature of utilitarian culture is an impetus to social science knowledge of a theoretical as well as a pragmatic kind. For what is unbearable in utilitarian culture is the grotesque separation of values and power which undermines its moral and political authority, predisposing the culture to anomie, utopianism, and psychedelic revolt. I think Gouldner would not deny that it is Parsons' merit to have pointed to the culture of utilitarianism as the matrix of the social sciences, even though this is greater news in Academic than in Marxist sociology where Hegel's *Phenomenology of Mind* and the description of Civil Society in the *Philosophy of Right*, as well as Marx's relentless critique of classical utilitarian economists, is well known. Parsons' procedure, however, was consciously to set aside the sociology of sociology in favour of the development of an analytic and general theory of action in which the substantive areas of economics, politics, and sociology are integrated as constituent features of any social action. Again, Gouldner regards Parsons' analytic intention as well-founded in the light of the crisis of conduct in the utilitarian culture of world capitalism which called for theoretical as well as pragmatic adjustments.

Unlike so many other critics of Parsonianism, Gouldner does not argue that its analytic intent is directly ideological; rather, it becomes so through the stipulation of criteria of autonomy and professionalization which reflect a failure of political will whereby the bourgeoisie rejects its historically revolutionary role in favour of order. It is the historically contradictory role of the bourgeoisie as a revolutionary force unable to universalize its revolution which provides the orientation for the various systems of sociology from Comtean positivism to Marxism and the structural functionalist absorption of all these developments into a system-oriented theory of social consensus, marginalizing internal counter-sociologies while proposing convergences at the level of advanced industrial societies regardless of ideology. The ahistorical functionalist theory of professional sociology is marvellously suited to the 'end of ideology' which professional academic and Marxist sociology alike welcome in the face of Third World ideologies of revolt against international stratification and industrial domination. What produces the impending crisis of utilitarian culture is the inability of the multi-national corporation to alter its overprivatized agenda which results in a peculiar imbalance of international and public squalor combined with private affluence.[1] For want of any ability to alter its corporate agenda capitalist culture is increasingly unable to absorb the young, old, sick black, and poor but prefers instead to expand its own political and economic space through war and para-military space programmes. The result is an internal migration on the part of youth and the Blacks into a hairy and tribal counterculture which aims at a reality bust with capitalism and its experts.

The liberal state has, of course, attempted to adjust to the need to re-define its membership otherwise lost to it by the exclusiveness of the corporate agenda. The result has been the Welfare (warfare) State which has in turn forced academic sociology to rework its notions of sociological autonomy, change, and intervention. Gouldner argues that these developments have forced structural functionalism into a merger with Marxist theory, in particular with respect to notions of conflict, change, and the role of technology as a cultural universal. But he misses the anti-communist manifesto which is the real implication of the neo-Marxist dress of Parsonianism. For what is actually happening here is a return to a technological historicism which Karl Popper first denounced in his *Poverty and Historicism* more than twenty years ago in favour of the liberal concept of piecemeal social engineering.[2] The Parsonian revision is a part of a new combination of holism and historicism which passes under the guise of systems and future thinking, grounded upon what Clark Kerr, Rostow, Aron, Bell, and Kahn would call the 'logic of

[1] See chap. 3.
[2] Karl R. Popper, *The Poverty of Historicism*, London, Routledge and Kegan Paul, 1957.

industrial society'.[1] The latter functions to make ideology irrational
within advanced industrial societies while at the same time dictating
an ideology of development to the so-called uncommitted world.
What Gouldner perceives as the Marxianizing of academic sociology
is rather the becalming of social thought through the vision of 'post'
industrial society, the dream of a truly establishment and administrative social science which far exceeds anything Comtean positivism
might have proposed.

Unfortunately, the transition to 'post' industrial society is not
smooth but passes by way of tribal visions and the Kafkesque
nightmares of contemporary bureaucratic life. Suddenly, the whole
morality of utilitarian culture is up for grabs. The goal is the Age of
Aquarius but the way is darker than the moon. Meantime sociology
has gone underground.

Gouldner's treatment of the new sociology is surprisingly lopsided.
It misses altogether the new sociology of C. Wright Mills and for the
same reasons that Gouldner criticizes Parsons' ignorance of Marxism.[2]
Neither of them has much knowledge of Marx.[3] I need say no more
here since my own response to Gouldner should be taken in a
Marxist vein. In some ways more disturbing, because less expected, is
the imbalance of sensitivity which Gouldner displays in his treatment
of Goffman and Garfinkel. Incidentally, here again he misses Peter
Berger and this I imagine is because Gouldner is ignorant of Schutz's
phenomenology and thus, of course, incapable of dealing with
Garfinkel whom he imagines to be something of a street artist like
Jerry Rubin.[4] If this were not ignorance on Gouldner's part then it

[1] Clark Kerr, *Marshall, Marx and Modern Times: The Multi-Dimensional Society*,
Cambridge, 1968; W. W. Rostow, *The Stages of Economic Growth*, Cambridge, 1960;
R. Aron, *Dix-huit leçons sur la société industrielle*, Paris, Gallimard, 1962; Daniel
Bell, 'Notes on Post-Industrial Society', *The Public Interest*, 6 and 7, 1968; H. Kahn
and A. J. Weiner, *The Year 2000*, New York, Macmillan, 1967.

[2] I. L. Horowitz(ed.), *The New Sociology*, New York, Oxford University Press, 1965.

[3] It would be an interesting exercise to compare the pale life of Marxist concepts
in American sociology with their original context. Using Weber to by-pass Marx
is a widely used strategy. What Parsons and Gouldner treat as Marxist sociology
is confined to Soviet Academic sociology and is ruled by Parsons' 'convergence'
thesis. Gouldner recognizes recent developments in Marxist sociology in France,
Poland, and Yugoslavia but, unless this is the aim of a later volume, he attempts
no theoretical discussion of these developments other than to treat them as
symptoms of a crisis.

[4] Peter Berger, *Invitation to Sociology*, New York, Doubleday-Anchor, 1963.

deserves contempt for its blindness if not cruelty. It is in any case, an abuse of the task of reflexive sociology to confuse it with one's sociological memoirs.

All the same, Gouldner's appraisal of Goffman is superb even while maintaining a critical stance with respect to its ultimate failure of nerve. 'Goffman is to the sociology of fraud what Fanon is to the sociology of force and violence.' This observation seizes upon the basic response to the experience of the separation of power and morality in modern society which produces the revolt of youth and black rage at its hypocrisy and merchant morality. The underlying crisis of authority which drives youth into migration and pushes sociology underground is simultaneously the sorrow of the modern self, choking in roles, screaming at offices.

With Berger and Goffman we have to choose between sociology as an underground exploitation of impotence or a parlour-game of one-upmanship. The vision of 'post' industrial society must be set in the context of the new sociological scenarios of the modern self, in its prisons, theatres, and asylums where the only resort is the crippled transcendence of underworld tricks of status inversion, a mental carnival of muttering and making out. Here sociology has to pay the price of its autonomy but in ways that it could not foresee. The predicament of the sociological self arises from the contraction of its life space constricted by class opportunities or eked out in the confines of bureaucratic settings. The sense of the vastness of social space opened up by the market and the destruction of the feudal word was essential to the liberal conception of individual freedom, although its edges were darkened by the absence of God. Nowadays the ratio of self to social space is radically diminished so that the centre of its experience warps in its shrunken landscape. The typical settings of the modern self are the underground, the tiny room, the prison, mental hospital, and concentration camp. These scenes produce a critical disturbance in the ratio of self and world experience. Thus in Goffman's scenarios, like those of Beckett, the self is trapped in primitive social scenes which force it to account for itself as an object, obsessed with the degrees and form of distance between itself and other social objects, bewildered by the knowledge that others anticipate the slightest deviation in standards of spontaneity, cleanliness, generosity, and courage.

Where Goffman provides for 'cooling out' devices such as absenteeism or defaulting on a prescribed self, Berger advocates the permanent possibility of organizational sabotage, daydream, and the ecstasy of negative thinking which reduces every social given to a possibility only. Berger adapts Goffman's concept of role-distance to the practical recommendation that we seek sociological authenticity by treating what others take to be an essential identity as a convenient disguise. Where Goffman inverts bureaucratic white affluence with the everyday sociology of the crippled and insane Berger turns it into a threepenny opera of swindlers, charlatans, and social Machiavellians.

Gouldner's attempt to bracket Garfinkel's ethnomethodology with the possibilitarian sociology of Goffman and Berger, who must be included here despite Gouldner's silence, is a woeful misunderstanding of transcendental sociology which is the aim of his own final effort to produce a 'reflexive sociology'. The possibilitarian is potentially a crackbrain, a dreamer, a fool, and a god who like Musil's man without qualities risks the possibilities of reality in the reality of possibility. But we cannot be above society or outside of it *and* part of it by means of a simple schizophrenic copulation or momentary improvization. The whole point of Garfinkel's incongruity procedures is to show that the sense of possibility and its technique of impression management is false to the naïve intersubjectivity which is the unarticulated structure of our everyday trust in and competence with social reality.[1] So far from putting commonsense knowledge of social structures up for grabs, Garfinkel's experiments are intended to show that our mundane experience of the self and its definition of the situation is given to us through the same set of typifications, role-conceptions, and course-of-action patterns which are the convenience of anyone. It is only by some incongruity of experience that I discover that my self is not synonymous with selves in general, or that what I take to be the perceivedly normal and typical features of my situation are not in fact available to anyone like me. In other words, and in stark contrast with the ecstatic and possibilitarian thesis, the universality of consciousness is prior to the particularities of the personal biography which becomes its expressive vehicle.

In the fourth and last part of his theoretical odyssey, Gouldner

[1] For Garfinkel's explicit critique of Goffman's dramaturgical model see, *Studies in Ethnomethodology*, pp. 165–180.

The Theorist Pulls Himself Together, Partially. Once again, where the need is for deep reflection upon his own methodology such as one might have expected to preface an undertaking of a kind that so risks partiality and the bitterness of argument *ad hominem*, Gouldner stops short only to see himself in a glass darkly. For how shall we hold a mirror to nature when it is human nature that is in question? In any case, Gouldner is easily convinced that our way with the world is the way of the world, and were it not so then our ineluctable theorizing would convince us of it. In essence Gouldner's use of theory serves his own ambitious theoretical potency with which he seeks to slay Minotaur, to end the Myth of a Value-Free Sociology.[1] Gouldner's conclusion is a self-portrait done in the name of Reflexive Sociology, an unusual attempt to document the sociology of sociology out of the history of a successful career. Such an exercise is necessary if the professional sociologist is to escape the snares of opportunism and the disenchantment that only success breeds. It is the dream of a fresh start, the frontier and the American version of innocence, half fight, and half vision. Reflexive Sociology proves to be defiantly romantic, a quest for transcendence rejecting the conventional sociological celebration, embracing action and responsibility. Its *habit* is to see itself as it sees others, to break with the self-conceit of sociology and its way with the world. But the larger purpose of this therapeutic conception of reflexive sociology is to renew the connection between self awareness and awareness of the social world which is broken by the adoption of the neutral observer paradigm of scientific knowledge. We need to abandon the preconception of the world and certain knowledge as the construction of an unsituated rationality whose technological success has benumbed the subjective linkages of practice and responsibility. The recognition of sociological knowledge as subject-bound to a self-interpreted field of experience is the first step in assuming responsibility for social science knowledge at the same time that it renews the necessity to inform it with moral vision. Sociological detachment built upon the methodological dualism of subject and object must yield to a Reflexive Sociology more concerned with 'soul searching' than the professional vulgarities of 'soul-selling'.

1 Alvin W. Gouldner, 'Anti-Minotaur, the Myth of a Value-Free Sociology' in I. L. Horowitz (ed.), *The New Sociology*, New York, Oxford University Press, 1965.

Reflexive Sociology takes its leave of liberals and radicals alike, for their knowledge is warped with domination and is ignorant of art. Theirs is the saying of yay and nay, the one at home, the other abroad. Reflexive Sociology sweats in the stables of Academic sociology where its labours are needed most. It is hardly any surprise then that Gouldner's Reflexive Sociology should provide us with a work ethic to make Parsons smile and the young writhe. The aim of this ethic is to make men out of boys and sociologists, to give them confidence in their own ideas, perhaps amid tea and cakes and ices to force the moment to a crisis, or in a room where the women come and go to talk to Talcott Parsons.

For my part, there can never be any question of the transcendence of sociology; it is given with my relation to the world and others around me without flight beyond this touch or talk. Socially, our universals lie between heaven and earth, in the toss of the clown, not on the tightrope of pompus metaphysical generalities but in the face-evident relations between myself, others, and the world around me. But the way of this transcendental epiphany is more patient than Anti-Minotaur, more like the way of Hegel, Marx, Husserl, and Merleau-Ponty, in the surrender of mind to the catch of embodiment. The reflexivity of sociology does not arise from the corruption of its youth but from the puzzle that its own topic is the everyday resource of social life. We may wish that our daily lives were more just, more honest and less violent. Some of us work towards that end, but in this none of us is at all special, least of all the sociologist. Indeed he should be last to strike postures on this issue. For sociology has yet to earn the people's trust.

In raising the question of a reflexive sociology Gouldner comes to the limits of his discipline as a form of theoretical life. Because he has neglected to consider the philosophical foundations of reflexive sociology he is obliged to make his choice of a sociology a political choice. This is a result which appears to follow from the Marxist sociology of knowledge upon which Gouldner leans in tying sociologies to infrastructures of sentiment and power, while at the same time trying to reconstruct his own intellectual biography as a left thinker. I am critical of Gouldner in this, rejecting his Marxism, while affirming my own understanding of it as well as of recent decent developments in phenomenology and ethnomethodology which I think render Gouldner's exercise obsolete, and worse still, since it comes so late after Mill's *Sociological Imagination*, without any moral appeal.

Gouldner's theoretical concern is properly the reflexive concern with how it is we wish to live as sociological theorists. He rejects the paths of 'high science' theorizing and its methodologies, or rather he undertakes a critique of the sociological practices that follow from it. The task of such a critique is to articulate the way in which sociological theory is reflexively a theory of biography and history, as Mills would have put it. It is to reach for the promise in sociology by conceiving of sociological theory as the same thing as the method of utopian thinking discerned in its present practices. The classical example of this is Marx's critique of classical economics and its utilitarian culture. On this conception of theory the goal of sociology theory cannot rest at the half-way house of professional agreements; its true collective is the practice of a humane society. For this reason, or because its matter is human history, sociological theory cannot identify itself with the conquest of methodological scepticism; it can only explain its purposes to the community which is its anchorage.

15: Can Phenomenology be Critical?

What is the task that I mean to set for myself in asking whether phenomenology can be critical? I am raising the question whether we can be authentically aware of the reflexive limits of the corpus of social science knowledge due to its implicit ties with the order of history and politics. The very question is evidence of a certain uneasiness, but also of a determination to dwell within its circle at least as much as to drive for a solution. How shall I proceed then? For to begin, I cannot settle for you the nature of phenomenology. Of course, I am aware that I might attempt to set out some of the principal features of Husserlian phenomenology. But the nature of the auspices for such an exposition should not be confused with its method of historiography and reference whose very intention of making its appeal public invites criticism and reappraisal, and is ultimately the same thing as philosophical argument. The question of the authoritative procedures for introducing phenomenology is made even more problematic by the developments in phenomenology from Husserl to Heidegger, Scheler, and Jaspers; or through Sartre and Merleau-Ponty; not to mention Schutz and the ethnomethodology of Garfinkel and Cicourel. Faced with a similar problem, Merleau-Ponty has remarked that 'we shall find in ourselves, and nowhere else, the unity and true meaning of phenomenology. In other words, we must take our own context, namely, our gathering out of mutual concern with the contemporary issues in the social sciences, as the topic for phenomenological theorizing.

What is the occasion, then, which provides the resource for my own theoretical effort? I take it that it is not simply a by-product of my academic *curriculum vitae* which yields a certain kind of documentary evidence of my concerns with the topic of our symposium. I want also to assume that this occasion is not the simple production of a symposium under the rule of dialectical or trinitarian postures of argument and torture of the truth. However, I would not deny that these may well be contingent features of performances such as a symposium. Clearly, though, there is some kind of rule which is a constitutive feature of our symposium. It is the rule which provides for the dramatization of the assumption that there are issues in the social sciences which are philosophical and which are as such in dispute from a variety of standpoints, but in a manner which does not preclude exchange and mutual exploration of common concerns. This is an enormously important assumption which is threatened nowadays by certain highly subjectivist and solipsistic postures as well as political ideologies which invade classrooms and conferences and threaten to turn the modern mind into an armed camp, a result which, as Camus has remarked, would separate us from the Greeks.

I want to develop a phenomenological conception of critique and argument under a rule of limit and cosmic order which is simultaneously the ground of political order and rebellion. Habermas has argued[1] that Husserl's critique of positivist science does not go far enough in simply denying the separation between knowledge and the life-world. In so far as science and philosophy, including the social sciences, separate the activity of theorizing from the world of human interests, both rest upon a positivist ontology. The prescriptions for this separation constitute the rule of methodological objectivity or segregation of subjective interests and values. The unfortunate practical consequences of the separation of science and values can only be corrected through an understanding of the true relation between knowledge and interest, in other words, of *praxis*. Husserl's critique of the objectivism of science and the natural attitude which is its pre-scientific ground, may be taken as an obvious sense in which phenomenology is critical. But it does not go far enough to free transcendental phenomenology itself from practical interest. Habermas invokes the etymology of θεωρία in order to trace a development in the concept of theory from the original activity of

---

[1] Jürgen Habermas, 'Knowledge and Interests: *A General Perspective*', appendix to his *Knowledge and Human Interests*, translated by Jeremy J. Shapiro, London, Heinemann Educational Books, 1971.

the representative sent by a polis to witness the sacred festival of another city to the philosopher's μίμησις or representation in the order of his soul of the natural κόσμος.

Husserl rightly criticizes the objectivist illusion that deludes the sciences with the image of a reality-in-itself, consisting of facts structured in a lawlike manner; it conceals the constitution of these facts, and thereby prevents consciousness of the interlocking of knowledge with interests from the life-world. Because phenomenology brings this to consciousness, it is itself, in Husserl's view, free of such interests. It thus earns the title of pure theory unjustly claimed by the sciences. It is to this freeing of knowledge from interest that Husserl attaches the expectation of practical efficacy. But the error is clear. Theory in the sense of the classical tradition only had an impact on life because it was thought to have discovered in the cosmic order an ideal world structure, including the prototype for the order of the human world. Only as *cosmology* was *theoria* also capable of orienting human action. Thus Husserl cannot expect self-formative processes to originate in a phenomenology that, as transcendental philosophy, purifies the classical theory of its cosmological contents, conserving something like the theoretical attitude only in an abstract manner. Theory had educational and cultural implications not because it had freed knowledge from interest. To the contrary, it did so because it derived *pseudo-normative power* from *the concealment of its actual interest*. While criticizing the objectivist self-understanding of the sciences, Husserl succumbs to another objectivism, which was always attached to the traditional concept of theory.[1]

Whether or not Husserl neglected the original connection between θεωρία and its consequences for the philosophical way of life, as Habermas argues, it is important to stress the ambivalence in classical philosophical knowledge with respect to the idea of Beauty and Goodness. Habermas tends to overlook this tension. Miss Hannah Arendt, however, has argued that the subordination of life in the pursuit of human affairs (βίος πολιτικός) to the 'theoretical way of life' (βίος θεωρητικος) is a result of the Platonic subordination of the contemplative love of the true essence of Being, under the idea of the Beautiful, to the idea of Good, or an art of measurement which provides a rule to the philosopher's potential disorientation

[1] *Ibid.*, pp. 305–306.

in everyday political life.[1] In other words, there is an essential ambivalence in western knowledge between the values of the recognition and domination of Being which has been consequential for its political tradition, particularly when the pattern of domination is based upon modern scientific knowledge which breaks once and for all the connection between κοσμος and θεωρια.

Modern social science knowledge has reduced its independence as a form of theoretical life to a rule of methodology founded upon the auspices of technical rationality. This results in a disenchanted objectivism or rationalization of the interests and values which guide technological domination as a form or 'conduct of life', to use Max Weber's phrase. However, Weber's formal rationality, so far from resting upon 'value-free' auspices, is in fact an historical constellation whose precondition is the separation of the orders of knowledge, work, and politics. In the period of the bourgeois ascendency, the value-free conception of rationality furnishes a critical concept of the development of human potential locked in the feudal world of 'traditional' values. Weber makes a fatality of technical rationality, thereby identifying its historical role with political domination as such,[2] whereas Marx's critique of class political economy showed the critical limits of economic rationality.[3] Social science knowledge needs to be grounded in a limited but authentic reflexivity through which it recognizes its ties to individual values and community interests, notwithstanding its attempts to avoid bias and ideology. Habermas himself furnishes five theses which I shall interpret as the auspices of a limited reflexivity responsible to the project of *homo faber*.

(i) The achievements of the transcendental subject have their basis in the natural history of the human species.

(ii) Knowledge equally serves as an instrument and transcends mere self-preservation.

(iii) Knowledge-constitutive interests take form in the medium of work, language, and power.

(iv) In the power of self-reflection, knowledge and interest are one.

(v) The unity of knowledge and interest proves itself in a

[1] Hannah Arendt, *Between Past and Future*, Six Exercises in Political Thought, Cleveland and New York, Meridian Books, 1963, pp. 112–115.

[2] Herbert Marcuse, 'Industrialization and Capitalism in Max Weber', *Negations*, Essays in Critical Theory, Boston, Beacon Press, 1968.

[3] See chap. 16.

dialectic that takes the historical traces of suppressed dialogue and reconstructs what has been suppressed.

Together these five theses reveal the axiological basis of human knowledge as a pattern of communication, control, and decision, predicated upon man's self-made and thus largely symbolic project of creation and freedom. The human project is a structure of biological, social and, I would add, libidinal values, which are institutionalized through the media of language, work, and politics. The vehicle of the human project is a common tradition and identity tied to speech, creation, and citizenship which relate individual expressions to everyday social life and culture.[1] In each of these realms there is practical metaphysics of the relation of particulars to universals, within the limits of common speech, the exchange of labour and the pursuit of the common good. Moreover, there is, as Habermas argues, an essential relation between the orders of language, work, and politics. The man who is not free in his labour is not free to speak and thus freedom of speech presupposes an end of economic exploitation as well as of political repression. Dialogue and poetry are therefore the primary expressions of the bond between speech and politics; it is through them that knowledge achieves reflexive awareness of the values of the human community to which it belongs and is thus able to play its role in the constitution of the body politic.[2] I have mentioned the work of the poet in the politics of freedom because he, as well as the novelist and musician, is the guardian of tradition and creativity. I think it is necessary to relate the knowledge-constitutive interests to the expressive, libidinal interests of the body politic in order to extend political dialogue into the street, the songs and everyday confrontations within the body politic. For these are the life-world understandings of the traditions of need and rebellion.

Modern consciousness is tied to the standpoints of anthropology and historicism which reveal that all knowledge about man, including scientific knowledge, presupposes some metaphysical position on the relation between human facticity, knowledge, and values.[3] Thus we can only speak of the reflexive ties between subjec-

[1] See chap. 11. [2] See chap. 6.

[3] Ludwig Landgrebe, *Major Problems in Contemporary European Philosophy*, From Dilthey to Heidegger, translated by Kurt F. Reinhardt, New York, Frederick Ungar Publishing Co., 1966, p. 11.

tivity and the regional ontologies of the worlds of science, economics, politics, and everyday life, and not of a naïve realist, subject/object dichotomy.

It may help to clarify the conception of limited reflexivity which I am proposing as the auspices for a mode political theorizing which has its community in the body politic, if I contrast it with the consequences of a total reflexivity of absolute knowledge. There is, for example, a conception of reflexivity which is very close to the limited notion I am fostering, but which is quite alien to it in its consequences for the orders of language, thought, and politics. I have in mind the sociological conception of reflexivity as the awareness of the infra-structures of knowledge in culture, class, and biography. At first sight, the consequences of the sociology of knowledge and ideology might appear to make for a moderation of political argument through an understanding of the intervening circumstances of class and history. But in practice it has brutalized political awareness and obscured the science of politics for which Mannheim had hoped. It was to these issues that both Husserl and Weber addressed themselves in their reflections on the vocations of science and politics. Both were concerned with the nihilism that was a potential conclusion from historicism and the sociology of knowledge. Husserl and Weber approached these problems in terms of an inquiry into the very foundations of western knowledge or science. Let us recall briefly Weber's reflections, which are perhaps better known to sociologists and political scientists, and then turn to Husserl's struggles with these problems in *The Crisis of European Sciences*.[1]

At first sight, the connection between Weber's reflections on the vocations of science, politics, and capitalism are not evident. Superficially, modern economics, politics, and science present us with an exotic competition of goods and values without a rational standard of choice. We accumulate knowledge much as we do money, and the result is a vast obsolence of commonsense knowledge and values. Any attempt to introduce order into this process is as disturbing to it as the occasions for these very attempts, so that our politics is snared in a polytheism of value. 'And with this,' says Weber, 'we

[1] Edmund Husserl, *The Crisis of European Sciences and Transcendental Phenomenology, An Introduction to Phenomenological Philosophy*, translated by David Carr, Evanston, Northwestern University Press, 1970.

come to inquire into the meaning of science. For, after all, it is not self-evident that something subordinate to such a law is sensible and meaningful in itself. Why does one engage in doing something that in reality never comes, and never can come to an end.'[1] Weber's question about the auspices of modern science is simultaneously a question about the grounds of modern community and personality in a world from which God is absent and order thereby an enigma to a disenchanted world of value accumulation. Weber compares his own questioning of the meaning of science with Tolstoi's question about the meaning of death in the modern world, where man is pitted against himself in a self-infinitude of want and desire. 'And because death is meaningless, civilized life as such is meaningless; by its very "progressiveness" it gives death the imprint of meaninglessness.'[2] In this way Weber made sociology aware of its own reflexive need to embed in a community of purpose whose institution is as much a charismatic hope as a goal of rationality.

Weber's conclusions, though they do not satisfy Marcuse's conception of critical theory, are in striking contrast with the Parsonian interpretation of Weber which serves to make sociological knowledge an irony of functionalist practice. That is to say, the Parsonian version of sociological knowledge invents a utopia of social system and pattern variable action congruence in order to embed its own instrumentalist rationality as a precipitate of utilitarian culture. Whether it starts from Hobbes's nasty vision or from Luther's excremental vision, Parsonian sociology reduces the problem of its own reflexivity to the anodyne of instrumental knowledge, hoping thereby to substitute affluence for the glory of love's risen body. While we cannot dwell upon Parsonian sociology in any detail, it may not be amiss, in view of its adoption into political science, to comment that Parsons' latest generalization of the instrumentalist vision based upon the master metaphor of money as the most generalized means of exchange and efficacy, only serves to further mystify the grounds of political order by neglecting the ways in which the behaviour of money is nothing else than the algebra of the system of stratification and exploitation for which Parsons pre-

---

[1] Max Weber, 'Science as a Vocation', *From Max Weber*, Essays in Sociology, translated, edited, and with an Introduction by H. Gerth and C. Wright Mills, New York, Oxford University Press, 1958, p. 138.

[2] *Ibid.*, p. 140.

tends to account. In short, and in contrast with the critics of
Parsonian ideology, I would argue, that it is Parsons' conception of
theorizing as an activity grounded in the means-end schema which
generates his intrinsic notions of social structure and personality as
a functionalist utopia of congruent orders of individual and collective reality.[1] Yet the unconscious merit of Parsons' classical study
of the corpus of utilitarian social science knowledge[2] is to have
focused on the ambivalence of the instrumental and ritual values of
human knowledge, subordinated to the *a priori* of individual interest.

I have turned my argument towards the topic of sociological
reflexivity not for the purpose of engaging in criticism as it is con-
ventionally understood, but for the purpose of coming to terms with
the very phenomenon of sociological reflexivity, namely, *how it is
that we can show the limits of sociology and still be engaged in authentic
sociological theorizing*. This is the question that I began with when I
set myself the task of asking whether phenomenology could be
critically aware of its own limits and its implicit ties with history
and politics. I shall now pursue this topic in Husserl's later writings,
acknowledging that my reading of them is a continuation of an
earlier reading by Merleau-Ponty. More concretely, my reading
of Husserl and Merleau-Ponty is essentially a borrowing from
them both, continuous with everything else we borrow in life. For,
indeed, as Merleau-Ponty remarks, 'I borrow myself from others; I
create others from my own thoughts. This is no failure to perceive
others; it is the perception of others.'

We need a conception of the reflexive grounds of social science
knowledge which will be grounded in the facts of institutional life
and yet remain equally true to the claims of science and poetry, or
to what is general as well as what is unique in our experience. Reflecting upon the crisis of the European sciences, Husserl remarked
that '*the dream is over*' of there ever being an apodictic or rigorous
science of philosophy. Some have thought that it is only those who
set such goals for philosophy who are likely to turn to philosophical
disbelief and despair. In such circumstances, it is the task of
phenomenological philosophy to take its historical bearings, to

[1] See chap. 13.
[2] Talcott Parsons, *The Structure of Social Action*, A Study in Social Theory with
Special Reference to a Group of Recent European Writers, New York, The Free
Press of Glencoe, 1964.

acknowledge its debts to the life-world which it presupposes so long
as there is no total threat to civilization, but which must then concern it.

The philosopher, says Husserl, 'takes something from history'.
But history is not a warehouse, or a rummage heap from which we
can take 'things', because facts, documents, philosophical, and literary works, are not palpably before us, apart from our own indwelling
and interpretations. Furthermore, we do not, strictly speaking,
transmit or hand down a scientific, literary, or historical tradition.
We may be Renaissance historians without having read or researched
every aspect of the Renaissance, just as we may be Platonists without
a concern for every word of Plato, so that we might as well speak
of a 'poetic transmission' which owes as much to us as to fact.
And yet none of this need imperil the teleology of knowledge, of
science, history, or philosophy.

> Let us be more precise. I know, of course, what I am striving
> for under the title of philosophy, as the goal and field of my
> work. And yet I do not know. What autonomous thinker has
> ever been satisfied with this, his 'knowledge'? For what auto-
> nomous thinker, in his philosophizing life, has 'philosophy' ever
> ceased to be an enigma? Everyone has the sense of philosophy's
> end, to whose realization his life is devoted; everyone has certain
> formulae, expressed in definitions; but only secondary thinkers
> who in truth should not be called philosophers, are consoled by
> their definitions, beating to death with their word-concepts the
> problematic *telos* of philosophizing. In that obscure 'knowledge',
> and in the word-concepts of the formulae, the historical is con-
> cealed; it is, according to its own proper sense, the spiritual in-
> heritance of him who philosophizes; and in the same way, obvi-
> ously, he understands the others in whose company, in critical
> friendship and enmity, he philosophizes. And in philosophizing
> he is also in company with himself as he earlier understood and
> did philosophy; and he knows that, in the process, historical
> tradition, as he understood it and used it, entered into him in a
> motivating way and as a spiritual sediment. His historical pic-
> ture, in part made by himself and in part taken over, his 'poetic
> invention of the history of philosophy', has not and does not
> remain fixed—that he knows; and yet every 'invention' serves
> him, and can serve him in understanding himself and his
> aim, and his own aim in relation to that of others and their

'inventions', their aims, and finally what it is that is common to all, which makes philosophy 'as such' as a unitary *telos* and makes the systems attempts at its fulfilment for us all, for us (who are) at the same time in company with the philosophers of the past (in the various ways we have been able to invent them for ourselves).[1]

Merleau-Ponty remarks how well Husserl's term *Stiftung*, foundation or establishment, captures the fecundity of cultural creations by which they endure into our present and open a field of inquiry to which they are continuously relevant.

It is thus that the world as soon as he has seen it, his first attempts at painting, and the whole past of painting all deliver up a *tradition* to the painter—*that is*, Husserl remarks *the power to forget origins* and to give to the past not a survival, which is the hypocritical form of forgetfulness, but a new life, which is the noble form of memory.[2]

Through language, art and writing, what was only an ideal meaning in the mind of an individual, achieves an objective and public status, enters a community of thinkers, which is the presupposition of truth. Thus we witness the event of that circuit of reflection in which what was first recognized as neither local nor temporal 'according to the meaning of its being', comes to rest upon the locality and temporality of speech, which belongs neither to the objective world nor the world of ideas.

Ideal existence is based upon the document, not, of course, as a physical object, or even as the vehicle of one-to-one significations assigned to it by the language in which it is written, but upon the document in so far as, again by an 'intentional transgression', it solicits and brings together all lives in pursuit of knowledge—and as such establishes and re-establishes a 'Logos' of the cultural world.[3]

We need, then, a conception of the auspices of philosophical reflexivity that is consistent with 'poetic invention' (*Dichtung*), as well as with the community in which we philosophize. Such a notion may be present to us in the concept of *reflexivity as institution*

[1] *The Crisis of European Sciences and Transcendental Phenomenology*, pp. 394–395.
[2] M. Merleau-Ponty, *Signs*, translated by Richard C. McCleary, Evanston, Northwestern University Press, 1964, p. 59.
[3] *Ibid.*, pp. 96–97.

rather than as transcendental constitution. By means of the notion of institution we may furnish a conception of reflexivity which, instead of resting upon a transcendental subjectivity, is given in a field of presence and coexistence which situates reflexivity and truth as sedimentation and search. We must think of reflexivity as tied to the textual structures of temporality and situation through which subjectivity and objectivity are constituted as the intentional unity and style of the world.[1] 'Thus what we understand by the concept of institution are those events in an experience which endow it with durable dimensions, in relation to which a whole series of other experiences will acquire meaning, will form an intelligible series or a history—or again those events which sediment in me a meaning, not just as survivals or residues, but as the invitation to a sequel, the necessity of a future.'[2] The institution of reflexivity is founded upon a series of exchanges between subjectivity and situation in which the polarities of means and ends or question and answer are continuously established and renewed, no less than the institution of ideas, truth, and culture. Reflexivity, therefore, is not an *a priori*, but a task which we take up in order to achieve self-improvization, as well as the acquisition of a tradition or style of thought which is the recovery of an original auspices opened in the past. To this we bring a living expression, or the inauguration of a world and the outline of a future, which is nothing else than ourselves, 'borne only by the caryatid of our efforts, which converge by the sole fact that they are efforts to express'.[3]

The notion of *critique* which we may derive from the concept of reflexivity as institution is one which is grounded in a contextual environment which lies open horizontally to the corpus of social science knowledges rather than through any transcendental reflection. This notion of critique is the result of abandoning Husserl's attempt to construct an eidetic of any possible corpus of knowledge as the correlative of a universal and timeless constituting reflexivity and the problems it raises for intersubjectivity, rationality, and philosophy itself. The corpus of the historical and social sciences is

[1] See chap. 7.
[2] M. Merleau-Ponty, *Themes from the Lectures at the Collège de France 1952–1960*, translated by John O'Neill, Evanston, Northwestern University Press, 1970, pp. 40–41.
[3] *Signs*, p. 69.

not, properly speaking, constituted through any object or any act of reflection. It arises from a continual production or verification (*reprise*) which each individual undertakes according to his situation and times. Thus each one's work must be continually reviewed to unearth its own auspices sedimented in the archaeology of human science. This is not a simplistic argument for eternal starts, any more than a crude rejection of the accumulation of human knowledge. It is rather an attempt to interpret the *rhetorical* nature of the appeal of knowledge and criticism through which tradition and rebellion are made.

'Reading' a text is inevitably an essay in rhetoric, that is to say, if we follow Aristotle, leaving aside Plato's insistence on the mastery of truth, it requires a profound knowledge or care for the souls one seeks to persuade. This concern to suit one's speech or argument to the other person's soul is the anthropological ground of all talk, argument, and criticism. It is at the heart of what is serious in our concern to discuss with one another, to correct and to persuade. It is for this reason that we elaborate upon one another's speech and thought. And we never argue so fiercely as between ourselves, because what is at stake is the utopian connection between truth, justice, and beauty. We sense implicitly the style of the world from a manner of speaking and thinking, so that we are drawn by its resonance, or else confused and repulsed. The error in modern communication and information theory is that it overlooks the rhetorical vehicle of speech, reading, and writing. It does this because in turn it lacks any conception of the intention to institute solidarity and a just social order in the relations between the partners to human speech.

What emerges from these examples is that the universality and truth aimed at by theoretical consciousness is not an intrinsic property of the idea. It is an acquisition continuously established and re-established in a community and tradition of knowledge called for and responded to by individuals in specific historical situations. Understood in this way, history is the call of one thought to another, because each individual's work or action is created across the path of self and others towards a *public* which it elicits rather than serves.[1] That is to say, history is the field which individual effort requires in

---

[1] 'Materials for a Theory of History', in *Themes from the Lectures at the Collège de France*, pp. 27–38.

order to become one with the community it seeks to build so that, where it is successful, its invention appears always to have been necessary. Individual action, then, is the invention of history, because it is shaped in a present which previously was not just a void waiting to be determined by the word or deed, but a tissue of calling and response which is the life of no one and everyone. Every one of life's actions, in so far as it invokes its truth, lives in the expectation of an historical inscription, a judgment not of its intention or consequences but of its fecundity, which is the relevance of its 'story' to the present.

> True history thus gets its life entirely from us. It is in our present that it gets the force to refer everything else to the present. The other whom I respect gets his life from me as I get mine from him. A philosophy of history does not take away any of my rights or initiatives. It simply adds to my obligations as a solitary person the obligation to understand situations other than my own and to create a path between my life and that of others, that is, express myself.[1]

The object of human knowledge is not, strictly speaking, an object; it is the institution within human space and historical time of artefacts, tools, services, institutions which are depositaries of what men before us have thought, needed, and valued. Cultural objects, in this sense, are the vestiges of embodied beings who live in society and communicate with one another as embodied minds.[2] It is such human beings who have opened up for us the hearth of culture and institutions, which it is our first duty to tender. And this we do, not as mere drudgery, but as the cultivation of our own growth, the basis for our departures and the source to which we return for fresh inspiration. Human institutions are the ground of our common and individual achievements, enriching us and impoverishing us with a legacy which was never quite intended for us and is yet never totally rejected by us, even when we refuse it. This human legacy is never fully ours until we learn to alter it through our own inventions, our personal style.

Human experience and vision accumulates only in the circle of social relations and institutions, which enlarge and deepen the sense

[1] *Signs*, p. 75.
[2] John O'Neill, *Perception, Expression and History*; The Social Phenomenology of Maurice Merleau-Ponty, Evanston, Northwestern University Press, 1970.

of our sentiments, deeds, and works through the symbiosis of solidarity and personality. Human action is essentially the unfolding of a cultural space and its historical dimensions, so that in a strict sense we never accomplish anything except as a collective and historical project. For the individual action involves, therefore, a constant dialogue with others, a recovery of the past and the projection of breaks which are never entirely successful. But this is not a source of irremediable alienation; it is the feature of our experience which calls for its completion through a collectivity, with a history that knows a tradition as well as a future. Such a collectivity or institution is never wholly reified; it is made and unmade, with a particular grain in each of us who lives and alters what he draws upon for his life. And this is a feature not only of human institutions, but of our thoughts, our sentiments and, above all, of human talk. Understood in this way, human institutions are the sole means that we have of keeping faith with one another, while being true to ourselves.

The ultimate feature of the phenomenological institution of reflexivity is that it grounds critique in membership and tradition. Thus the critic's auspices are the same as those of anyone working in a community of language, work, and politics. In the critical act there is a simultaneity of authorship and authenticity which is the declaration of membership in a continuing philosophical, literary, or scientific community. The critic does not alienate himself from his community, which would be the consequence of an absolute knowledge and ultimate nihilism. This is not to say that the critic is not rebellious; it is to remark upon the consequences of solitude and solidarity as the starting points of criticism.

Criticism in our sense is very close to Camus' conception of rebellion and order under the sun. Criticism reflects an aspiration to order under the auspices of the things that are present and of our fellow men, under a limit which is reflexively the recognition of solidarity and a rule of memory as an antidote to revolutionary absurdity.

> At this meridian of thought, the rebel thus rejects divinity in order to share in the struggles and destiny of all men. We shall choose Ithaca, the faithful land, frugal and audacious thought, lucid action, and the generosity of the man who understands. In the light, the earth remains our first and our last love. Our brothers are breathing under the same sky as we; justice is a

living thing. Now is born that strange joy which helps one live and die, and which we shall never again postpone to a later time. On the sorrowing earth it is the unresting thorn, the bitter brew, the harsh wind off the sea, the old and the new dawn. With this joy, through long struggle, we small remake the soul of our time, and a Europe which will exclude nothing. Not even that phantom Nietzsche, who for twelve years after his downfall was continually invoked by the West as the blasted image of its loftiest knowledge and its nihilism; nor the prophet of justice without mercy who lies, by mistake, in the unbelievers' pit at Highgate Cemetery; nor the deified mummy of the man of action in his glass coffin; nor any part of what the intelligence and energy of Europe have ceaselessly furnished to the pride of a contemptible period. All may indeed live again, side by side with the martyrs of 1905, but on condition that it is understood that they correct one another, and that a limit, under the sun, shall curb them all. Each tells the other that he is not God; this is the end of romanticism. At this moment, when each of us must fit an arrow to his bow and enter the lists anew, to reconquer, within history and in spite of it, that which he owns already, the thin yield of his fields, the brief love of this earth, at this moment when at last a man is born, it is time to forsake our age and its adolescent furies. The bow bends; the wood complains. At the moment of supreme tension, there will leap into flight an unswerving arrow, a shaft that is inflexible and free.[1]

I have tried, then, to outline a notion of criticism as a mode of theoretical life which is reflexively tied to the institutions of philosophy, art, and the sciences. The heart of this conception is its adherence to the presence of the things around us and of our fellow men in recognition of the institutional life which they share through the work of language, labour, and politics. It is a notion of critical theorizing whose auspices lie nowhere else than in the community of knowledge and value which are its claim to any contribution. The voice of such criticism is neither fanatical nor cynical, although it is in no way a simple affirmation of the claims of the community and tradition in which it belongs. What I have in mind is a conception of criticism which does not exploit the differences between the

---

[1] Albert Camus, *The Rebel*, An Essay on Man in Revolt, translated by Anthony Bower, New York, Vintage Books, 1956, p. 306.

way things are and how they might be but rather leaves itself open to the experience of their reversal, to the care for what is sublime as well as of what is desperate in the human condition and the times through which it passes.

For the reasons outlined above we cannot accept the paradigmatic value of the psycho-analytic conversation, at least in so far as the passive objectivity of the analyst is false to the dialogic search in which no member of the language community is absolutely privileged, and is therefore necessarily historical rather than clinical.[1] Moreover, we need to remember that human speech has no absolute goal of rational clarification, of disbelief, and rejection of prejudice. Human speech, dialogue, and conversation seeks just as well acceptance, or the understanding of what was already our belief, our native prejudice. This is the circle of language in which we dwell—the hermeneutic circle—which is not broken even when all come to understand our motives, our past experience. For there is nothing beyond death which alters what we have lived, although our understanding may return it to the silence of our being. There is, in other words, a naive dogmatism underlying the liberal social science conception of understanding which still draws upon the rationalist tradition of Enlightenment unmasking. But there is nothing behind the face of the man who speaks, beyond what else he has to say or how he keeps his silence. We find meaning between words and sentences and between men; there is nothing either in the back of this or beyond it.

[1] Habermas has himself provided for this conclusion in his essay 'Toward a Theory of Communicative Competence', in *Recent Sociology No. 2*, Patterns of Communicative Behaviour, edited by Hans Peter Dreitzel, New York, Macmillan, 1970.

16: On Theory and Criticism in Marx

Our times are characterized by a Marxism of fact and documentation which is in danger of becoming a revolutionary pastime if not a contribution to the counter-revolutionary structure of repressive communication which guarantees the success of liberal criticism. If this is not to be the case, then surely the phenomenal expansion of the Marx business and the thriving academic careers which it supports must provide a resource as well as an occasion for reflection upon the nature of Marxist critique. For unless we make Marx's own notion of critique thematic in the treatment of his work we shall risk reducing its unity and development to the contingencies of world politics and bibliographical discoveries which make of Marx an intellectual dope and of Marxism nothing but a series of historical and political pratfalls.

Like many others, I have contributed earlier to the argument on the unity of Marx's thought.[1] Looking back on my argument, I would say that what I was concerned with was the evident theoretical synthesis of philosophical and social science knowledge which is the heart of any reading of Marx. I was concerned to show this because whereas it is the feature of Marx's thought, together with his moral concerns, which converted me to Marxism, it is precisely the same feature which Marx's critics find it so easy to fault as an empty encyclopaedism. On another occasion,[2] I attempted to fend off an elaborate psycho-analytic reduction of Marx's economics to a Faustian drive in Marx which allegedly led him to project his split-personality upon the world through his reification of Capitalism and its schizophrenic counterpart, the Proletariat. Since these early skirmishes I have worked rather more in phenomenology than

[1] See chap. 9.   [2] See chap. 10.

Marxism, although through Hyppolite,[1] and especially Merleau-Ponty,[2] I have tried to keep these two concerns together, with an underlying attachment to Hegel rather than Husserl. The themes of my most recent concerns are all to be found in Hegel's *Phenomenology of Mind*. That is to say, I have tried to elaborate upon the structures of work, language, and violence in terms of the historical struggle between the principles of domination and recognition which expresses the alienation of technical and substantive rationality.[3]

I mention all this because I do not see any other way of bringing to bear my thoughts on the topic which I want to deal with now. And, as I see it, the topic arises by way of discerning within my various efforts the intention to be critical and the attribution of this feature to the essence of Marxist thought. By this, however, I do not mean to rest in the 'critical complacency' of the socialist gentleman. For, recently, I have been disturbed by the argument that phenomenology cannot be critical in the same sense as Marxism and that thus my earlier ambitions may have waned. In response to these difficulties I have attempted in another essay[4] to formulate a phenomenological approach to criticism. Now I am concerned with the argument from the other side, namely, that Marxism is not sufficiently critical because it lacks an adequate concept of reflection.[5] I think I can answer this argument by showing that the Hegelian and Marxist conceptions of critique are inseparably tied to the *apriori of embodied consciousness* and the reflexive structures of *language, work* and *recognition*. Moreover, so far as the unity of this conception is concerned, I think it can be shown to be the generative principle of Hegelian phenomenology and as such the legacy upon which Marx never ceased to draw.

I shall first try to defend the Hegel–Marx notion of critique against the arguments of two critical theorists, Habermas and Althusser. The latter is, of course, not usually considered a critical

[1] Jean Hyppolite, *Studies on Marx and Hegel*, translated with an Introduction, Bibliography and Notes by John O'Neill, London, Heinemann Educational Books, 1969.

[2] Maurice Merleau-Ponty, *Humanism and Terror*, An Essay on the Communist Problem, translated with Notes by John O'Neill, Boston, Beacon Press, 1970.

[3] See chap. 5.

[4] See chap. 15.

[5] Jürgen Habermas, *Knowledge and Human Interests*, translated by Jeremy J. Schapiro, London, Heinemann Educational Books, 1971.

theorist. But I would argue that Althusser's *problematic*,[1] namely, the nature of Marxist 'theory', lies precisely within the concerns of critical theory. I would then like to conclude with some remarks on the problem of the unity or totality of Marx's thought and the practice of Marxology in terms of a more general phenomenological approach to theory and criticism.

I shall argue for a notion of critique which derives the auspices of theoretical reflection in the social sciences from Hobbes rather than Kant, and from there to Hegel and Marx. I do not mean to ignore Kant; that is hardly possible. But I mean to show that *there is a materialist as well as idealist source of critical theory*. From the outset then, my own argument makes an appeal to a notion of critical reflection which is not to be decided and certainly can never be arrived at by reading texts in the ordinary sense. The criteria for the latter activity are something else and important enough in establishing the texts of Marx, for example, given his manner of work and the stray history of his publication. But it is a mistake to imagine that the question of Marx's own theoretical auspices can be established by stripping away all other interpretations through an appeal to texts overlooked, misconstrued, or only recently available. Now I cannot excuse myself from this confusion. But I would now argue that there is no escape from the phenomenon of the multiplicity of interpretations of Marx or Plato, or Christianity. The alternative is either to regard the history of thought as a colossal error or else as a gradual approximation to the truth in which everyone does his bit, so that although the whole labour is Sisyphean, it is manageable and even pleasant in parts. Conventional criticism in this case would amount to a series of minor labour disputes but not a babel of tongues.

The problem which must be the concern of critical theory is its reflexive awareness of the competing authoritative grounds for the recommendation of its own procedures. What makes Hobbes, Hegel, and Marx critical theorists is their awareness of the essential ambivalence in the authoritative grounds of the corpus of social science knowledge which takes *individual interest* as axiomatic in the treatment of man and nature. This central theme, which is generally

[1] Louis Althusser, *For Marx*, translated by Ben Brewster, New York, Vintage Books, 1970. It is important to consult the glossary to the text for the use of Althusser's basic concepts and his own interpretations of them.

known as the Hobbesian problem of order,[1] is set in the state of nature or civil society precisely because these are the conditions which portray the ambivalence of knowledge once a purely utilitarian conception of man and society is projected as a daily practice. I believe Hobbes interposed a divine fiat to solve the escalation of convention and the extreme subjectivization of the bases of social order inherent in his vision of the future of market society[2]. However, for a while at least, the Hobbesian problem was largely determined by metaphysical pathos. Thus, Locke and Smith appeared to settle the corpus of utilitarian knowledge upon the principle of the identity of interests, thereby launching the special sciences of psychology and economics, though at the expense of politics and sociology. So long as the authoritative grounds of the nature of theorizing as *instrumental rationality* held, then it provided for a self-interested conception of man and of nature and society as resources merely, or exchangeable utilities. In other words, the instrumental auspices of the utilitarian corpus of knowledge determined its basically reductionist conception of the nature of society and politics, strengthened by a nominalist epistemology which cleared the ground for individual agency. So much is clear (although, as we shall see, it is thoroughly obscured by Habermas) from even a preliminary conception of what Marx achieved in his critique of classical political economy and summarized in the theory of historical materialism. Moreover, it cannot be sufficiently stressed that the only science Marx dealt with critically was economics. Indeed, it is the principle contribution of what is called historical materialism to reveal critically the theoretical grounds of utilitarian economics.

Nor is it an accident that economics became an independent discipline under capitalism. Thanks to its commodity and communications arrangements capitalist society has given the whole

---

[1] See chap. 13.

[2] I am aware that this is a controversial assertion. Cf. A. E. Taylor, 'The Ethical Doctrine of Hobbes', and Stuart M. Brown, Jr., 'The Taylor Thesis; Some Objections', in *Hobbes Studies*, edited by Keith C. Brown, Oxford, Blackwell, 1965, pp. 35–55 and 57–71 respectively; as well as Michael Oakeshott, 'The Moral Life in the Writings of Thomas Hobbes', in *Rationalism in Politics and Other Essays*, London, Methuen, 1962, pp. 248–300; and Leo Strauss, *The Political Philosophy of Hobbes*, Chicago, University of Chicago Press, 1963; Howard Warrender, *The Political Philosophy of Hobbes*, Oxford, Clarendon Press, 1957.

of economic life an identity notable for its autonomy, its cohesion and its exclusive reliance on immanent laws. This was something quite unknown in earlier forms of society. For this reason, classical economics with its system of laws is closer to the natural sciences than to any other. . . . Its concern, as Engels put it, is with laws that are only understood, not controlled, with a situation in which—to quote Engels again—the producers have lost control of the conditions of life of their own society. As a result of the objectification, the reification of society, their economic relations have achieved complete autonomy, they lead an independent life, forming a closed, self-validating system. Hence it is no accident that capitalist society became the classical terrain for the application of historical materialism.[1]

I remarked earlier that I considered Hobbes more important than Kant in raising the question of the reflexive grounds of the corpus of social science knowledge.[2] Let me elucidate that comment briefly before considering Kant's claim and the respective arguments of Habermas and Althusser that Marx's positivism undermines his own critical effort. What I take to be the basis of the Hobbesian problem (why I do so must itself be open to reflection, and I shall return to this in my concluding remarks) is Hobbes's awareness, his nasty vision, that the axiomatization of individual interest had produced a conception of rationality which made insoluble the problem of *human recognition* except through such ironies as those of *Leviathan* itself with its mechanical metaphors and divine definitions. Indeed, the problem of recognition has remained endemic to the corpus of utilitarian knowledge since Hobbes and has defined the problematic of social science knowledge ever since. Thus, what makes Marx, Durkheim, Toennies, and Weber, for example, classical theorists is their pre-occupation with this particular problematic. What would show the differences between them would be the degree to which they achieve a reflexive awareness of the primacy of *the problem of recognition* in the determination of the role of knowledge in the

[1] Georg Lukács, *History and Class Consciousness*, Studies in Marxist Dialectics, translated by Rodney Livingstone, London, Merlin Press, pp. 231–232.

[2] Although he focuses upon the problem of recognition, as I would call it, and not the rational auspices of the corpus of social science knowledge, it is interesting to find some support for my thesis in Fred R. Dallmayr, 'Hobbes and Existentialism: Some Affinities', *The Journal of Politics*, XXXI, no. 3 (August 1969), pp. 615–640.

instrumental and ritual orders of conduct and society. I think that while we probably owe more to Parsons for the categorical distinctions involved, and for their analytic discrimination in the history of classical social theory, his naïve instrumental conception of knowledge leads him to play down the classical problem of recognition, of class struggle and alienation which have been basically Marxian themes, and thereby the concern of Durkheim and Weber.

So much for a first indication of the way in which the problematic of the authoritative grounds of the corpus of utilitarian knowledge, and specifically classical economics, is to be understood as essentially a problem of the relation between the cognitive and expressive interests in *domination, recognition and freedom*. In other words, the crisis of the positivist sciences has always been endemic to the utilitarian culture grounded in the authoritative auspices of instrumental rationality.

Kant's questions, What can I know? What ought I to do? What may I hope for? were raised from the very start in the tradition of reflexive theorizing since Hobbes, precisely because such questions are constitutive features of the culture through which they arise. More precisely, modern society consists of these questions as practical and theoretical procedures, as secularizations of alternately theological and epistemological questions which Kant settled by presuming upon the positivity of science. Nor should we overlook that Kant's Copernican revolution competes with the Industrial and French Revolutions as paradigmatic occasions for reflection upon the authoritative auspices of the corpus of social and political knowledge. However we read Kant,[1] Hegel and Marx could both argue

[1] Heidegger's reading of Kant would modify this judgment, putting greater stress on Kant's conception of the interplay between consciousness and the objects of experience. 'Kant's questioning about the thing asks about intuition and thought, about experience and its principles, i.e., it asks about man. The question "What is a thing?" is the question "Who is man?" That does not mean that things become a human product (*Gemachtes*), but, on the contrary, it means that man is to be understood as he who always already leaps beyond things, but in such a way that this leaping beyond is possible only while things encounter and so precisely remain themselves—while they send us back behind ourselves and our surface. A dimension is opened up in Kant's question about the thing which lies between the thing and man, which reaches out beyond things and back behind man.' Martin Heidegger, *What is a Thing?*, translated by W. B. Barton, Jr., and Vera Deutsch, Chicago, Henry Regnery Company, 1967, p. 244.

that Kant's separation between the noumenal and phenomenal worlds made it impossible for him to discover the concrete historical mediations for the transvaluation of human practice. The limits of science are the limits of abstract space and time which are outside of human time and place whose synthetic unity is constituted by human presence, through memory of the past and the projection of a future. In short, science itself presupposes the historicity of mind as set out in Hegel's *Phenomenology*. This does not mean, however, that scientific knowledge is not a major advent in the organization of human practice. But it can never furnish laws for human society of the same order as the scientific constitution of nature because of the distinctly reflexive features of human consciousness and its socially situated practices. Indeed, it is precisely the pretention of specific scientific rationalities, such as economics, to separate themselves from other substantively rational modes of knowledge and interest which Marx attached as *ideology*. Marx's distinction between the ideological superstructure and the substructure of relationships of production is not a reductionist argument for the simple reason that what Marx is concerned with is *human production* which is *as such* rational and moral. But this means that every mode of production is simultaneously a stage-specific mode of *domination and recognition*.[1] That is the critical core of the theory of historical materialism.

Nevertheless, Habermas has argued that whereas Hegel and Marx in their early work moved beyond Kant through the dialectic of recognition and its mediations in work and language, they respectively fell into the aberrations of the identity of absolute knowledge and historical materialism. The result, according to Habermas, is that Marxism reduces the fundamental conditions for human emancipation and critical reflection to the mode of technical rationality and instrumental control. The error of this reduction is allegedly clear in Marcuse's attempts to discover a basis for critical theory in the face of the ideological nature of modern technology and its social mode of repressive desublimation,[2] which appears to have becalmed any proletarian revolution. Althusser, on the other

---

1 Karl Marx, *Economic and Philosophic Manuscripts of 1844*, translated by Martin Milligan, edited with an Introduction by Dirk J. Struick, New York, International Publishers, 1964, Estranged Labor.

2 Jeremy Shapiro, 'From Marcuse to Habermas', *Continuum*, VIII (1970), pp. 65–76.

hand, is concerned with the political and philosophical consequences of Marxism governed by the alternations of ideological humanism and positivistic material determinism which allegedly are the endemic regressions of Marxian theorizing.

It cannot be my purpose here to show how Marx developed his account of the manner in which the features of bourgeois civil society, the split between public and private action in the pursuit of utilitarian values and the organization of the social relations of production around given modes of production, are consistent with the ideological essence of private property and its possessive individualism. The point that needs to be emphasized is that Marx's critical analysis is in no way outmoded by the findings, whether of Marcuse or Habermas, that the dominant mode of capitalist consciousness is now technical rationality. The corporate organization of capitalism remains attached to a subjective agenda[1] that simultaneously privatizes experience and dominates a multi-national world environment in a manner which is not intrinsically different from the operation of capitalism first grasped by Marx in the *Economic and Philosophic Manuscripts of 1844* and the *Communist Manifesto of 1847*.

Marx's critique of classical economics, by challenging the authoritative auspices of instrumental rationality on moral grounds, revealed the categorial structure of land, labour, and capital, or rent, wages, and profits to be destructive of the human forms of language, work and community. This is the sense of the paradox of the alienation of man through the universalization of his property of labouring which transforms the world and human nature itself into a calculus of being.

The *subjective essence* of private property—*private property* as activity for itself, as *subject*, as *person*—is *labour*. It is therefore evident that only the political economy which acknowledged *labour* as its principle (Adam Smith), and which no longer looked upon private property as mere *condition* external to man—that it is this political economy which has to be regarded on the one hand as a product of the real energy and the real *movement* of private property. (It is a movement of private property become independent for itself in consciousness—the modern industry as Self.)—as a product of modern *industry*—and on the other hand, as a force which has quickened and glorified the energy and

---

[1] See chap. 3.

development of modern *industry* and made it a power in the realm of *consciousness*.[1]

Marx, as we can see, was perfectly aware of the ideological and reflexive features of modern industry constituted through the subjective auspices of labour and property. In the continuation of the passage I have just quoted, he concludes with a vision of the subjective grounds of capitalist property which is just as surely the intuition that later made Weber's fortune.

To this enlightened political economy, which has discovered within private property the *subjective essence* of wealth, the adherents of the money and mercantile system, who look upon private property *only as an objective* substance confronting men, seem therefore to be *fetishists, Catholics*. *Engels* was therefore right to call *Adam Smith the Luther of Political Economy*. Just as Luther recognized *religion—faith*—as the substance of the external world and in consequence stood opposed to Catholic paganism—just as he superseded *external* religiosity by making religiosity the *inner* substance of man—just as he negated the priests outside the layman because he transplanted the priest into laymen's hearts, just so with wealth: wealth as something outside man and independent of him, and therefore as something to be maintained and asserted only in an external fashion, is done away with; that is, this *external mindless objectivity* of wealth is done away with, with private property being incorporated in man himself and with man himself being recognized as its essence. But as a result man is brought within the orbit of private property, just as with Luther he is brought within the orbit of religion. Under the semblance of recognizing man, political economy, whose principle is labour, rather carries to its logical conclusion the denial of man, since man himself no longer stands in an external relation of tension to the external substance of private property, but has himself become this essence of private property. What was previously being *external* to oneself—man's externalization in the thing—has merely become the act of externalizing—the process of alienating.[2]

Habermas traces the defects in Marx's conception of social theory to a relapse on the part of both Hegel and Marx with respect to Kant's critical achievement of revealing the antinomy of certain

---

[1] *Economic and Philosophic Manuscripts of 1844*, p. 128.
[2] *Ibid.*, pp. 128–129.

knowledge and the irrationality of its content. Kant himself was unable to grasp the nature of the historicity of knowledge and action which is the ground of the antinomy of rational knowledge. This was Hegel's contribution, revealing the weakness of Kant's positivist assumption of the certainty of Newtonian science. Hegel's development of Kant consists in his conception of critical knowledge as the historical genesis of self-reflexive knowledge in the context of the cultural formation of the human species. Kant started from the positive *a priori* of an unhistorical subject whose cognitive formation is axiomatically that of Newtonian science. The weakness of the tradition of doubt from Descartes to Kant, as Hegel sees it, is that the tradition of methodical doubt is removed from the dialectical life of the self-knowledge of reason determined by specific historical praxes, and thus falls inevitably into the positivist assumptions of a specific category of knowledge, namely, science. Ultimately then, Kant's critical theory remains phenomenologically naïve from Hegel's standpoint because it fails to raise the question of the practice of science *in itself* to a question *for us* as reflexive theorists of human knowledge and practice. Hegel's transcendental phenomenology, unlike Kant's, is thus a wholly historical reconstruction of the processes of individual development, the universalization of the history of mankind, and the reflection of the cultural forms of absolute mind in religion, art, and scientific knowledge.

Habermas's remarks on the transition from Hegel to Marx are important for their difference with Althusser over the significance of Marx's *Theses on Feuerbach*. At the same time, Habermas introduces his own version of an epistemological disjunction—in this case with critical theory—within the *Economic and Philosophic Manuscripts*, which results in Marx's progressively positivist conception of social theory. In the first thesis on Feuerbach, Marx corrected previous materialist theories with the Hegelian comment that materialism overlooks that objects are the product of human praxis. But then, according to Habermas, Marx understood praxis solely as the 'process of material exchange', without any relation to other symbolic syntheses, in particular, ideology, science, and politics. 'On the one hand', he says,

> Marx conceives of objective activity as a transcendental accomplishment; it has its counterpart in the construction of a world in which reality appears subject to conditions of the objectivity

of possible objects of experience. On the other hand, he sees this transcendental accomplishment as rooted in real labour (*Arbeit*) processes. The subject of world constitution is not transcendental consciousness in general but the concrete human species, which reproduces its life under natural conditions. That this 'process of material exchange' ('*Stoffwechselprozess*') takes the form of processes of social labour derives from the physical constitution of this natural being, and some constants of its natural environment.[1]

Habermas succeeds in cutting off Marx from critical theory by reducing the synthesis of symbolic structures contained in the theory of historical materialism to a crude form of technological and biological determinism. Once again, it would be tedious to marshal texts for this criticism. To put it as sharply as possible, let us simply say that Habermas' argument involves reading the *Economic and Philosophic Manuscripts* in a totally reductive sense, that is to say, as a *literally* materialist synthesis of economics and philosophy! The result of Habermas' materialist reduction is to deprive Marx's conception of the critique of political economy of any claim to constitute critical theory.[2] As Habermas presents it, historical materialism is a strictly materialist synthesis achieved solely at the level of the material production and appropriation of products. Habermas is clear enough that Marx regarded nature as a category of human praxis, and that Marx is in this sense more Kantian than materialist. 'But *nature* . . . taken abstractly, for itself—nature fixed in isolation from man—is *nothing* for man.'[3] But he reduces the transcendence of human praxis to the invariant relation of the species of a tool-making animal to its natural environment, despite the historical restructuring of that relation through ideological critique and class-conscious revolutionary action which together constitute what Marx understood by historical materialism. By insisting that Marx tied the reflexivity of social science knowledge to the system of instrumental action, Habermas is able to argue that historical materialism

[1] *Knowledge and Human Interests*, p. 27.

[2] Lest my argument seem to rely too much on the early writings, whereas Habermas draws freely from early and later writings, see Marx's discussion of the method of political economy in *The Grundrisse*, edited and translated by David McLellan, New York, Harper and Row, Publishers, 1971, pp. 33-35; 65-69.

[3] *Economic and Philosophic Manuscripts of 1844*, p. 19.

lacks any adequate conception of critical theory and rests ultimately on a positivist epistemology.

> Thus in Marx's works a peculiar disproportion arises between the practice of inquiry and the limited philosophical self-understanding of this inquiry. In his empirical analyses Marx comprehends the history of the species under categories of material activity *and* the critical abolition of ideologies, of instrumental action *and* revolutionary practice, of labour *and* reflection at once. But Marx interprets what he does in the more restricted conception of the species' self-reflection through work alone. The materialist concept of synthesis is not conceived broadly enough in order to explicate the way in which Marx contributes to realizing the intention of a really radicalized critique of knowledge. In fact, it even prevented Marx from understanding his own mode of procedure from this point of view.[1]

Habermas and Althusser arrive by different paths at the same conclusion with respect to Marx's faulty grasp of the nature of critical theory. In the case of Habermas, the question is whether we need to accept his reductionist account of the materialist synthesis.[2] Similarly, we shall need to question whether Althusser's positive interpretation of historical materialism as a theory of the over-determination of social structures really adds anything to Marx. With respect to both critics we shall have to ask whether the different ways in which each professes to complement Marx's conception of economics with a theory of politics, allegedly lacking in Marx, constitutes the full development of critical theory needed to ground Marx's conception of the relation between philosophy and praxis.

Although Habermas does not explicitly confront the question of the significance of Marx's *Economic and Philosophic Manuscripts*, his interpretation of certain passages, and the progression which he derives from them, is tantamount to a stand on the debate which they have inspired and allows for a comparison between himself and Althusser. If Habermas is right, there can be no question of any

---

[1] *Knowledge and Human Interests*, p. 42.

[2] For a non-reductionist account of Marx's critical theory, see Trent Schroyer, 'Toward a Critical Theory for Advanced Industrial Society', *Recent Sociology No. 2*, edited by Hans Peter Dreitzel, New York, The Macmillan Company, 1970, pp. 210–234.

critical role for the *Economic and Philosophic Manuscripts* with respect to the industrial praxis of socialist society because the only critique contained in them is the substitution of an instrumentalist or pragmatic theory of knowledge for Hegelian idealism. It follows that Marx could not formulate any critical reflection upon the status of the natural sciences in relation to the science of man called for in the *Manuscripts*, because Marx insisted on reducing human science to the positivist study of the laws of social development along the path of human emancipation.

Having stripped Marx's argument of its political framework, Habermas then argues that the materialist synthesis needs to be combined with a moral synthesis of critical-revolutionary action. Thus Habermas succeeds in separating Marx from Hegel to point out the necessity of rejoining Marx with Hegel in order to produce an adequate critical theory. A number of comments are called for with regard to these two moves. In the first place, Habermas suppresses the connection between Marx's analysis of alienation and class struggle, which is pervasive of the early writings, central to the *Economic and Philosophic Manuscripts* and never set apart either in the *Grundrisse* or *Capital*, not to mention the *Communist Manifesto*, which deserves more serious consideration than that of a pamphlet. But Hegel fares no better in Habermas's hands when it comes to putting Marx and Hegel together again. Whereas it is obvious that the dialectic of recognition is central to the *Phenomenology of Mind*, Habermas insists upon restricting its role to Hegel's early theological and political writings. Thus we have a very special version of the young Hegel and young Marx, each separated from the totality of their respective corpus.[1] It is on the basis of this reading of the Hegel/Marx relationship that Habermas formulates his own claim to a comprehensive critique of social science knowledge:

> Unlike synthesis through social labour, the dialectic of class antagonism is a movement of reflection. For the dialogic relation of the complementary unification of opposed subjects, the re-establishment of morality, is a relation of *logic* and of *life conduct* (*Lebenspraxis*) at once. This can be seen in the dialectic

---

[1] I have argued earlier that the 'existentialist' reading of Hegel destroys the unity of the *Phenomenology of Mind* and the basic complementarity of Hegel's corpus with Marx's work. Cf. John O'Neill, 'History as Human History', in Jean Hyppolite, *Studies on Marx and Hegel*.

of the moral action developed by Hegel under the name of the *struggle for recognition*. Here, the suppression and renewal of the dialogue situation are reconstructed as a moral relation. The grammatical relations of communication, once distorted by force, exert force themselves. Only the result of dialectical movement eradicates this force and brings about the freedom from constraint contained in dialogic self-recognition-in-the-other; in the language of the young Hegel, love as reconciliation. Thus, it is not unconstrained intersubjectivity itself that we call dialectic, but the history of its repression and re-establishment. The distortion of the dialogic relation is subject to the causality of split-off symbols and unified grammatical relations; that is, relations that are removed from public communication, prevail only behind the backs of subjects, and are thus empirically coercive.[1]

[1] *Knowledge and Human Interests*, pp. 58–59. Actually, Habermas's complete theory also depends upon making Freud's notion of surplus repression the real basis of the revolutionary–critical theory of communication. Since it would require another essay to deal with this argument, I can only cite the passage in which Habermas gives everything to surplus repression and nothing to Marx's theory of the historical structures of surplus value. 'Marx was not able to see that power and ideology are distorted communications, because he made the assumption that men distinguished themselves from animals when they began to produce their means of subsistence. Marx was convinced that at one time the human species elevated itself above animal conditions of existence by transcending the limits of animal intelligence and being able to transform adaptive behaviour into instrumental action. Thus what interests him as the natural basis of history is the physical organization specific to the human species under the category of possible labour; the tool-making animal. Freud's focus, in contrast, was not the system of social labour but the family. He made the assumption that men distinguished themselves from animals when they succeeded in inventing an agency of socialization for their biologically endangered offspring subject to extended childhood dependency. Freud was convinced that at one time the human species elevated itself above animal conditions of existence by transcending the limits of animal society and being able to transform instinct-governed behaviour into communicative action. Thus what interests him as the natural basis of history is the physical organization specific to the human species under the category of surplus impulses and their canalization: the drive-inhibited and at the same time fantasizing animal. The two-stage development of human sexuality, which is interrupted by a latency period owing to Oedipal repression, and the role of aggression in the establishment of the super-ego make man's basic problem not the organization of labour but the evolution of institutions that permanently solve the conflict between surplus impulses and the constraint of reality. Hence Freud does not investigate primarily those ego functions that develop on the cognitive level within the framework of instrumental action. He concentrates on the origins of the motivational foundation of com-

It would be tiresome to document the misinterpretations and fundamental alteration introduced by Habermas into the relationship between Hegel and Marx. Indeed, in general I prefer to document more intensively the arguments of Habermas and Althusser, respectively, since I imagine these are frequently more difficult to many than the notorious Hegel and Marx. All the same, I cannot simply counter in a declarative way that Habermas's improvement upon Hegel and Marx is superfluous, any more than I think this of the questions raised for Marxian theory by Althusser. On the contrary, I think both are adding babies to the Marxian bathwater which then becomes even more and not less essential to their displacement. The fundamental question, then, is the critical status of the theory of historical materialism. Habermas argues that Marxian social theory reduces the nexus of communicative interaction to instrumental action, which is then understood to determine reflection ideologically, so that critical theory is nothing but a critique of ideology lacking any positive phenomenological basis for a science of man and human value. According to Habermas, 'Marx did not develop this idea of the science of man. By equating critique with natural science, he disavowed it. Materialist scientism only reconfirms what absolute idealism had already accomplished: the elimination of epistemology in favour of unchained universal "scientific knowledge"—but this time of scientific materialism instead of absolute knowledge.'[1]

Habermas's conclusion must be confronted at least briefly with an attempt to formulate the theory of historical materialism as a critical expression of the antinomy of the mathematical and value concepts of nature governing bourgeois natural science, which through the institution of the reification of commodities and human relationships furnishes the model of classical economics. Of course, such an interpretation involves the rejection of Engels' much disputed positivistic formulation of historical materialism. The passages which I quoted earlier from the *Economic and Philosophic Manuscripts* are fundamental to the revelation of the subjective

---

municative action. What interests him is the destiny of the primary impulse potentials in the course of the growing child's interaction with an environment, determined by his family structure, on which he remains dependent during a long period of upbringing.' *Ibid.*, pp. 282–283.

[1] *Ibid.*, p. 63.

sources of the massive objectivity of commodity production and the laws of economics. Furthermore, they illustrate the dependency of the ontological abstraction of exchange values upon the subjective reduction of human nature to the single value of labour. The other side of this, clearly, is the implicit theory of value, that is to say, of human nature and social organization, contained in the notion of use-value and its historical production.[1] Marx's critique of classical political economy is methodologically in no way below the level of reflexive critical theory. It rests upon the same intuition of the limited nature of the formal presuppositions of objective knowledge. But instead of bringing its argument to bear on mathematics or physics, it deals with the science of economics and the relativity of the institutional arrangements that make the natural sciences an analogue for economics. The error contained in Engels' positivist endorsement of scientific praxis is that he overlooks the alienation of objectivity separated from its subjective sources in the historical decision to treat nature, as Heidegger would say, 'mathematically',[2] an error, which Marx and Engels made patent when it came to the status of the economic laws of capitalist society. In other words, Marx and Engels ordinarily were very clear that the 'objectivity' of capitalist conduct depended upon the reification or alienation of the motives for accumulation and class oppression internalized as the objective bases or situated vocabularies of economic action. Thus, between Adam Smith and Hegel the subject of historical action is latent with the dialectical possibility of the humanization of nature as the larger project, into which the naturalization of man enters as a necessary secondary but alienated structure. This is the final positive conclusion of the *Economic and Philosophic Manuscripts* and it remains the philosophical underpinning of all of Marx's work which is inseparable from his critique of political economy.

Industry is the *actual*, historical relationship of nature, and there-fore of natural science, to man. If, therefore, industry is con-ceived as the *exoteric* revelation of man's *essential process*, we also gain an understanding of the *human* essence of nature or the *natural* essence of man. In consequence, natural science will lose

---

[1] Lezek Kolakowski, 'Karl Marx and the Classical Definition of Truth', in his *Toward a Marxist Humanism*, Essays on the Left Today, translated from the Polish by Jane Zielonko Peel, New York, Grove Press, Inc., 1968, pp. 38–66.

[2] *What is a Thing?*, B I, 5.

its abstract material—or rather, its idealistic—tendency, and will become the basis of *human* science, as it has already become the basis of actual human life, albeit in an estranged form. *One* basis for life and another basis for *science* is *a priori* a lie. The nature which develops in human history—the genesis of human society—is man's *real* nature, hence nature as it develops through industry, even though in an *estranged* form, is true *anthropological* nature.[1]

With these last remarks I should now turn to Althusser's argument which is raised in the first instance, obviously, by my insistence on the unity and significance of Marx's early works and thus the denial of any effective epistemological break (*coupure epistémologique*).[2] I do not intend to respond to Althusser's argument over the epistemological break in Marx by means of a fresh analysis of the sequence of Marx's texts.[3] This is in part because, despite its length, Althusser's own argument is only apparently so derived and is in reality much more dependent upon the larger question of the Marxian problematic[4] and the relation between theorizing and ideology which, for the rest, joins with my own broad concern with the reflexive grounds of the corpus of social science knowledge.

Althusser's *For Marx* is concerned with the 'critical death' of Marxist philosophy in the Soviet Union and the French Communist Party, the latter's milieu being as narrowly construed as to allow for no references to Kojève, Jean Wahl, Jean Hyppolite, or Maurice Merleau-Ponty and only scant remarks on Sartre's *Critique de la Raison Dialectique*.

Perhaps most glaring is Althusser's silence with respect to the works of Lukács and Korsch, both available in French and thus once again central to the present argument. Korsch's *Marxism and Philosophy*, as well as Lukács *History and Class Consciousness* of course, make patent Althusser's strange combination of critical theorizing and theoretical regression. But, once again, it is hardly to the point to cite different textual sources against Althusser, for this no longer responds to the sense of the grounds of theorizing, which I want now

---

[1] *Economic and Philosophic Manuscripts of 1844*, pp. 142–143.

[2] *For Marx*, p. 249.

[3] For Althusser's organization of Marx's writings around the epistemological break of 1845, see *ibid.*, pp. 33–38, 256–257.

[4] *Ibid.*, pp. 51–86, 253–254.

to invoke in a final understanding of the notion of critique. This would require that we display our differences with Althusser as conjunctures of biography and politics, that is to say, as essays in the phenomenology of mind, determined retrospectively yet committed to the human contingency.

Althusser's own conception of his earlier approach to Marxist theorizing is self-consciously aware of the positivist fallibility which subtly pervades the concept of Marxist critique based upon the scientific reduction of its philosophical auspices. He states this in the following introspection in which we need to sense the interweaving of philosophical beginnings with Marx's own youthful proclamation of the death of philosophy.

So we contorted ourselves to give philosophy a death worthy of it: a philosophical death. Here again we sought support from more texts of Marx and from a third reading of the others. We proceeded on the assumption that the end of philosophy could not but be *critical*, as the sub-title of *Capital* proclaims that book to be of Political Economy: it is essential to go to the things themselves, to finish with philosophical ideologies and to turn to the study of the real world—*but*, and this we hoped would secure us from positivism, in turning against ideology, we saw that it constantly threatened 'the understanding of positive things', besieged science and obscured real characteristics. So we entrusted philosophy with the continual critical reduction of the thread of ideological illusions, and in doing so we made philosophy the conscience of science pure and simple, reduced it completely to the letter and body of science, but merely turned against its negative surroundings as its vigilant conscience, the consciousness of those surroundings that could reduce them to nothing. Thus philosophy was certainly *at an end*, but it survived none the less as an *evanescent* critical consciousness for just long enough to project the positive essence of science on to the threatening ideology and to destroy the enemy's ideological phantasms, before returning to its place amongst its allies. The critical death of philosophy, identified with its *evanescent* philosophical existence, gave us at last the status and deserts of a really philosophical death, consummated in the ambiguous act of *criticism*. Now philosophy had no fate other than the consummation of its critical death in the *recognition* of the real, and in the return to the real, real *history*, the progenitor of men, of their acts and their thoughts. Philosophy meant retracing on our own account the Young Marx's critical Odyssey, breaking through the layer of illusion that was hiding the real world from us, and arriving at last in our native land: the land of history, to find there at last the rest afforded by reality and science in concord under the perpetual vigilance of *criticism*. According to this reading, there could no longer be any question of a history of philosophy; how could there be a history of dissipated phantasms, of shadows traversed? The only history possible is that of reality, which may dimly arouse in the sleeper incoherent dreams, but these dreams, whose only continuity is derived from their anchorage in these depths, can never make up a continent of history in their own right. Marx said so himself in *The German Ideology*: 'Philosophy has no history.' When you come to read [my] essay 'On the Young Marx' you will be able to judge if it is not still partly trapped in the mythical hope for a philosophy which will achieve its philosophical end in the living death of a critical consciousness.[1]

Who has not read Marx this way? All that separates us from Althusser, surely, is only his ulterior motives in locating this Promethean reading of Marx in *Capital*, instead of throughout Marx from the time of his dissertation, *On the Difference Between the Democritean and Epicurean Philosophy of Nature*. Is there, then, no progression in Marx's thought? There is indeed; and on this Althusser has written with very genuine phenomenological insight, if I may say so without intention to convert. Let us leave aside Althusser's ulterior motive, namely, his desire to stem the tide of revisionism since the Twentieth Party Congress, although this may be a suggestion which is thoroughly inimical to the unity of theory and praxis. However that may be, Althusser's arguments for the *specificity of Marxist theory* can just as well be treated in terms of his proposed 'reading' of the shift in the problematic of Marx's thought which makes for a radical separation between its *ideological humanism* and its theoretical formulation of the *historical structures of overdetermined contradictions*.[2] This epistemological break, as Althusser calls it, represents a decisive departure from Marx's early dependence upon Hegel's critique of bourgeois civil society, as well as Feuerbach's materialist critique of Hegel which so enchanted Marx and Engels

---

[1] *For Marx*, pp. 29–30.   [2] *Ibid.*, pp. 200–216, 255.

prior to the *German Ideology*, when they 'settled' their philosophical consciousness. Actually, Althusser wants to argue that the young Marx '*was never strictly speaking a Hegelian*', and that the first dependency, so obvious, I would think, in the dissertation and the *Economic and Philosophic Manuscripts*, belongs only to the very early period of his 'disordered' consciousness, and then only functioned to produce the 'prodigious "abreaction" ' required for its dissolution. To be exact, according to Althusser, Marx's philosophical consciousness was first Kantian-Fichtean and then Feuerbachian, that is to say, ideological until 1845 and thereafter scientific.

The potential regression of Marxist theory arises more than anything else from its interpretation in terms of the Hegelian notion of unity or totality. In this respect Althusser's argument is far below the level of Habermas's treatment of the relation between Hegel and Marx. However, Althusser also argues, as does Habermas, that there is a permanently positivist deficiency in Marx's concept of social theory and that there is a critical necessity to revive Marxist philosophy without which the demise of theoretical Marxism or its subordination to political opportunism is a certainty.

According to Althusser, though this is hardly news, and is certainly more Hegelian than he seems to think, the specific theoretical advance which belongs properly to Marx is his theory of the over-determination of social structures which accounts for their features of simultaneous complexity and unity. Such 'structures in dominance' are the only proper referents of the notion of unity or totality in Marx's thought. Marx's theoretical advance in the analysis of social structures allows us to account for the relative autonomy of super-structures while nevertheless attributing determination in the last instance to the substructure, according to the overdetermination or value-added effect of the specifically antagonistic or non-antagonistic contradictions which dominate the system at any stage of its development. The theory of the overdetermination of social structures has nothing in common, therefore, with the Hegelian unity of essence through its alienated appearances or with the monistic causality of material determinism. The Hegelian unity relentlessly negates differences which never exist for themselves and therefore can never determine any practical policy which would materially affect the development of the spiritual unity of the Hegelian essence. 'My claim', argues Althusser, is that the Hegelian totality: (1) is not really, but only apparently, articulated in 'spheres'; (2) that its unity is not its complexity itself, that is, the structure of this complexity; (3) that it is therefore deprived of the structure in dominance (*structure à dominante*) which is the absolute precondition for a real complexity to be a unity and really the object of a *practice* that proposes to transform this structure: political practice. It is no accident that the Hegelian theory of the social totality has never provided a basis for a *policy*, that there is not and cannot be a Hegelian politics.[1]

It hardly bears comment that a simplistic theory of economic determinism makes an enigma of the whole notion of Marxist political practice. What does deserve to be noticed is that Althusser's attribution of the theory of structural overdetermination to Marx, which is easily enough found in Marx, is derived much more from a gloss on *Lenin's political practice*, that is to say, it harks back to a time when Soviet political and economic life had not yet frozen in the grip of Party dictatorship. However, I shall return to Althusser's interpretation of Lenin's political philosophy in my concluding remarks on critical biography.

I should now take up Althusser's more important plea, whatever its derivation, for a reflexive theoretial awareness or philosophical consciousness in Marxism. It is the role of theory, he argues, to formulate problems which already exist in Marxian political practice. However, a theoretical transformation requires a genuine theoretical labour in which there is an advance in knowledge and simultaneous critique of illusions. Thus it is the proper task of reflexive theory to examine the conditions which constitute the validity of its relevance to political practice, i.e., the transformation of social relations, or to economic practice, i.e., the production of goods and services. Now it is essential to recognize that theory itself *qua theoretical practice* falls among the economic, political, and ideological practices to which it is relevant. As such, theoretical practice includes ideological and pre-scientific theoretical practices, as well as scientific knowledge. It is therefore the specific task of theoretical practice to advance by means of distinct epistemological breaks with pre-scientific and ideological practices, in which it generally inheres.

[1] *For Marx*, p. 204.

The explicit consciousness of the transformation of the domains of knowledge is what Althusser calls *Theory*.

> So theory is important to practice in a double sense: for 'theory' is important to its own practice directly. But the *relation* of a 'theory' to its practice, in so far as it is at issue, on condition that it is reflected and expressed, is also relevant to the general Theory (the dialectic) in which is theoretically expressed the essence of theoretical practice in general, through it the essence of practice in general, and through it the essence of the transformations, of the 'development' of things in general.[1]

Whereas Feuerbach denounced the speculative illusion in Hegel, Althusser argues that the essence of Marx's critique of Hegel is that Hegel denies the reality of theoretical practice, i.e., the genuine labour of the Notion. Thus, Hegel inverts the orders of autogenesis between the levels of abstract and concrete reality, reducing the concrete generalizations of experience to the purely ideological universality of the Idea. However, Marx understood that the transformations of the concrete generalizations of fact or experience (Generality I) require particular theoretical transformations (Generality II) of the special sciences in order to be raised to the level of knowledge or science (Generality III). For these reasons, it is absolutely essential that Marx's theoretical advance over Hegel not be expressed as the *inversion* of Hegel's dialectical method, for this would leave Marxian theoretical practice essentially ideological and cut its roots with political intervention or the joining of knowledge and freedom.

> To sum up: if we recognize that scientific practice starts with the abstract and produces a (concrete) knowledge, we must also recognize that Generality I, the raw material of theoretical practice, is qualitatively different from Generality II, which transforms it into 'concrete in thought', that is, into knowledge (Generality III). Denial of the difference distinguishing these two types of Generality and ignorance of the priority of Generality II (which works) over Generality I (which is worked on), are *the very bases of the Hegelian idealism* that Marx rejected: behind the still ideological semblance of the 'inversion' of abstract speculation to give concrete reality or science, this is the decisive

[1] *For Marx*, p. 169 and the qualification of this definition of Theory in the glossary, p. 256.

point in which the fate of Hegelian ideology and Marxist theory is decided. The fate of Marxist theory, because we all know that the deep reasons for a rupture—not the reasons we admit, but those that act—will decide for ever whether the deliverance we expect from it will only be the expectation of freedom, that is, the absence of freedom, or freedom itself.[1]

We see then that both Habermas and Althusser find Marxian theory liable to a positivist regression from which it can be rescued only by a critical conception of theorizing able to deal with the relative autonomy of symbolic and communicative structures. The source of these criticisms lies in the concern with the one-dimensionality of experience in industrial societies, whether capitalist or socialist, which forces an ideological unity of theory and practice that threatens to absorb genuine critique. The problem here, I suggest, is that of *the end of history* in the sense that the corporate economy, on the one hand, and the Party bureaucracy, on the other, destroy the space–time coordinates of genuine political action, dialogue, and criticism. But these are the essential elements of political life, the enduring Hellenic ideal which pervades Hegel's thought and Marx's ideal of the Commune. Althusser is able to twist these theoretical developments around the notion of *historical delay*[2] by which he means that Marx, Engels, and Lenin, as well as Lukács and Gramsci, were all philosophically premature in their views. The same concept, according to Althusser, allows us to understand that the union of Marxian theory with the workers' movement was likewise premature for previous stages of socialist history. In each case the deviations involve the attempt to push philosophy ahead of Marxist science. However, Althusser will render justice where history denied it by reinstating the philosophical and political unity of Lenin's thought! The rest of Althusser's argument can only be summarized. It results in the reduction of philosophy to the zero point of the epistemological intervention contained in the eleventh thesis on Feuerbach: 'Die Philosophen haben die Welt nur verschieden *interpretiert*; es kommt darauf an, sie zu *verändern*.' Althusser interprets this thesis to deprive philosophy of any proper domain. Having lost its one-sidedness, philosophy acquires the task of representing the class

[1] *Ibid.*, pp. 191–192.
[2] Louis Althusser, *Lénine et la Philosophie*, Paris, François Maspero, 1969, pp. 30–31.

struggle in the realm of *theory* (the theoretical systems of particular sciences). Thus philosophy is neither (critical) theory nor science, but a political–theoretical intervention on behalf of the interests of the class struggle, a

> pratique sauvage au sens où Freud parle d'une analyse sauvage, qui ne fournit pas les titres théoriques de ses operations, et qui fait crier la philosophie de 'l'interpretation' du monde, qu'on peut nommer philosophie de la dénégation. Pratique sauvage tant qu'on voudra, mais qu'est-ce qui n'a pas commencé par être sauvage?[1]

We have reached two opposing conclusions as to the nature of political life and the role of critical theory. Althusser returns theory to the savage practice of the Hobbesian state which provided the very occasion for political theorizing. Habermas, on the other hand, returns to the moral dialectic of recognition as the framework of a theory of political dialogue and communication. In each case what we witness is an appeal to different theoretical grounds in the determination of the corpus of social science knowledge. The argument has proceeded in terms of a variety of interpretations of Marxian social theory and its Hegelian sources, including my own attempt to display historical materialism as a critique of the 'mathematical' auspices of classical political economy and its imputations of individual conduct and social order.

Althusser argues that it will not do to display a variety of interpretations of a man's thought, or of the corpus of social science knowledge, as though there were any stage that was ideologically neutral. The development of social science thought must be determined by its own internal problematic, i.e., to understand its answers we must understand the *question of its questions*. That question is always the question posed to knowledge by its times—or the problem of order and recognition, as we have called it, determined according to the specificity of its historical and political context. But I think that 'the question of its questions' for social science knowledge is also a biographical question which determines each theorist's conception of the bases of order and recognition. Thus, the task of critical theory is the recognition of the processes of individual as well as social self-formation (*Bildung*). For this I believe Hegel's *Pheno-*

---

[1] *Lénine et la Philosophie*, p. 55.

menology of Mind still serves as a paradigm of the integration of the structures of biological, social, and libidinal values which constitute the human project. It is this Hegelian legacy which is the treasure of Marxist critical theory. I hold Hegel in this regard for the reason that it was he who took over Hobbes's vision of man's bodily organization and its competitive felicity and built its capacities of reason, fear, and speech into a covenant with the whole of humanity and not just a convenient article of peace in an essentially unstable social order.

The differences I have referred to in the interpretations of Marx, must, as I have said earlier, be treated as problematic. Not, of course, in the sense that they invite despair over the trained stupidity of commentators. Such a reaction would not simply be unkind; it leaves totally unresolved what it is to read a text. Although I have disagreed with Althusser's procedures with respect to Marx, I do believe, that apart from its restriction to Marxist theory, the following statement of Althusser's expresses superbly the intentionality of criticism.

That this definition (of Marxist theory) cannot be *read* directly in Marx's writings, that a complete prior critique is indispensable to an identification of the location of the real concepts of Marx's maturity; that the identification of these concepts is the same thing as the identification of their location; that all this critical effort, the absolute precondition of any interpretation, in itself presupposes activating a minimum of provisional Marxist theoretical concepts bearing on the nature of theoretical formations and their history; that the precondition of a reading of Marx is a Marxist theory of the differential nature of theoretical formations and their history, that is, a theory of epistemological history, which is Marxist philosophy itself; that this operation in itself constitutes an indispensable circle in which the application of Marxist theory to Marx himself appears to be the absolute precondition of an understanding of Marx and at the same time as the precondition even of the constitution and development of Marxist philosophy, so much is clear. But the circle implied by this operation is, like all circles of this kind, simply the dialectical circle of the question asked of an object as to its nature, on the basis of a theoretical problematic which in putting its object to the test puts itself to the test of its object. That Marxism can and must itself be the object of the epistemological question, that this epistemological question can only be asked as a function of the Marxist theoretical problematic, that is necessity itself for a theory which defines itself dialectically, not merely as a science of history (historical materialism) but also and simultaneously as a philosophy, a philosophy that is capable of accounting for the nature of theoretical formations and their history, and therefore *capable of accounting for itself*, by taking itself as its own object. Marxism is the only philosophy that theoretically faces up to this test.[1]

The intentionality of criticism, as I see it, is a structure of reading and writing, of second-order speech, which is never a simple correction of what was said but a contribution in the same direction of meaning through which the critic memberships his own sense of a text in a community of truth. The anonymity of knowledge is in this sense never a goal but a means only of the establishment of truth. Hence disputes, errors, persuasions, and corrections are never neutral, for what is at stake is the claim to embeds in a community of knowledge. Of course, none of this is acceptable to the one-world epistemologists who look upon Marxism and its squabbles as the latest or most widespread of human follies. But this overlooks that the claim to truth is a call to the freedom of the other and is inseparable from its dialogic constitution. That is why we read and think and talk and argue—not endlessly but because of the inexhaustible depth and variety of human culture to which we are always latecomers.

In terms of these general remarks, we can look upon the differences between Althusser, Habermas, and myself, as well as our intellectual developments, revisions, and the like, as different institutions of a community of knowledge determined by theological, political, and sociological valencies which alternate between the extraversion of method and the introversion of self-understanding. These are not simple contradictions; we never cease to make of our moods objective frameworks and these in turn never hold without enthusiasm. This is the hermeneutic circle within which the question of the unity, youthfulness, and maturity of Marx's thought, arises only as the question of the significance of the life of *any* thinker. For there is no privileged standpoint from which either Marx himself or ourselves as interpreters could see or fail to see what he had in mind, except as the production of its sense within this same hermeneutic circle

[1] *For Marx*, pp. 38–39.

and the conjuncture of meaning and facticity which makes it impossible for us ever to foreclose upon its sense. But that is the very same thing as the opening of thought or the opportunity it provides each of us for our inscription, our place in the work of the culture of truth, beauty, and justice, which is the determinate opening of philosophy to practice.

Introduction

How did I bring you here? Was it out of habit that you began where I must leave or did you, and why did you, reach here by way of what went before? I would understand both. Of course, there is no real end here, nor any real beginning, just a going on. I needed this and perhaps you did too. Why does one write or anyone read? What are the lines of connection, the bonds between us? These are not separate questions. I leave you thoughts, words, essays—struggling to be a book so that they can be kept together somewhere. They have always had a certain sense, a kind of belonging in me. But now they are like old loves, remembered gently for the times one could not but belong to them, although already leaving.

I am a sociologist, God help me. Better say I am one of the people, born without difference, dying now of rage, of beauty, of love, of pain, but for work and its hopes and passions that tie me to my fellowmen. What is the word that will touch them? Too many words, certainly, or the wrong words, will only separate me from them. I am a Marxist without a revolution, though my mother and my father still work. My mother's hands. My father's hands. How shall I separate what is cruel from what is beautiful in the story of their lives? The rest of my family I do not know: they are workers.

Index